WHAT I SEE?

D0112901

Also by Russell Targ

The End of Suffering: Fearless Living in Troubled Times
(2006, with J. J. Hurtak)

Limitless Mind: A Guide to Remote Viewing
and Transformation of Consciousness
(2004)

The Heart of the Mind: How to Experience God without Belief
(1999, with Jane Katra)

Miracles of Mind: Exploring Nonlocal
Consciousness and Spiritual Healing
(1998, with Jane Katra)

The Mind Race: Understanding and Using Psychic Abilities
(1984, with Keith Harary)

Mind at Large: Institute of Electrical and Electronics Engineers
Symposium on the Nature of Extrasensory Perception
(1979, 2002, with Charles Tart and Harold Puthoff)

Mind Reach: Scientists Look at Psychic Ability
(1977, 2005, with Harold Puthoff)

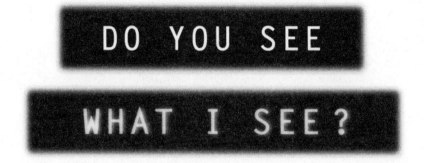

MEMOIRS OF A BLIND BIKER

RUSSELL TARG

HAMPTON ROADS
PUBLISHING COMPANY, INC.

This edition first published in 2010 by Hampton Roads Publishing Company
www.hrpub.com

Copyright © 2008
by Russell Targ

Cover design by Bookwrights Design
Sketch of the author © 2007 by Patricia Targ

Credit: Lady Godiva, c.1898 (oil on canvas) by John Collier (1850–1934)
© Herbert Art Gallery & Museum, Coventry, UK
The Bridgeman Art Library
Nationality / copyright status: English / out of copyright
PLEASE NOTE: The Bridgeman Art Library works with the owner of this image to
clear permission. If you wish to reproduce this image, please inform us so we can clear
permission for you.

Hampton Roads Publishing Company, Inc.
www.hrpub.com

Library of Congress Cataloging-in-Publication Data for the hardcover edition

Targ, Russell.
  Do you see what I see? : memoirs of a blind biker / Russell Targ.
    p. cm.
  Summary: "The autobiography of a noted scientist who made significant
contributions to the field of optics and lasers, and participated in the
government's top-secret psychic spy program. Includes the author's
encounters with well-known authors, actors, scientists, and other
recognizable figures"--Provided by publisher.
  Includes bibliographical references and index.
  ISBN 978-1-57174-559-0 (hc : acid-free paper)
  1. Targ, Russell. 2. Physicists--United States--Biography. 3.
Parapsychologists--United States--Biography. I. Title.
  QC16.T355A3 2003
  530.092--dc22
  [B]
                                                  2007052155

ISBN 978-1-57174-630-6
10 9 8 7 6 5 4 3 2 1
Printed on acid-free paper in Canada

For Patricia Kathleen, my life partner,
lover, companion, and dharma buddy;
and for Alexander and Nicholas,
my dear sons who are mensches
and a pride to my father's heart.

CONTENTS

What was seen as correct in one generation is realized as incorrect in the next generation. Within every generation there is a huge blind spot. When you look back at slavery, you cannot help wondering how it is possible that this horror could have occurred, and it occurred with the acceptance of good people! We have to be willing to see what is occurring in our own lives, just as horrible as slavery, that we have been blind to . . .

> *It is not that people won't betray you. It is not that your heart won't break again and again. Opening to whatever is present can be a heartbreaking business. But let the heart break, for your breaking heart only reveals a core of love unbroken.*
> —Gangaji

> *Nothing can bring you peace but yourself.*
> —Ralph Waldo Emerson, *Self-Reliance*

FOREWORD

In 1963, with wife, daughter, newly born son, and a freshly minted degree in psychology, I left the respectable but conservative University of North Carolina in Chapel Hill and drove west toward an exciting new life in exotic California. I had a vague feeling that I would meet new and exciting people—after all, California was about as romantic and exotic as one could imagine to those of us who grew up on the East Coast—but little realized just how interesting some of these people would be. You're about to learn about the life of one of these people, Russell Targ. Who else do you know who can honestly joke, while being quite serious, that he found God while spying for the CIA?

And why is Russell important as well as interesting? Let me start with some historical background.

Like Russell, I had been interested in parapsychology since I was a teenager. By 1963, I was already well-read in studies of things like telepathy and clairvoyance, had conducted a couple of experiments, and occasionally visited the world-famous laboratory of Dr. Joseph Banks Rhine at Duke University, less than an hour's drive from Chapel Hill. Rhine had pioneered rigorous laboratory research into extrasensory perception (ESP), which covered telepathy, clairvoyance, and precognition, and mind-over-matter, or psychokinesis (PK). Collectively, ESP and PK are nowadays referred to as psi phenomena. When I studied this laboratory evidence, I was convinced that the case for the existence of ESP and PK was excellent, better than for many accepted mainstream phenomena, yet it was clear that many establishment scientists rejected it, and rejected it for irrational, prejudicial reasons, rather than good scientific ones.

Even before leaving for California, I was already convinced that it was pretty much a waste of time to collect more evidence to prove the existence of psi; it would just be prejudicially ignored, too. What was needed was a way of getting strong, reliable amounts of psi to manifest in the laboratory, and then we could study what affected it and how it worked. A better understanding of how it worked would lead to more progress in getting psi to happen and practically applying it. In turn, strong, reliable psi effects would bypass the problem of prejudiced scientists not paying any attention to psi effects, which would allow more research to happen, hopefully leading to better understanding. But the few scientists (parapsychologists) working on psi back then almost always found what I often termed "statistically significant but practically trivial" psi effects.

An analogy I started using back then and still like, particularly apt for the autobiography of a physicist like Russell, is that the study of psi was where the study of electricity had been for most of humanity's history. We had lightning strikes, powerful and spectacular, but over in the blink of an eye and therefore hard to study. This was like the occurrences of psi in everyday life, sometimes very striking but over and gone, therefore hard to study. We had static electrical effects. If you rubbed a piece of amber on some fur, sometimes it would pick up a feather and many times, for reasons not at all understood, nothing at all happened. These were our laboratory psi tests, statistically meaningful but practically teensy and often not working at all for unknown reasons.

The science of electricity took an incredible leap forward with the invention of the battery. It was way less spectacular than lightning but far more powerful than amber rubbed on fur, and it was reliable; you could work with it whenever you wanted to. Now we could study how electricity worked, what affected it—and in a very short time, compared with the full scope of human history, we have a civilization run on electricity and electronics! In parapsychology, we needed a psi battery, a method to get moderately strong and reliable psi from people, then we could study it efficiently, strengthen it, and develop practical applications.

You can anticipate where I'm going with this if I describe Russell Targ as a "battery development pioneer," who would soon be in my future as colleague and friend.

After arriving in California, we settled down in Palo Alto, and I began postdoctoral training at Stanford. Through an earlier parapsychology contact, I soon met Russell, and we hit it off. A physicist by training, he was working at Sylvania Electronics at the time. We had many interests in common: We had both independently been thinking about the need to get strong, reliable psi to happen in the lab so we could study it, and we had both decided that seeing parapsychological studies in training terms as an opportunity to learn what you need to do to get psi (through getting immediate feedback) looked like a profitable route to research, rather than just testing how much psi someone could show. Even more importantly to me, I liked Russell's attitude. As a developer of a then new device, the laser, he was immersed in a physics and engineering culture that thought of lasers as inherently weak—like those statistically significant but practically trivial ESP effects? But, undeterred, he went on to develop a laser that would burn a hole through a brick! That was my kind of colleague and friend.

Back in the 1960s, Russell occasionally expressed a little interest in more spiritual things, compared to technical parapsychology research, but then and for the next several decades I did not think of him as really interested in spirituality. He was a brilliant and highly logical person who thought about the world as physicist and engineer.

As you will read in the following pages, Russell and his colleagues at the Stanford Research Institute (SRI) went on to develop a method of eliciting ESP—remote viewing—that was a lot more exciting and successful than the traditional multiple-choice guessing methods, the card guessing tests, that we had originally tried to turn into learning situations by giving people immediate feedback. Trying to see the location where someone is hiding, perhaps anywhere in the world, is just plain "sexier" and more intriguing than guessing numbers or cards over and over again.

Many remote viewers, as you will read here, were so good at it that government organizations like the CIA supported the research for decades because the practical intelligence-gathering results were so useful—and yes, most of those results are still classified so we can't talk about them. During the Cold War, our "psychic spies" were very helpful in supplementing other sources of intelligence and so kept down tension from possible surprises. Politics, of course, eventually caught up, and the CIA was embarrassed to become known for supporting such far-out research, so they admitted they had supported it but claimed nothing had come of it. So they kept supporting it for twenty years when nothing was happening? Really . . .

And finding God while spying for the CIA?

I saw Russell less frequently after I stopped consulting on the SRI remote viewing projects in the 1970s, and was then surprised in the '90s when I would hear him mention ideas from, say, Dzogchen, an esoteric form of Tibetan Buddhism, or the profound channeled material of *A Course in Miracles*. These things had always interested me in my life work of trying to build bridges between the best of science and the best of spirituality, but my oh-so-logical physicist friend Russell talking about them?

Hmmm . . . Here was a whole, deeper layer of Russell emerging and going in a most interesting direction. "Spirituality" powerful enough to burn a hole in a brick, rather than just be an interesting but trivial spot of light?

So read on, dear reader, about a man who has led—or could we better say created?—a most interesting life with some lessons for us all.

—Charles T. Tart
Berkeley, California, November 2007

ACKNOWLEDGMENTS

First and foremost, I want to thank my wife Patricia Kathleen for encouraging me to undertake this memoir, with the idea that it might be helpful to other visually handicapped readers, or any seekers endeavoring to find a spiritual path without giving away his or her mind. I also want to thank her for her patience and loving care in reading, re-reading, and correcting the manuscript.

I am also very grateful to my editor Phyllis Filiberti Butler who patiently and skillfully edited the evolving book in its many manifestations; and also my dear friend Susan Harris for her many insightful suggestions throughout the manuscript—just what I would hope from a loving psychiatrist. Additionally, I want to express my sincere appreciation to my publisher Jack Jennings for his vote of confidence that the book was not only an interesting read, but might even make sense for Hampton Roads. I want to thank Jane Katra, with whom I have co-authored two previous books, and whose many original and creative ideas have informed this book as well. And I am grateful to my dear friend Judith Skutch Whitson, publisher of *A Course in Miracles,* for introducing me to the *Course* and for her wise and supportive friendship for these many years.

Finally, I want to express my heartfelt thanks to my teacher Gangaji, for her pristine transmission of love and wisdom that guided me during this past decade to the surprisingly joyful and peaceful path where I now find myself. And as a disclaimer, I must add that Gangaji does not necessarily endorse or recommend any of the ideas or behaviors described herein.

INTRODUCTION

I am legally blind and always have been. I have to be two feet from a painting or blackboard to see it with the detail and clarity that you or anyone else sees it with at twenty feet—otherwise it's pretty Impressionistic. That's the meaning of 20/200 vision. I also have been a magician, an enthusiastic motorcycle rider, a laser physicist, and an extrasensory perception (ESP) researcher and psychic spy for the CIA.

Strange, say you? On the contrary, it seems natural to me for a person with very poor vision to be interested in optics and perception—even extrasensory perception. I learned from thirty years of ESP experimentation and meditation that it is no more difficult to see *psychically* across the planet than it is to see across the room. One of the themes of this book and my recurring life experience is that "things are seldom what they seem," as Gilbert and Sullivan tell us in *HMS Pinafore,* "skim milk masquerades as cream." Although my physics professors at Columbia University gave me a wonderful grasp of modern physics, they told me less than half the story of the reality of life. They left out the fact, for example, that it is possible to experience a world where everything is made of love. And, with the help of wonderful loving teachers, that's the world I have been blessed to discover in my seventy-four trips around the sun.

Aldous Huxley's *Perennial Philosophy* describes such a world and the many levels of awareness that we can experience. "Perennial philosophy" is Huxley's term for the highest common elements of all the major wisdom traditions and religions. This philosophy has as its first principle that *consciousness* is the fundamental building block of the universe—the world is more like a great thought than a great machine. The Buddhists teach that nothing is actually happening in our world, except for the meaning we give it. That, too, is one of the profound truths that I have come to embrace about life. Great writers have long recognized this. For example, three of the great romantic heroines of the nineteenth century, Anna Karenina, Madam Bovary, and Gwendolyn, in George Eliot's *Daniel Deronda,* were literally bored out of their minds "by the dullness of it all"—even as they were surrounded by wealth, beauty, revolutions, and social upheaval during one of the most tumultuous times in world history. They all became mad housewives because they could find no meaning in their lives. We're not going to do that.

When, at the late age of sixty, I finally internalized the idea that "I give all the meaning there is, to everything I experience," I profoundly reduced my own suffering, heartache, and loneliness. I began to understand that things may indeed be happening, they are just not happening *to me.* For example, the car didn't actually cut me off on my motorcycle, it just moved in front of me. I can give it any meaning I like. Maybe the driver doesn't see me or just doesn't like tall nearsighted Jews on motorcycles. More likely, it had nothing to do with me—he probably didn't even know I was there. We *can* learn to let go of the idea that things happen *to us.* That is another theme that runs through this memoir. If you want to *really* suffer, try personalizing everything. Even though I have no Buddhist credentials—I have not spent time as a monk. I am not even a chipmunk. But I have spent many years working on the problem.

Indeed, at this stage of my life, I am much more interested in questioning answers, than my previous specialty of answering questions. This questioning is what led to my interest in what the Buddhists call emptiness or *sunyata*. The short summary here is that when this basic principle—that we are largely making it all up—is internalized, we can greatly reduce our suffering from all causes. Thus, the title for my previous book, *The End of Suffering*. When we catch on to this fact, I have found that we can make the decision to deliberately move our awareness from fear, resentment, judgment, and craving, to gratitude, peace, love, and spaciousness. And that spaciousness, freedom, and fearlessness are real and available to us.

Generally, freedom appears when we finally become unbearably bored with the repetition of the story of our suffering. For me, it appeared when I noticed that I no longer needed anything, especially not even applause. That is to say, no-thing will ever make me happy. Happiness ensues—it's an inside job. Inside our mind, that is.

Our principle source of suffering is our defense of the story of who we think we are—the story of Me. We defend our business card whether or not we actually carry one. This is not an abstraction. I recently saw a public television documentary on the condition of our prisons. One of the prisoners interviewed was a well-spoken young black man who had recently killed a man. The prisoner explained, "I had to kill him. He dissed [disrespected] me right on the street." The idea behind *emptiness* teaches us that we can't be disrespected unless we have made ourselves available to be insulted. The *self* is just another part of our story of who we think we are.

The world around us may look finite, but thirty years of research into psychic abilities and verified out-of-body experiences have convinced me that *our awareness is limitless* in space and time—and therefore *we* are limitless. This is the basic finding from our two decades of remote viewing research at Stanford Research Institute (SRI). Through my work in this area I have taught thousands of people all over the world how to get in touch with the part of themselves that is psychic. And I am convinced by the data and my own experience that some aspect of our personality survives bodily death—as I describe in the final chapter of this book.

Understand me, please. I have come to realize that science, history—especially recent historical events like September 11—make it clear that no-thing exists and no event occurs independent of profoundly interconnected causes and conditions. Things that appear locally are often affected globally. And vice versa. It's part of the nondual, nonlocal view that separation is an illusion.

Huxley knew this, too. He tells us that we human beings can access all of the universe through our own consciousness and our nonlocal mind—that it's the mind that fills all of space and time. Physicist David Bohm's idea of quantum-interconnectedness has been the hottest topic in physics for the past two decades. Before that, *separation is an illusion* was first described in physics by Nobelist Erwin Schrödinger in 1927—and in the Hindu *Vedas* thirty-five hundred years earlier—teaching that one's *self* (or awareness) is one with the entire physical and nonphysical universe (*atman* equals Brahman). This philosophy also maintains that we have a nature that is both local and nonlocal, both material and nonmaterial.

Finally, the "Perennial Philosophy" teaches that the purpose or meaning of our lives is to become one with this universal nonlocal consciousness that is available to us, that is, to become one with our Divine, loving, spacious nature (which some call God), and to then help others to share this transcendent experience of who we are. This is also the nondual teaching of Jesus, that "The Kingdom of God is *within* you," rather than separate or up in Heaven. I have been exploring the nature of consciousness and trying to pierce the illusion that this material reality is all there is for many years, and if you bear with me, I just might convince you as well.

I am very comfortable talking publicly about areas where I have some expertise, such as lasers, magic, or ESP research. But recently I was asked to speak at a large book-signing event in New York City, right across the street from Town Hall. I know for a fact that New Yorkers do not suffer fools gladly, if at all. So I was nervous about my forthcoming talk on the concept of emptiness. I whined to my wife that I was concerned about embarrassing myself in my old hometown. But as soon as I said the words, I remembered that the whole essence of the teaching is that there *is* no *self*—certainly not one that can be embarrassed. It's all just a story. I felt entirely relieved, spoke easily, and sold lots of books. Once one has experienced emptiness, he is not likely to fall back to egoical thinking, unless he has an impulse to ignorance.

Back to what *this* book *is* about. Blind as I am, I have been riding motorcycles for more than thirty-five years—a bit of a maverick riding the hills and byways of hi-tech Silicon Valley and loving it. The most important thing I learned from this precarious existence is that it's wise to question reality—question what we think we are seeing and experiencing. This questioning is what has kept me alive while flitting in and out among the cars, busses, and potholes for all these years. In due time I will explain how I managed to cloud the mind of the Department of Motor Vehicles year after year, so that they would continue to give me a driving license even though I couldn't read their silly eye chart.

ME AND MR. MAGOO

The bumbling, nearsighted cartoon character Mr. Magoo has been a somewhat bruising role model for me ever since he appeared in movie cartoons in the 1940s. Last summer on a paint-ing adventure to Tuscany with my artist wife Patty (Patricia Kathleen), I especially identified with Magoo as I tripped through Italy with its historical, crumbling, and uneven pavements. It's always been a sort of French impressionist world. But much bet-ter I admit, than with a white cane, I'm sure! From a normal viewing distance of a couple of feet, Monet, Degas, and Renoir paintings look perfectly realistic to me. (Before the Ronald Reagan "tax reform," my vision was good enough—bad enough—to get me a federal income tax deduction "on account of blindness." But the Great Communicator decided to crack down on all those blind tax cheats, and the deduction is now gone.)

I have found that *focus of attention* is much more important than ordinary seeing. I learned this as I struggled through the humiliations of my gawky nearsightedness in elementary school. Exams were especially problematic for me at around age ten. I had to parade back and forth in front of the entire class with my notebook in hand, copying the questions from the blackboard before I could sit down to answer them. Then as a teenager I dealt with painful embarrassments of not recognizing my high school classmates—a continuing lifelong problem. I couldn't see the blackboards in college either. And there were often no text-books in physics courses taught by fancy Nobelists at Columbia during my graduate study years.

Whose reality is this anyway? Perhaps out of loneliness I became a proficient stage magician in my spare time, and got to create my own reality in the world of science fiction. My sensibilities espe-cially resonated with A. E. van Vogt's inspiring short novel *Slan*—a hair-raising teen adventure story with two super-bright, evolutionarily advanced, telepathic children, a boy and a girl, being pursued by the police and government of a corrupt and decaying state who wanted to rid themselves of the psychic, Slan. What lonely teenager would not identify with that?

After leaving Columbia, I soon found exciting work in the earliest development of the laser, and much later I created a ten-year laser program at Lockheed—my last corporate job—to detect invisible air turbulence and prevent airplane crashes with a premonitory windshear sensor. It seems natural to me that a guy with bad vision would try to make sense of reality by becoming first a student of magic, and then an optical engineer—eventually an ESP researcher.

Between two optics research careers, I sought this clarity by co-founding an ESP research program at Stanford Research Institute, now SRI International. This amazing $20 million program (the *real* X-Files) was supported by the intelligence community of the U.S. government—Central Intelligence Agency, Defense Intelligence Agency (DIA), Army Intelligence, etc.—for almost twenty-five years. And magic, lasers, and ESP are all part of the illusion that we call reality. With lasers of course, it's *all* done with mirrors.

Questioning reality is the essential first step in the greatest opportunity we have as a species—the *evolution of consciousness.* I believe we have completed our physical growth. Our brains are big enough. I am proposing that species *transcendence* is the next evolutionary step for us to take: starting first as animals looking for food, then to moderately self-aware humans trying to understand nature, and finally to our destiny as beings with personal awareness of our spacious and nonlocal consciousness transcending space and time. Every society before the so-called Enlightenment revered its prophets who had this larger view. Today, when we need such prophets, they are ridiculed, or turned into sideshow attractions—think of Al Gore, Linus Pauling, the Dalai Lama, and Albert Einstein. The suffering, wars, depression, and confused search for meaning we are experiencing are manifestations of our inner selves sensing, and crying out for, but not yet grasping our true nature. The hardware is fine, it's the software that must be upgraded—and quickly, I believe.

Mystics get a bad rap in modern Western society. A mystic will never ask you to believe anything. He or she will describe to you his or her life-changing transcendent experience and the instructions allowing you to explore that path yourself. It's like a lab experiment. Try this and report back in a few weeks, and let me know what happened. I have had such a totally unexpected experience twice without drugs, while sitting quietly with powerful spiritual teachers (my teacher Gangaji, and also with Yukio Ramana), both Americans in the *Advaita* (nondual) lineage of the great contemporary Indian Saint Ramana Maharshi. (Advaita means "not two" in Sanskrit.)

In these almost indescribable experiences, I felt as though my body were suddenly filled with warm loving syrup—love without an object. I could see clearly through eyes of love that there was no separation in consciousness between me and the other people in the room—many bodies, one consciousness. It's like in a dream, when you experience many dream characters, some loving, some frightening—but in reality you can notice that there is only you—the dreamer. In the epiphany, I was overcome, almost faint, with tears, love, laughter, and joy in the sudden blissful experience of seeing with crystal clarity the perfection of my life and the world. I have come to understand that who we are, our fundamental nature, *is* this flow of loving awareness. In describing this experience of unconditioned awareness, the contemporary Buddhist teacher Yongey Mingyur Rinpoche writes in *The Joy of Living* that: "Clarity, like emptiness, is infinite. It has no starting point and no end." My writing since then has been in service to this vision and these experiences.

Students occasionally fall in love with beautiful and charismatic Gangaji. I was once present when she explained the situation to an overwrought, love-struck male student in a large meeting. She said in effect: "It's okay to be in love with me. I frequently reside in love, and you are welcome to reside there with me. Just don't get attached to this body or this form. As you know, bodies and forms change, they come and go." Such an awakened person can and does spend increasing amounts of time peacefully "residing in love" and crystal clarity. In this book I will describe some of the paths that lead to this experience, and some of the many hindrances as well.

I will also describe my laser research where I had the opportunity to work with the visionary physicist Gordon Gould, who became the patent holder for the invention of the laser. Interestingly, though Charles Townes and Arthur Schawlow received the Nobel prize, Gordon got all the financial proceeds from the invention. In our work at Technical Research Group Inc. (TRG) on Long Island, our little band from Columbia University did not build the first successful laser, though we were on the right track, but we did pioneering research. The first laser was successfully operated by Ted Maiman at Hughes Research Labs, in Malibu, California, on May 16, 1960. I well remember the date because it is my mother's birthday, and also the birthday of my former girlfriend of many years, who through her deep love rescued me from spending my life living with the persona of the nearsighted cartoon character Mr. Magoo. But more of that later.

I spent fifteen years of my life working on the development of lasers. I then went on to devote a dozen years to designing, building, and flying airborne laser wind sensors for Lockheed and NASA—an invention to protect airplanes from air turbulence and windshear hazards that killed hundreds of people in several crashes in the 1980s. These systems were called premonitory sensors because they could see into the plane's future, allowing them to avoid windshear instead of flying into it and crashing. Although the Air Force and NASA liked and supported this highly successful and innovative research, the airlines and the

Federal Aviation Administration (FAA) decided that "safety doesn't sell," so our system has not been mandated or put into general service. It also worked excellently at the Cape to measure winds aloft to 80,000 feet for the shuttle. I believe it could have prevented the Challenger accident in 1986.

In my other parallel life, I co-founded SRI's research program, where we studied remote viewing (or ESP), which is an ability we all have to quiet our minds and describe and experience objects and events that are blocked from ordinary perception, either in the distance or in the future. Our program ran successfully for an incredible twenty-three years with a budget of $25 million, teaching U.S. Army officers on the East Coast how to be psychic, while at SRI in California we were using remote viewing to spy on Russian and Chinese weapon systems. We also looked in on our hostages in Iran, searched for and found downed U.S. and Soviet airplanes for the CIA, and were the first to describe an enormous new Soviet submarine for other parts of the U.S. Defense Intelligence Agency. We even found a crashed Soviet plane in Africa, still carrying secret codes. President Jimmy Carter gave us unwanted public commendation for this, thereby blowing the secrecy of our program.

From 1972 to 1995 we were the real "X-files." You could say that I had a metamorphosis from Magoo to Mulder. Although our main responsibility was remote viewing—ESPionage for the government—we also published our findings in the world's most prestigious scientific journals. Our work has been well replicated in international laboratories. And our exciting nonlocal findings show that it is no more difficult to describe a hidden object or person across the globe, than it is to describe something across town. And most surprising of all is the fact that the future is also available to a remote viewer *just as clearly* as the present.

In this memoir I describe how we became very skillful in helping a wide variety of people come into contact with the part of themselves that is psychic, as well as the changes that have taken place in my own awareness. In 1995 the CIA decided that since the USSR had collapsed, the United States no longer faced any serious enemy threats, and our program was ended. Since then, I have been teaching remote viewing to groups of people all over the world.

We at SRI never had an opportunity to search for Osama bin Laden, but my good friend Stephan Schwartz and a team of remote viewers at Virginia Beach produced a remarkably accurate description of Saddam Hussein's hiding place in a "spider hole" four months before his capture. Stephan's team published a report saying that: "Saddam will be found beneath an ordinary-looking house on the outskirts of a small village near Tikrit. The house will be part of a small compound that is bordered on one side by a dirt road and, on the other, by a nearby river." This document included a drawing of the building with a square hole dug in the courtyard. CNN's report said: "Saddam was found near the village of Adwar in the Tikrit area in a small compound . . . a river runs nearby, and a road is in front of the compound" (CNN, 16 December 2003).

Although remote viewing is not a spiritual path, the hindrances to spiritual awakening are very similar to those that interfere with remote viewing. They come from our conditioning, which teaches us that we are nothing but bits of talking meat, that there is no ESP, and that who we are is fully described by our story of who we *think* we are. I have learned to move from this conditioned awareness to spacious (naked) awareness. We have to give up our ego-based, self-centered, rigid, and grasping mode of life, and move into a flexible, unconditioned, nonjudgmental, and joyful space. In order to be psychic, it is essential to find a way to wake up and learn to recognize how much of what you experience is the result of conditioning by parents, teachers, and the cult we all belong to, which is called society. Another hindrance to living in unconditioned nondual awareness is that one has to learn to live with the seemingly paradoxical notion that most things you encounter *are neither true, nor not-true.* "Neither this, nor not-this" is the essence of giving up judgment and also suffering, as taught by the second-century Buddhist genius, Nagarjuna.

I recently took part in a ten-day lucid dreaming workshop where the teacher, Stephen LaBerge, taught us to awaken ourselves from sleep during a dream or nightmare and thereby recognize that it is only a dream. Similarly, to overcome our societal conditioning we must learn to wake up from the dream of our daily lives. That is, we must awaken from the dream the world is dreaming for us. I have found that it *is* possible to wake up and not be sleepwalking—at least some of the time.

SINS OF THE FATHERS

Renowned science writer and skeptic Martin Gardner wrote a regular monthly column called "Mathematical Recreations" in *Scientific American* magazine for more than twenty-five years. During that time he was unstinting in his slings, arrows, and vituperation—all directed toward me and my ESP research at Stanford Research Institute. However, in the March/April 2001 issue of *Skeptical Inquirer* magazine, Gardner wrote an amazing and amusing long article describing the history of three generations of my family called, "Distant Healing and Elisabeth Targ." The following abstract of Gardner's piece makes a nice little introduction to this memoir.

"I never cease to be amazed by how easily a set of beliefs, no matter how bizarre, will pass from parents to children, and on to grandchildren . . . Readers of *SI [Skeptical Inquirer]* will recall how the team of [Russell] Targ and his paraphysicist friend [Dr.]

Harold Puthoff made a big splash in parapsychological circles in the 1970s. They claimed to have established beyond any doubt that almost everybody is capable of 'remote viewing,' their term for what used to be called clairvoyance. . . . Russell inherited his psi beliefs from his father, William Targ.

"When I lived in Chicago I used to visit the father's bookstore on North Clark Street, a store he opened when he was twenty-two. It had a large section devoted to books about the paranormal and the occult. After working for a time as an editor for World Publishing Company, in Cleveland, Targ moved to Putnam in Manhattan where he rose to editor-in-chief. His entertaining autobiography, *Indecent Pleasures,* was published in 1975. At Putnam, Targ was responsible for many best-sellers, including Erich von Däniken's notorious *Chariots of the Gods.* Under his editorship Putnam also published a raft of books about psychic phenomena, such as Susy Smith's *Book of James* in which she reports on channeled messages from the spirit of William James. [He also published *The Godfather* and the Pulitzer Prize–winning *Andersonville.*] Targ died in 1999, at age ninety-two. His original name was William Torgownik, taken from his parents when they came from Russia [Poland] to settle in Chicago where he was born.

"William Targ's beliefs in the paranormal trickled down to his son Russell, and now they have descended on Russell's attractive and energetic daughter Elisabeth. Her mother Joan, by the way, is the sister of chess grandmaster Bobby Fischer. Elisabeth is a practicing psychiatrist with an MD from Stanford University, and psychiatric training at UCLA's Neuropsychiatric Institute. Ms. Targ is firmly convinced that persons have the power to use psi energy to heal the sick over long distances even when they don't know the sick but only see their photographs and are given their names.

"Elisabeth Targ is now the acting director of the Complementary Medicine Research Institute (CMRI). It is part of the California Pacific Medical Center (CPMC), in turn part of the University of California School of Medicine. Her institute is devoted to investigating such alternative forms of healing as acupuncture, acupressure, remote healing, therapeutic touch, herbal remedies, meditation, yoga, chi gong, guided imagery, and prayer.

"Ms. [Dr.] Targ has received $800,000 from the Department of Defense to head a four-year study of the effects of alternative healings on patients with breast cancer."

The report of Elisabeth's pioneering and highly significant distant-healing study with sixty San Francisco AIDS patients was published in the prestigious *Western Journal of Medicine,* December 1998, as "A randomized double-blind study of the effect of distant healing in a population with advanced AIDS. Report of a small scale study by F. Sicher, E. Targ, D. Moore II, and H. S. Smith." This work has now led to other National Institute of Health (NIH)-funded investigations of the efficacy of intercessory prayer.

My beloved and multitalented daughter Elisabeth tragically slipped from this plane of existence in July 2002, as the result of a brain tumor, at age forty. It's too soon to tell just what the legacy of the remaining Targs will be, but I am honored to share with you my little portion of the story . . .

I trust this memoir will help you see that we can become aware of how much we ourselves make up our experience as a result of our psychological projection. Yes, things happen, but we give them all the meaning they have for us. That's why I think of this book as *Questioning Reality.* As Prospero declaims in Shakespeare's *The Tempest:*

The solemn temples, the great globe itself,
Yea, all which it inherit, shall dissolve
And, like this insubstantial pageant faded,
Leave not a rack behind. We are such stuff
As dreams are made on . . .

(*Note:* Rather than litter this volume with footnotes, I have gathered together all the citations to books and technical papers in the bibliography at the end of the book, where they can be found listed alphabetically by author.)

CHAPTER ONE

An American, Chicago Born

Fourteen billion years ago, at the heart of the universe,
An explosion occurred that we call the creation of space and time.
The fragments from that explosion fled their quintessential origin and
Raced in every direction at greater than the speed of light.
We, of course, you and I, are the condensation of
these star-borne fragments:
Matter aware of itself.
Star children with brains and consciousness,
who can look back across
All of space and time,
To re-experience and almost comprehend the moment of our birth.
—Russell Targ

I am an American, Chicago born, as Saul Bellow says in the opening lines of *Augie March*. My story begins with a surprising spring blizzard on Chicago's Near North Side. It's April 11, 1934 (ironically, the hottest year in U.S. history), and my slim and trim mother is in Woodlawn Hospital trying to give birth to a nine-pound baby boy while snow lashes the windows and piles into six-foot drifts outside. To help with the pain, my mother is given the ever-popular scopolamine as a childbirth anesthetic. But as every doctor knows, it's not really an anesthetic; it's a pretend amnesiac, producing so-called "twilight sleep"—which is to say, the delivery still hurts like hell, but you are not supposed to remember it. My mother *did* remember it—and screamed her head off. Which is why I am an only child.

Both my parents and two grandparents were also born in Chicago. In fact, this writing celebrates the one-hundredth birthday anniversary of my parents. My grandfather Max Torgownik, a tailor from Krakow—and a gambler—was a character straight out of *Fiddler on the Roof*—beard, *yarmulke,* and homilies to match. He could have called his little shop "God and Me," whereas the Fifth Avenue version in New York was already widely known as "Lord and Taylor." His tiny curly haired wife Esther was the family saint, also the first woman buyer for a major Chicago department store—Goldblat Bros. Max and Esther came to the U.S. in 1905, a few years before Max's cousins, the brothers Max and Sam. These highly intelligent and energetic men quickly learned English and became an active part in the growing interface between the Yiddish and American life of Chicago. They started buying and selling used violins—a very important part of the immigrant community. Over two decades they grew from being instrument peddlers, to becoming partners in the largest music publishing and wholesale instrument business in the Midwest—a firm called Targ and Dinner, which later gave millions of dollars for the construction of a music library in Israel. (This generosity, together with there being two Max Targs, created serious problems for me and the FBI in the 1950s. But I'm jumping ahead.)

In 1937 the two brothers returned to Krakow in Poland to urge their extended family to come out of harm's way and join them in safe and prosperous Chicago. I have a photo from that visit, showing eighteen successful-looking men and attractive women sitting around the dining table set with candles and crystal as part of their Krakow reunion. Max and Sam were unable to convince a single person to come back to the U.S. with them, and within two years all these cheerful and loving people had been murdered by Nazi troops sent to Poland specifically to exterminate the Jewish population. Historically, it has always been the wealthy, well-integrated ones who feel they are part of the community and stay behind to be killed; while the young ones, who

Extended Torgownik family in Krakow, 1937

were sent by their loving families to get an education and have nothing to lose, get the hell out while there is still time.

Even Jews who tried to come to the U.S. often didn't make it to our shores. In May of 1939, the German transatlantic liner *St. Louis* left Hamburg, Germany, with 937 Jewish refugees on board. This was one year after *Kristallnicht* (the night of broken glass) when the Nazis coordinated an attack on all Jewish people and their property in Germany. The hopeful refugees from "the final solution" were sailing to Cuba, as a sanctuary. But as the ship entered Cuban waters, the government caved in to widespread anti-Semitism, fanned by the pro-Fascist newspapers, and turned them away. Our president, Franklin Roosevelt, and the U.S. Congress (in another day of infamy) also expressed no willingness to accept them—as did England. Everyone felt they already had enough Jews. So they had no choice but to sail back to Nazi Germany to meet their fate. My grandfather, Max, was lucky to have come to the U.S. on this same ship, landing at Ellis Island in 1905.

Probably my earliest memory, at the age of about nine months (walking but not talking), was of climbing out of my high, slat-sided crib. Despite having pajamas with feet sewn in, I managed to climb over the top rail and slide safely down the slats to the floor. I then padded across the living room to surprise my mother, who was having coffee with a girlfriend in the kitchen. I remember how shocked she was at my appearance. For weeks after that, I was safety-pinned to the sheets of my crib. (For those interested in such things, I have distinct mental pictures of the dark red Oriental carpet on the floor and the low windows to my left.)

Other early Chicago memories include going to Oak Street Beach with my mother and splashing in the deeply rippled sand of chilly Lake Michigan; and later, as an eager three-year-old fishing for goldfish—difficult for me to see—with a little net in the window of my maternal grandfather Ben Jesselson's South Side fish market. His parents came from Baden-Baden. Grandpa Ben would occasionally throw a handful of quarters onto the sawdust-covered floor of his shop to give me practice crawling around and locating things that were hard to see.

Thank God I finally got glasses at age four, and learned to read soon after, using giant-size flash cards with my patient and encouraging mother, Anne Jesselson Targ, by the fireplace in the evening—just like young Abe Lincoln. At that age, I also loved to get up at six o'clock, put on my warm bathrobe and fuzzy slippers, and go for a ride in the cool light of dawn helping the Borden's milkman carry eggs, cheese, and bottles of milk from his horse-drawn, ice-filled delivery wagon to the front porches of houses in our South Side neighborhood. This would be right after I heard the morning hillbilly music and hog and grain prices from WLS, Chicago talk radio with National Farm Radio reports. At this point readers may begin to wonder, "Is this guy still alive?" This simpler pre-war world has a strong nostalgic pull for many of us older Americans.

I identified with the "Elephant's Child" of Kipling's *Just So Stories,* which my mother read to me when I was five. I was the baby elephant with "insatiable curiosity," who put his nose into everything and got it pulled very long by the crocodile—searching for truth, love, understanding, perhaps even God. It was not only a burning desire to understand the way of the world, but also to *do it*—to try it for myself, even if I had to get my nose in it to see it, which was often the case. Even today, I must read close-up with my nose in the book, but I generally read quite rapidly.

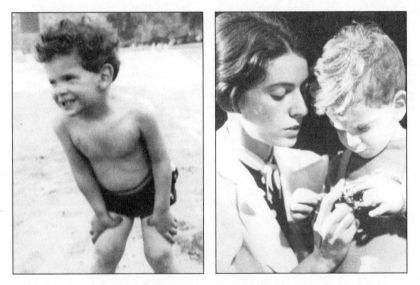

The author at his best, three-years-old, at Oak Street Beach in Chicago, 1937; and as a two-year-old with his mother for an Ovaltine commercial.

Face blindness was another continuing and very perplexing problem for me—still is. It's a perceptual defect where people all look more or less alike—two eyes, a nose, and mouth. What more is there to see? This face blindness (prosopagnosia) is a developmental problem of the visual cortex. In my case this lack of what developmental researchers call neural sprouting was probably the result of congenitally very poor vision. It can even affect people with so-called normal vision, who have had strokes, brain injury, or other congenital defects. The exact cause is not known. You not only don't recognize people you have met, they don't even look familiar if you meet them out of context! This is a particularly confusing disability for a child on the playground where he is supposed to be learning how to make friends. At least in the classroom, I could memorize which person was sitting in which chair—back when the desks were screwed to the floor. Today, face blindness is a new hot topic in digital image processing and computer face recognition research. An excellent website devoted to this subject is maintained by Bill Chaisser, a face-blind San Franciscan who describes the situation as follows:

> Researchers several years ago isolated facial recognition to a part of the brain known as the right temporal lobe, and recently they have pinpointed it to a more precise area known as the "fusiform face area." The precise point is not relevant to someone who can't recognize faces, but what is relevant is this: Researchers have isolated recognition of most patterns other than faces to a different part of the brain on the left side. Since an injury or malfunction can occur in one spot and not the other, this situation establishes a physical explanation for the occurrence of face blindness.

Cecilia Burman is another face-blind Internet writer. She has a very interesting site full of explanations and examples of living with the problem. She writes:

> Most people think that if you can see something like a face, then you must also automatically know who you are seeing. The problem with this approach to *prosopagnosia* is that you do see the face. You see it as an image using the brain's image center. You can also see it using any of the other intact centers. This means that you can see the person's gender, age, etc. But you just cannot see who it is. These symptoms are very confusing for someone who has them, and they are probably the reason why many face-blind people go through all their entire life not knowing that their problems are caused by *prosopagnosia*.

A blind friend, who is a sociology professor at Stanford, once told me that he has an easier time than I do. When he is at a conference, he just stands aside with his white cane in his hand, and if someone wants to talk to him, they come by and pull his sleeve and announce their name. Nobody expects him to recognize anyone. However, my face blindness continues to cause frustration, loneliness, and confusion for me because my colleagues of many years simply can't believe that I don't recognize their unique and very special faces. This has created many challenging situations in my life—some of the more interesting will follow. (Dating identical twins was probably the most confusing. Throughout my life, I have found relations with women to be profoundly intricate— whether real or imaginary—even when complex conjugation wasn't involved.) My really good friends usually tell me who they are at once.

The opposite situation is seen throughout my favorite novel *Anna Karenina,* where Tolstoy depicts dozens of dinner parties and cocktail parties. These are the major concern of most of the characters in the book—since the men only pretend to work, and the women only pretend to love them. The preoccupation of all of the women is what they will wear and whom they should invite. It is an example of the wasted lives of people utterly trapped in their social conditioning. (Of course Tolstoy knew the revolution was soon to come—as it always does when the poor get tired of supporting the idle rich.) But at these parties, people are not face blind, rather they are clairvoyant! All the players seem to have the ability to tell from the briefest glance across the room if a woman is about to divorce her husband, if a man has a new mistress, or if the woman on the balcony wants to meet you in the garden at eleven. My highly psychic dear friend and remote viewing partner Hella Hammid could do that, but I have never seen anyone else own up to such talent. She could read people like a book, right down to their underwear—or CIA credentials. I, on the other hand, don't even recognize *myself* in the mirror, with my gray hair and my new rimless glasses. The image feels only vaguely familiar.

However, my eyesight notwithstanding, as a child I did have surprising success assembling Erector sets and taking apart alarm clocks—even adjusting tiny set screws on the wheels, because I could hold them as close to my face as necessary. Later, I designed and hand-wired (and sold) a number of very high-quality vacuum-tube-driven music amplifiers—with a magnifying glass in one hand, a soldering iron in the other, and a surgical hemostat holding the parts together.

It seems I learned early that we all have awareness and possibilities which are not limited by the physical body. That is how I dealt with the ongoing celebration of what I call "National Mock the Handicapped Week"—in school, in films, and even from teachers who should know better. I remember telling a teacher that she should be ashamed of herself for calling me "four eyes" in front of the class. For my boldness I was taken to the principal's office—and privately commended by the very enlightened woman in charge. I had somehow already figured out that I was not available to be insulted by someone for whom I had no respect, even if she was a teacher. Again, it's very important for kids to develop self-esteem, before they can give the self away.

In the Eightfold Path, Right Intention informs such compassion and goodwill toward others. Buddhism teaches that there are many bodies and one consciousness. And what we call love is part of that universal consciousness. Puppy love for the girl across the classroom aisle is pure openhearted love at six. For me at six, this love—wanting and needing nothing—was focused on a little round-faced girl with blond braids named Jane Lynch, to whom I have never spoken one word. This is probably a direct experience of sexual energy, or more likely love energy—a kind of omnipresent radiation without a radiator. At that age, or younger, I had a strong sense of aesthetic awareness. I would cry real tears, again and again, overcome with the beauty of Degas' pirouetting dancers, their diaphanous cloud-like tutus floating about them, in the big folio art books in my father's library. Even now, I don't know why the child in me was so deeply touched by these impressionist figures.

Childhood is perhaps the last time for decades that we are in touch with our own delicious flow of pure loving awareness, which is, of course, who we really are. It is what the Indian sage H. W. L. Poonja (a disciple of Ramana Maharshi) would call "love, loving itself, your own self." He says, in his book *The Truth Is,* "You are always in love. Bliss is not an experience, it is your nature."

Love is a place to reside. *Love is who you are,* rather than something to do.

"*Of course I love you—I'm programmed to love you. I'm a goddam lovebird.*"

A bit older love appeared for me at ten, when my little girl-friend Virginia and I almost set fire to the school, having been given freedom to roam because we were such good students. We were both in a sight-saving class, and the teacher was trying to encourage our independence. From the top of the school building, we made and flew paper airplanes, dripping with balls of fire from burning highly flammable celluloid, which we had stripped from the edge of our wooden rulers. A neighbor across the street called the police, and we got a "U" in citizenship on our report cards. But it was a great adventure—long remembered.

About this time I found the magic stores in the Chicago Loop near my father's popular Dearborn Street bookshop, Targ's Books. I began to practice card tricks in front of the mirror. I loved to fool adults. The reason that magic tricks can be done close up is that there is absolutely nothing (no moves, no sleights of hand) for the observer to see in a properly done trick, whether it's cards or cups and balls. I'll have more tales of magic to tell as we go along. Before the Dearborn Street shop, my father had had another bookstore on Clark Street in Chicago's North Side. Many famous and soon-to-be famous writers from the 1930s congregated there: Nelson Algren, James T. Farrell, Richard Wright, Mario Puzo, John Reed, and Fred Dannay are just a few who come to mind—all this literary activity was from a man who never graduated from high school. My father was very welcoming to all, communist and non-communist alike, though he was personally highly allergic to any sort of dogmatism. At eighteen, he had left his West Side Polish neighborhood to become a copy boy, manuscript reader, and salesman for McMillan Publishing. He was allowed to be a first reader for submissions because of his already prodigious knowledge of American literature—even as a teenager. While I was reading science fiction at his age, he was reading real books. It was his boss at McMillan who suggested he change his name from Torgownik to the more American sounding Targ. "Torg" or Targ is the Indo-European word for center, as in "target." All the family adopted "Targ" at that time. A torgownik was a person with a shop in the town center or square. (In Sweden, the buses returning to the center of town all display the word "Torg," as their destination.) I guess being a square was my cultural heritage.

I often went with my parents to the Rosenwald Museum of Science and Industry near the little lake in Jackson Park. Rowing boats could pull right up to the museum's back entrance. I loved to visit its large complex replica of a coal mine, complete with a rickety elevator plunging down a seemingly endless shaft, ending with a surprise gas explosion! My other Sunday museum treat was the Art Institute, with the two large stone lions at the entrance. They were said to roar whenever a virgin entered the museum. My favorite and best-remembered pictures at the museum were the beautiful, soft, impressionist paintings of Mary Cassatt, showing the loving interaction between mothers and their children, often in little idyllic boating scenes. Lake Michigan features large in the thoughts of a Chicago eight-year-old.

My other great childhood memory that's uniquely Chicago is going to school in the dim morning light on my little wooden skis with leggings and ski poles. I made my way dashing between snow drifts blown high over my head by the blizzard wind, often in sub-zero temperature, howling in from the frozen lake.

Just before we left Chicago, I experienced the shock of Pearl Harbor on a Sunday drive to Grandma's house. We had just finished dinner at a Chinese restaurant—where I learned to use chopsticks for the first time and cracked open my first lichee nuts. I remember the somber "December 7, 1941" announcement over the radio of my father's little Chevy coupe. My father instantly said to my mother and me that the attack meant that Roosevelt would finally be able to declare war on the Nazis. In my youth, everything on the world stage derived its meaning from what effect it would have on the Jews—especially at large family gatherings.

The war was underway, and we were aware of it in many ways besides the daily news flashes. We flattened tin cans for the scrap metal and saved bacon grease in a can on the stove for the fat drive. My mother helped me make a victory garden in our back yard, where we successfully grew carrots and remarkably sharp and crunchy radishes. Near the garden, we had a large flowering lilac bush, which filled the house with sweet, purple perfume all through the spring. The whole childhood scene is completely restimulated for me whenever I encounter a lilac bush in bloom.

When we moved to Cleveland the following year, I finally learned to keep up with the boys. I'd follow my running Cub Scout pals, crawling on my hands and knees on fallen trees high above the rocks and rushing water in the ravines of Cleveland Heights where we lived. I again attended a one-room school for visually handicapped children. But learning was no problem for me and soon I was able to skip the fifth grade by sitting in on lessons of the upper grades. I learned to touch type because it was uncertain if I would ever be able to write legibly—a very valid concern. In moving to Cleveland, my father William Targ sold his bookstore and became an editor at World Publishing Company. But he retained his large library of occult and magic books. I like to recall the day he took me to see the great American magician and illusionist, Blackstone. It was a huge education for me—sitting in the front row, watching a beautiful woman vanish right before my eyes. That's where I first learned to ask myself, "How must that have been done?"

Father also took me to World's huge publishing plant to see the magic of bookmaking, with the giant noisy presses, the intricate paper folding machines, and the bindery. My love of books doubtless dates from those days. I still remember the surprisingly pungent smell of the ink that filled my nostrils as soon as I walked into the sprawling printing plant. Someone even created a hardcover Cub Scout manual for me.

My father was a tall, handsome man, with wavy dark hair and beautiful hazel eyes. He was very quick witted, humorous, and always teasing. My own little children didn't understand him, and they didn't like the teasing. He was, of course, extremely well read and had at his fingertips most of what he had encountered in a long literary life. One whole wall of his study at home was papered with the brightly colored covers of the books he had published at World. He would say, "When you have read as many books as I have, you don't need to pretend to have read the ones you haven't." He was scathing wherever he felt he saw pretentiousness. I am sorry to say that both my parents were very judgmental, and it caused them both a lot of suffering—as it usually does for us all.

CHAPTER TWO

Now You See It, Now You Don't

In New York City, where we next lived, I learned to play tag on the rooftops. Somehow, I've always been willing to take chances. The other kids and I would jump from building to building over the yawning five-story-high, five-foot-wide gaps between buildings on the block where I lived for three years. The roofs were covered with many different colors of tar paper and a scattering of gravel, so you were never sure where your feet would land. But we have all seen those rooftop chases in the movies. That was in the Village—on Eighth Street between Fifth and Sixth Avenues, across from the enthralling Whitney Museum of Art. I loved Greenwich Village and the Whitney—which has now moved Uptown to Madison Avenue, leaving only shoe stores and tattoo parlors on Eighth Street. Sorry to say the book-shops are also gone—and so close to New York University (NYU).

The week after we moved to New York, I learned about both Trotskyites and dipsomaniacs—a big thing for an eleven-year-old. I'll never forget the day my father and I visited James T. Farrell and his wife Hortense. Farrell was the well-known author of *Studs Lonigan* and many other realistic novels of Chicago. He and my father were good friends from the old days in that city. I remember they chatted and drank scotch from thick tumblers in Farrell's book-cluttered apartment filled with cigar smoke and comfortable bent-wood chairs. They reminisced about their friend Richard Wright, the author of *Black Boy* and *Native Son,* who was about to move permanently to France to avoid American racism. That was the first time I had ever heard of an interracial marriage.

A decade later I had a memorable meeting with Wright and his writer/literary agent wife Ellen when I visited Paris for the first time. They were very hospitable and gave me my first taste of a really ripe Camembert—about to jump off the plate—on a crispy French baguette. After lunch, they guided me to the Mistral Bookstore, right across from Notre Dame Cathedral, where I bought a finely made paperback edition of *Lady Chatterley's Lover*—which I then smuggled into the U.S. and had bound with beautiful red boards and gold stamping. I still have the book.

(I realize that many of the events described in this memoir are presented in an order determined by their meaning to me, rather than by their chronological order. I hope we can all just relax, have a nonjudgment day, and enjoy the stories.)

Back in the apartment, Farrell was describing to my father his fear that the Stalinist Communists were about to carry out their threat to kill him. He was a well-known Trotskyite and said that he too was thinking of leaving the States. After all, they had killed Trotsky in Mexico six years earlier and literally *erased* him from photos and statues where he had appeared with Lenin and Stalin—thus rewriting history to *make it as it should be.* This is what Nietzsche called *monumental historicism*—"the use and abuse of history." Time for another reality check.

It seems to me this is not unlike dressing up George—"I'm the decider"—Bush in flight-suit drag and putting him on the deck of an aircraft carrier under a huge banner proclaiming "MISSION ACCOMPLISHED." We all know that more than 4,000 American soldiers and 500,000 Iraqi civilians have been killed needlessly and senselessly since then—thus creating an utterly bogus iconic moment in this catastrophic presidency. There is a famous painting by Jacques-Louis David, showing Napoleon galloping across the Alps on a fiery white charger (1801), whereas, it is well known that he actually crossed the Alps in winter on a mule (on his ass, as they say). Revisionist history, I call it.

(I promise that this book is not going to be a rant about the president. But while Anne Frank was writing about her life as a girl in Amsterdam, she really could not ignore the Holocaust going on outside her window—could she? . . . well neither can I!)

Author Farrell was also concerned that our benevolent post-World War II government under Truman was conspiring much too closely with both industry and agriculture, and heading toward American fascism—government for the benefit of the industrialists and agro-business. Eight years later, Eisenhower made the same concerns public in his famous farewell address to the nation about the dangers of the "military industrial complex." I guess I must have become a radical at my father's knee during such afternoons in New York. Today we have to deal with the military-corporate-religious complex—more fearsome than ever.

On another score in New York, our upstairs neighbor on Eighth Street was frequently found partially clothed and asleep on our third-floor landing, having not quite made it up to her fourth-floor apartment. My mother, a teetotaler, called her a "dipsomaniac." I thought that was unfriendly of my usually generous mother—I very much liked cheerful, young Nancy. Who cared that she occasionally fell asleep in the hall? I thought she was cool, although the word probably didn't have that meaning yet. She was my lovable little twenty-six-year-old baby-doll playmate, with springy blonde curls. And I liked playing with her eleven-year-old son, Hoppi, on our connecting fire escapes.

Hoppi and I also played king-of-the-mountain at lunchtime with our classmates on the coal barges tied up at the wharf on the

Hudson River. I felt like Tom Sawyer on the Mississippi—everywhere I turned was a new and exciting way to get into trouble. Lunch was a delicious hot dog with mustard and sauerkraut, or maybe a potato knish and a bottle of chocolate egg cream. The unforeseen danger of playing king-of-the-mountain on the coal barges was that if you were knocked to the bottom of the huge coal pile, some kids might untie the barge and push you out into the river. I never thought that this was a good idea. You would then either have to swim to shore, or risk being beaten up by the very angry barge owner. It never happened to me personally, but I saw it happen to others.

My junior high school, P.S. 3, was only two blocks from the waterfront on Christopher Street. It was a huge, four-story, prison-like building with bars on all the ground-floor windows. The cafeteria was in the basement from which we exited single file up a narrow wire-covered steel stairway, directly onto the street. (The school was also attended by my first wife Joan Fischer and her brother Bobby, as well as my stepmother Roslyn. Joan and Bobby were expelled when Bobby kicked the sarcastic and always grumpy principal, Mr. Sallen, whom I also remember well.) I didn't personally have a problem with *that* principal. The one that *I* hit was in high school, but only when he decided to shake me because he thought that my extremely poor spelling was some kind of acting out—evidence of bad character. He grabbed me from behind to shake the badness out of the skinny fourteen-year-old. I happen to be very ticklish and responded to his shaking by vigorously elbowing him in his corpulent midsection. He outweighed me by a hundred pounds, but I almost decked him. I must admit, it still gives me pleasure to think about it.

In the winter, I loved the sting of the cold air with the mixed smells of salt, fish, and creosote. For a nickel, we could take the Lackawanna Ferry across the river to Hoboken. The ferry would crunch through the heavy ice floes in the river, which would always slow down the old wooden boats. Sometimes it would get stuck, and we would miss a class, but it really wasn't our fault. Ah! The freedom of those days.

Christopher Street had a surprise for me in every block. Across from my school, the old Hudson movie theater was being turned into the Theater de Lys for the first American performance of Kurt Weill's *Threepenny Opera*. Even a twelve-year-old knew that it was a big deal. The original star Lotte Lenya came all the way to the U.S. from Vienna to star again in this famous production celebrating the struggles and foibles of the down-trodden poor. I was to see this show many times in the following

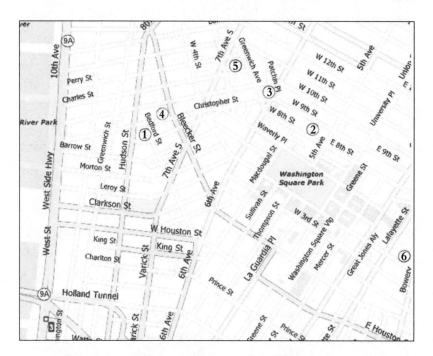

Russell's Greenwich Village in the 1940s: 1) P.S. 3 on Christopher and Hudson; 2) Russell's house on Eighth Street and Macdougal; 3) Woman's penitentiary on Sixth Avenue; 4) Theatre de Lys on Christopher Street; 5) Village Vanguard on Seventh Avenue and Eleventh Street; 6) John Simon's house on East Fourth Street and Bowery

years. Two blocks east was the Village Vanguard with sounds of jazz floating out the open doors every afternoon as I walked past on my way home. Although many famous people and bands performed there, my favorites at that time were the Modern Jazz Quartet, the powerful black folk singer Odetta, the Weavers with Pete Seeger, and the creepy but highly imaginative monologist, Theodore, who would sit in the dark, illuminated only by a candle, telling stories about life in the netherworld. Thelonius Monk was also often there, but his jazz was too advanced for me at that time. Right next door, I got to see Beckett's memorable play *Krapp's Last Tape* and Albee's *Zoo Story*.

Along Christopher Street, there was the stinging aroma of fresh-roasted dark coffee from the Italian coffee wholesaler on the left side, and on the right side, the powerful vapors from the Italian cheese shop with huge piles of three-foot round cheeses ripening in the sun. Just down the street was a Sicilian pizzeria, where the old mama in the black kerchief and papa in his cap would cut their delicious thick pizza into garlic-scented steaming squares covered with clams. This was my first taste of pizza of any description. I often felt as though I were in a foreign country. Even many of the street signs were in Italian. At several of the smaller intersections were green and white signs that said something like *passaggio pedonale,* which I assumed meant pedestrian crossing. And, of course, *Zoo Story* is set in Washington Square Park.

At the end of the block was the imposing brick women's federal penitentiary (now a library), with its twelve-foot-high brick walls enclosing the prison yard where we could hear the women and the guards yelling at each other. Once during the McCarthy years, a friend was rounded up during a demonstration and thrown into that establishment. The woman trustee bringing my good-looking young friend to her cell asked her, "Are you in for 'pros,' Honey?" My friend replied, "No. They say I'm a Red," at which the guard shrieked, "Oh my God," and pushed her roughly into the cell and slammed the door. (I'm reminded of the fact that today there are now 2.2 million Americans in our U.S. prisons—seven times the rate for Western Europe—the new poorhouse and asylum. And 60 percent of these people are incarcerated for nonviolent offenses related to using or selling drugs—mainly marijuana.) But back to Eighth Street and Sixth Avenue. One more block past the prison and I was home. Every day was something new.

From that same corner, I could take the D-train all the way to Coney Island. I loved the beach, the boardwalk, and the little drive-it-yourself bumping scooter cars. For a nickel, I could have complete control of an electrically driven car surrounded by a rubber bumper, and crash into anything I pleased. And I became skillful at hitting the back edge of hapless drivers, so as to spin them around, making them head against the flow of traffic—that's freedom for a twelve-year-old (boy). I'm sure the reason I particularly liked this game was because I knew that my poor vision would never allow me to drive a real car. Little did I imagine that one day I would be riding a full-sized motorcycle down Palo Alto's El Camino Real or through the rolling foothills.

On my way to school each day, I passed many beautiful fancy new cars, together with a vast preponderance of junkers. I invented a game, which statisticians would call "optimal stopping"—which, if you ask me, is really the game of life. I pretended that I could have any car I passed, but once passed, it was gone. Only one a day. How many cars do I have to sample in a block before I make a choice, since once a choice is made, that's it for the day? To carry the idea further, how many women does a high school graduate have to date before he has enough information about what's available, to sensibly get married? One is obviously too few, because at that age you don't even know who *you* are. And a thousand is beyond a man's normal life span. You get the idea. If a big jar is filled with folded up checks made out to you, and you can have any one that you are presently looking at, how many do you have to see before you get a useful measure of the sample space? A statistician might have you look at about a third of the checks, discarding each in turn. Then, keep the first one you see of the next two thirds that's larger than the largest you saw in the first third—realizing that there may be no such larger check, and you will be stuck with the last one (the Old Maid) in the bottom of the jar. On the other hand, *maturity* is "knowing when you have enough." If the first check is for $10 million, or the first car is a Bentley, most of us could stop right there. We don't care what else is in the jar. I believe it is important to avoid obsessively looking for something better, in order to avoid making a decision or choosing at all—then *you* become the Old Maid. It's been said before: Don't let your knowledge of the "best" prevent you from accepting the "good." The "best" is often a nonexistent abstraction or ideal that prevents us from making any decision at all. The purpose of this digression is to mention the all-too-common example of this decision process: How long should you continue doing something that is not working, before you give it up? Albert Einstein famously said: "The definition of insanity is doing the same thing over and over and expecting different results." My childhood game was an early exploration of this very important principle.

In life, we always have to make a decision with incomplete information as to which path we should take. In a business situation, even the copy boy could make a correct decision if all the essential information was at hand. In the old days the CEO who is paid the biggest bucks is the one who has developed an intuition that allows him to be correct with the *least possible* information. As for me, I have generally chosen to take the more adventurous path as Robert Frost suggests in "The Road Not Taken":

Two roads diverged in a yellow wood,
And sorry I could not travel both
And be one traveler, long I stood
And looked down one as far as I could
To where it bent in the undergrowth;

Then took the other, as just as fair,
And having perhaps the better claim,
Because it was grassy and wanted wear;
Though as for that the passing there
Had worn them really about the same,

And both that morning equally lay
In leaves no step had trodden black.
Oh, I kept the first for another day!
Yet knowing how way leads on to way,
I doubted if I should ever come back.

I shall be telling this with a sigh
Somewhere ages and ages hence:
Two roads diverged in a wood, and I—
I took the one less traveled by,
And that has made all the difference.

In the summer I would often walk with a friend all the way across the city and cross the Brooklyn Bridge to go swimming at the Olympic-size saltwater pool in the Hotel Saint George. The bridge seemed as though it were from another era—with rough wooden planking on the walkway and on either side, a spider web of steel cables cutting the bright blue sky and the Manhattan skyline into oblique little diamonds. Since there were very few pedestrians, it always seemed like a path into an unknown land—always the promise of something unexpected on the horizon. At the pool, as twelve-year-olds, we thought it was exciting that they had signs all over the pool area, proclaiming, "No Horseplay, No Petting," whatever that was. We had an idea—but then again, would they really put that up on the walls?

My other great love in Brooklyn was the Brooklyn Dodgers. I followed them religiously on the radio. The legendary team had class and style. Every player had a story, and the greatest story of all was Jackie Robinson, the first Negro player in the Major Leagues. The only baseball game I ever attended was at Ebbets Field in Brooklyn, in 1947, to celebrate Robinson's entry into the majors and his amazing base stealing—he could even steal home. I couldn't see much from the stands, but my thirteen-year-old sensibilities already were aware that this was an historic occasion. Now, sixty years later, my strongest memories of that afternoon in the sun are the brilliant green of the field, the already dilapidated stands, and the overpowering smell of hot dogs, mustard, and sauerkraut—probably oozing out of the ancient bleachers. I was an enthusiastic radio fan and for many years kept box score in a spiral bound notebook, recording every pitch, ball, strike, hit, and error, as the wonderfully humorous, folksy Red Barber broadcast them over the radio from his catbird seat high above Ebbets Field. To this day I can tell you the name and position of every man on that team. I even recorded Cookie Lavagetto's game-winning, pinch-hit double, to win a World Series game that season for the Dodgers in the ninth inning against the Yankees. I think he did it by breaking up a no-hitter. But the Dodgers did not win the series. They had to wait until 1955 for that happy day. Three years later they unaccountably moved to L.A. Probably the legendary and beloved players were getting too old to play. (And I got married, so I also had other things on my mind.)

In seventh grade, I still couldn't see the blackboards, but I was able to skip another grade at P.S. 3, because the Cleveland schools proved well ahead of the New York schools. Our rapid-advancement class spent a semester at the Museum of Natural History, making pottery, visiting the Hayden planetarium, and looking at its collection of fabulous gemstones, including the Star of India, in the dimly lit rooms padded with velvet from floor to ceiling. (That experience very likely explains why I have a Burmese sapphire ring on my finger as I write this.) But my real learning was in the many magic shops on Forty-second Street. And as a twelve-year-old I was allowed to go to Hubert's Flea Circus in the basement of the Penny Arcade. Upstairs at the shooting gallery, I could fire real 22s at moving tin ducks and candles, while downstairs were Albert/Alberta the hermaphrodite, the armless girl who could write with her toes, and JoJo, the strong man bending railroad spikes, which he would give to me to take home. There were also actual fleas pulling tiny chariots, and some carrying parasols. (Large magnifying glasses were available.) But best of all were tricks performed close up by the magician. No matter how closely I watched, I couldn't see which ball went into which cup, and how the ball disappeared.

I would then go upstairs to the office buildings and talk to real magicians at Holdens, D. Robbins, or Tannens, which were professional magic shops. I might even buy the trick, or a book explaining it. Hubert's is gone, although its neon sign and several of these same acts appear in the recent film *Fur,* which dramatizes the tragic life of the gifted and quirky New York photographer Diane Arbus, who shared my fascination with freaks. I call her life tragic, because she committed suicide the year before the 1972 opening of her one-woman show at the Museum of Modern Art.

Tannens has moved downtown, doubtless taking with it its great magic catalog. At twelve, I had the run of the city—quite a change from Cleveland. And I thank my courageous mother, Anne, for not keeping me tied to her apron strings. In spite of her continuing illness and depression, I experienced our family situation as basically hopeful and promising. My father was being promoted and money no longer appeared to be the problem it had been the years before in Cleveland. And I literally had this new and fantastic city at my doorstep.

I know my mother was particularly worried for me when I would go off Boy Scout camping with a hatchet swinging from my belt. What she should have been concerned about were the many older homosexuals trying to seduce little Russ in my Greenwich Village scout troop. "Be my friend, and I'll pull your dick," right in the basement of the Christopher Street Synagogue where we met. And of course, finding "friends" is very important for a twelve-year-old. Much more of this went on in Boy Scout camp, where the older patrol leader, Jules, would invite the little tenderfoot scouts to crawl into his big sleeping bag with him on bitterly cold nights in our large open tent. I remember that his member was so long that it could be seen hanging down to the edge of his official Boy Scout shorts. As a twelve-year-old, I did not find any of this very appetizing. In fact, it kind of grossed me out, as the kids would say today. But I must say the Boy Scouts were otherwise a very important and basically positive experience for me. It taught me, in spite of my handicapped state, great self-reliance, to cook meals, pitch a tent, chop wood, make a fire, send and receive Morse code, and even sew on buttons. Most important was the experience of dealing with the ragtag collection of local boys who would show up for meetings or go camping with us. I was a Scout for four years, earning a "first class" rank and becoming a "Junior Assistant Scout Master" in my troop.

But spontaneous open-hearted love for my fellows was pretty much drained out of me by my junior high school experiences with gangs and threats of violence. P.S. 3, located in a poor, tough, Italian Catholic neighborhood, was a dangerous place for a refined, nearsighted Jew in a nice wool coat. It wasn't exactly Northern Ireland, but it was the time and place where I had to learn to stand and fight with my fists to avoid being bullied by the

Italian punks in the schoolyard. It didn't help that, often on Sunday, along with other annoyingly precocious children, I would be on an NBC talk show called Youth Builders broadcast from Rockefeller Center with host Bill Slater, discussing such things as "What can be done about juvenile delinquency"—this, a decade before *West Side Story.*

As a fourteen-year-old, I used this unique platform to argue to the best of my ability in favor of National Health Insurance, just because I felt it was the right thing to do. The opponents were already calling it socialized medicine. Today, sixty years later, the absence of national healthcare is a major distortion in our country. As I am sure you are aware, we are the only industrialized nation in the world that does not provide healthcare for its people. The situation is the most common cause of U.S. labor strife, and it raises the cost of U.S. cars as compared with Toyota, for example. Japanese health costs are borne by the government instead of the company. This discrepancy is the single most important reason that Toyota is profitable and GM is not.

My parents often had parties at our Eighth Street apartment in the Village. I was frequently asked to show off some of my latest magic tricks. (Even today kids love magic. I know two quite competent twelve- or thirteen-year-old aspiring magicians. All kids love to fool adults.) The reason for the magic this night was that a special guest was Fred Dannay, one of my father's authors, known to the world as the great mystery-story writer and master detective, Ellery Queen. I remember my mother had made a pilgrimage to the Cake Master bakery to bring home a special German walnut cake with exceptionally delicious bittersweet chocolate frosting, which I always saved for last to eat. I still remember the little cake topped with walnut halves and exuding its pungent chocolaty aroma. After performing my magic tricks, I went to bed around ten o'clock and then remembered that I had Scouts the next night, back at the *shule.* So, I thought this would be a perfect time to practice Morse code, on which I would be examined the next day for my First Class Scout achievement badge. As I lay in bed in my darkened third-floor bedroom facing Eighth Street, I used my little flashlight to send myself messages on the wall at the foot of my bed. I'll never forget that within five minutes there was a pounding at the door of our apartment. Two policemen were demanding to know who was in the room in the front of the apartment. The big cops walked right into the living room, past Ellery Queen, as my mother explained to the officers that it was just her little boy who was asleep in bed. It was the S.O.S. signals that really did the trick.

Another near-magical event that is still clear in my mind also occurred at home. My mother had been the original press agent of the fan dancer Sally Rand (a tale which I will share more fully later). Sally attended a New Year's party at our home, and after midnight she stayed on with my parents to talk about old times in Chicago. She sat on the couch—very glamorous in a black satin outfit with sequins and beautiful long blond hair. I loved it! As she settled back on the comfy sofa in front of a large wall mirror, saying, "Do you mind if I get comfortable?" she suddenly reached up and pulled off her hair, apparently a blond wig, revealing a short dark-brown crew cut! I was stunned—utterly unprepared for such a thing. I still remember, sixty years later, how she explained that the wig was "the greatest thing since sliced bread," because she didn't have to deal with long hair anymore. I thought it was a dirty trick. From my face-blind point of view, it's as though she had just pulled off her head. The thing that made her who she was for me was the great pile of golden hair.

My father was now editor-in-chief at G. P. Putnam in New York and the distinguished publisher of the novel *The Godfather,* written by his Chicago pal Mario Puzo. My father famously gave Puzo a $5,000 advance to write the book based only on his recitation of the plot, without a word yet written down. Father later framed the vituperative and now valuable letter he received from Walter Minton, the owner of the firm, who openly chastised him for giving away the company's money without getting an outline and a first chapter. We all know the successful result of my father's folly. About writing, in his autobiography *Indecent Pleasures,* he tells the prospective author, "There is no such thing as good writing. There is only good re-writing." The obvious corollary is, "There is no publishable first draft." Every editor would probably agree with this. Hemingway and Faulkner probably would not.

A nonobservant Jew, my father felt strongly that most of the problems and suffering in the world were caused by organized religion, so I did not have a Bar Mitzvah. But I didn't miss out on much else in my New York youth.

My father and mother took me, their only child, to plays and concerts to see many of the world's greatest musicians including Toscanini, Horowitz, Heifetz, Myra Hess, Walter Gieseking, and others. We usually had wonderful seats because of my father's friendship with Louis Biancolli, the music critic of the *New York Times.* Lucky for me, he didn't like to sit in the audience, but rather preferred to stroll in the back of the auditorium, making his pair of seats available to my family. I saw Toscanini's electrifying last performance, conducting with the NBC Symphony at Carnegie Hall. And, after his retirement at eighty-seven, I saw the next performance with no conductor—only a red light at the podium and high bowing by the first violin. I also heard the thrilling, dazzling, peerless Walter Gieseking playing a Mozart piano concerto at Carnegie Hall, looking to me like a German banker sitting at the piano straight and crisply sorting his letters, while outside on Fifty-seventh Street in the snow, a crowd of Jewish war veterans picketed his alleged Nazi connections. My father assured me that Gieseking was clean, which was later substantiated.

Once, after the opera, I had an opportunity to walk onto the great stage of the Metropolitan Opera following a performance of *Don Giovanni*. I felt as if it were still vibrating from the thrilling final scene. Much better than sleeping through most of *Parsifal*, which I had done the previous week. On another occasion, I experienced the magical heart-opening performances of the red-headed countertenor Russell Oberlin and the white-haired albino harpsichord genius Paul Maynard playing Purcell *(Come Ye Sons of Art)* at Town Hall. What a thrill for a teenager! (There was probably a little erotic component as well. I think countertenors always have a peculiar androgynous aspect—especially tall red-headed ones like Oberlin.) Many years later, as it turned out, Maynard married one of my college girlfriends, who was also a gifted musician. Unfortunately for me, I was not . . . much as I love music.

From my father's great friend George Jean Nathan, the very distinguished theater critic for the *New York Times,* our family would occasionally receive theater tickets to Broadway opening nights. I particularly remember *Flower Drum Song, Raisin in the Sun,* and *Waiting for Godot. Godot,* by Samuel Beckett, was probably my greatest and most memorable theater-going experience—with a breathtaking, bravura performance by Alvin Epstein as Lucky the slave, carrying a heavy suitcase and held on a leash around his neck by his blind master. More than fifty years later, it is still clear in my mind. In what must be a seven- or eight-minute show-stopping nonsense monologue, Lucky explains to the two tramps, Didi and Gogo, that they already have everything they could possible want, which is *nothing*. In the four-person play, the two tramps are waiting for Godot (God), who never comes and *will* never come, because he is always here. A child enters in Act Two to announce that "M. Godot will not be coming today." It's a play about the suffering caused by our unworkable dualistic view of a nondual world. For me, Godot was an utterly new, original, and unforgettable theatrical experience, with resonance even today.

The other memorable aspect of first night theater was going to Sardi's Times Square restaurant with the producers after the play (not *Godot*), to wait for the *New York Times* critics to write their reviews, which would come out around midnight. On more than one occasion, I remember seeing an exceptionally stupid, pointless, and badly acted play and wondering how it ever got to Broadway. For some reason, somebody had agreed to put up half-a-million dollars to mount such plays, that even a teenager could recognize as an absurdity. I was deeply puzzled and wanted to know why someone associated with the play wouldn't tell the producer that his play didn't make any sense and would be an immediate flop. This was an introduction to the teaching that "The Emperor has no clothes," and nobody will tell. My father explained to me that everyone associated with the play's production was making money from it as long as it lasted and therefore would never tell the truth about its chances on Broadway. "After all, even exceptionally stupid plays *have* made it before." (*Springtime for Hitler,* the play within a play in Mel Brooks's *The Producers,* would be an example of such stupidity.) This was probably one of my first moments of explicitly questioning the reality right in front of me, Sally Rand notwithstanding.

In high school, I was introduced to ESP by my classmate Robert Rosenthal, who eventually became a distinguished Harvard psychology professor. He went on to discover what's now called the Pygmalion Effect—the situation where psychology experimenters almost invariably create a covert self-fulfilling prophecy in the unconsciously biased way they conduct their experiments. For example, when San Francisco elementary school teachers were told that *certain* of their students (who were randomly selected) were supposed to be "late bloomers," the teachers subconsciously treated these kids with such positive affirmation that by the end of the school year, their performance in the classroom excelled and their objectively measured IQs were found to have significantly increased.

In our Newtown high school biology class, Rosenthal introduced us to J. B. Rhine's ESP test cards: circle, square, star, cross, and wavy lines—testing for ESP in the classroom. At age fourteen, I was hooked. I was enrolled at Newtown because my junior high school guidance counselor thought that because of my poor vision, I would be a good candidate for an agricultural high school. In fact, he thought I might make a good farmer. (In truth, I still can't tell a plant from a weed.) This was my sixth school because of all my family's moving. No wonder I didn't have many friends. It's also probably the reason I remained emotionally close to my mother, since she was the only fixed point in my life. From childhood, she would discuss with me what she was planning to wear in the evening, and whether I thought the colors went well together. At eight, she would still parade back and forth in front of me in her silk slip while dressing and introduce me to the secret world of differentiating fuchsia from mauve, and when to wear them.

As a result of Robert Rosenthal's input, I have now been doing psychic stuff since 1948—the year when I combined my stage magic interest with ESP research. I am sure that Prof. Rosenthal would be surprised—shocked—to learn that all my remote viewing research stemmed from his little ESP test almost sixty years ago. In fact, he was—when I ran into him at a recent conference at the University of British Columbia. It was my introduction to what I now think of as the Buddhists' Right Mindfulness—or spaciousness. This is what the eighth-century Buddhist master Padmasambhava called seeing with the clear light of naked awareness, rather than being hooked by our embellished passions. So by the end of high school I was reading the *Journal of the American Society for Psychical Research,* whose offices were conveniently located in New York City. It became totally clear to me from my reading that some people, at least, could expand their awareness and experience what was happening far away, or even in the future. We simply misapprehend the nature of the space and time in which we live. That's why we must question reality. The problem is that we are conditioned and brainwashed by the cult we belong to, which as I mentioned before is called society. It seems to me that we can demonstrate more courage by singing and dancing in freedom, rather than marching under orders imposed from without. An examined life allows you to notice that you are marching when you could be dancing—to notice that your life is free, and not contingent on others.

Of course, Buddhists don't often talk about ESP. They describe enlightenment as *moving your attention* from the conditioned awareness of the ego, rigidity, and self centeredness to naked awareness and the spaciousness of flexibility, joy, and love. In particular, enlightenment is the result of seeing the world without the lens of the ego. You have to let go of the idea that "I want" to sustain this experience. Who is this "I" after all? That's what Ramana Maharshi kept asking.

Only rarely does a really forthcoming book appear like *Buddhist Masters of Enchantment,* which describes metaphysical details including pictures of levitating yogis, such as the famous seventeenth-century "Flying Catholic Friar," Saint Joseph of Cupertino, who was reported to have levitated many times above his congregation. Of course, they don't have photos, but I have seen many woodblock prints of the period showing him airborne.

By my college days, I was doing stage magic, meditating, and beginning to experience some of this freedom. At sixteen, I was in my first year at Queens College, and playing bridge was by far my main interest. This was when I began to notice that it was always the older girls who took an interest in this immature sixteen-year-old—even if only for a bridge partner. We were still living in Jackson Heights in Queens, where my parents had moved to be close to my agricultural high school. But there was no good public transportation to Queens College. The result was that I would ride my new three-speed Raleigh bicycle, even though the route required a couple of miles along the Grand Central Parkway. Sometimes, in winter I would ride through the slush and snow on the Parkway which at least would slow down the cars. I remember slipping and sliding, peddling through the gloom and the falling snow, feeling that this is a very crazy thing to be doing. But we all know that sixteen-year-olds are immortal. I eventually found some connecting busses.

One day, my father asked me to do a little magic show for an art opening of his friend, the great watercolorist and war correspondent John Groth. I did some tricks for twenty minutes or so in Groth's brightly lit Madison Avenue gallery, with the arty crowd standing around drinking champagne from long-stemmed goblets. Often when I was standing on the stage with lights shining in my eyes, I would psychically pick up information about the trick I was doing, beyond what the trickery made available. (Even professional magicians who hate ESP, like Melbourne Christopher, agree that they sometimes get to supplement their tricks with a little flash of psychic information—like what a person's house or bedroom looks like. I have seen the famous psychic Peter Hurkos do exactly this in a large group ESP demonstration that I had organized for local friends and skeptics.) When I finished my act, John asked me to pull raffle tickets for two of his paintings out of a big glass bowl. He stirred them up and handed me the globe. The first one I pulled out was my father's ticket. There was some tittering, but people thought that was a pretty good trick, even though it was in fact pure chance. The second ticket I pulled out was my own. No one was amused, and I didn't get to keep the painting. This is the kind of *acausal synchronicity* that makes one feel that he's on a roll. But I had to pull a third ticket. Groth's beautiful first painting of GIs and Dutch orphan children is still on the wall of my stepmother Roslyn's art-filled penthouse apartment in the Village. Roslyn and my father were married for the better part of three decades after my mother died in 1965. She was the literary agent for my first books—along with those of Jackie Kennedy and many other notables.

All through school I had been reading only large-print books or using a powerful hand magnifier. Then, in my last year of high school I had my first encounter with a physics class. I knew I needed help . . . and soon realized that I would be able to read if I had the magnifier as part of my glasses. I persuaded an optometrist to give me an unheard-of six diopters of magnification in my bifocals, and that entirely solved my reading problem! Today I have eight diopters which is even better. Doctors don't usually like to give young people that much magnification. Tragically, they want to save it for later in life. This under-prescription particularly affects *albinos* like myself who are lacking retinal pigmentation and consequently don't have any acute central (foveal) vision. Older people with diabetic retinopathy have the same problem. It's shocking to know that optometrists are not taught the difference between a focusing problem (accommodation) such as nearsightedness (which I don't have) or farsightedness, and a resolution problem (*number* of pixels per square centimeters resolved) such as I do have to deal with.

Doctors are still publishing technical papers in medical journals erroneously stating that albinos cannot be corrected for reading. Even when I agreed to be examined by one such researcher at the NIH in Washington a few years ago, they didn't get it. They noticed that with my fancy specs, I could read at full speed (probably better than average). But they weren't interested in such details, because I was only a patient in a hospital gown. They were interested only in the genetic basis of my poor vision—called Hermansky-Pudlak Syndrome, HPS, found especially in Ashkenazi (Eastern European) Jews and Puerto Ricans. After all the physical exams of my body, eyes, blood, and endurance, they concluded that I was indeed one of the rare HPS cohorts who *did* have defective vision and serious blood coagulation problems (that almost killed me twice as a child), but did not have the lung disease which is the most deadly part of this annoying inherited problem. They also found that none of my forebears were carriers, nor were my children affected. So, I must have just been hit by an errant cosmic ray. In fact, my parents and children have all had exceptionally good vision. So, go figure.

Just before sending me home, the NIH geneticist in charge of my evaluation asked me if I would mind taking off all my clothes and sitting naked on a gurney cart, so that his class of first-year medical residents could take a look a me! I was, of course, grateful for the thorough weeklong medical work-up they had given me at government expense, but what sixty-year-old wants to be stared at by a bunch of punky medical students—for no personal benefit? I then had the insight that of course I would let them look at me, for after all, "it's only a body." It was actually quite liberating—a flash of freedom—to sit on a cold steel cart as just a skinny old man with a colostomy and no clothes, and not to care at all—totally understanding that this whole little drama had nothing to do with me. It reminded me of the aging raging King Lear (no delusions of grandeur here; he was mad after all), able to take off not only his crown, but all his clothes as well—"Expose thyself to feel what wretches feel." Some of us are just slow learners. I think we can eliminate a lot of our suffering if we bear that in mind. I notice that Nora Ephron's book, *I Feel Bad about My Neck,* has been on the *New York Times* bestseller list for thirty-three weeks.

So back in that sixteenth year, 1950, at least I could read—everything. I graduated and was finally finished with secondary education. What a relief. I began to devour science fiction, which was in its heyday. I card-indexed hundreds of stories by title and author, and loved the *Foundation* trilogy of Isaac Asimov. He created the great intergalactic semanticist Salvor Hardin, who taught planetary governments the fact of life that "Nothing has to be true. A thing just has to *seem* true." With the corollary that "A lie that's ashamed of itself cannot succeed." These are the fundamental principles of magic and illusion, as well as government. (Fifty years later, these ideas seem to be the foundation of the present administration that never admits an error, no matter how glaring, stupid, or obtuse. Hurricane Katrina comes to mind, with the president's ringing endorsement of the obvious incompetence of his buddy Michael Brown, "You're doin' a-heck-of-a-job, Brownie." The nation stood slack-mouthed with stupefaction. At least some of us did.) You could say that the president is "suffering from a serious irony deficiency." In fact we are all suffering from this illness, when we fail to laugh out loud at politicians who say on television, "I must have misspoken," when they are caught in a baldfaced lie. Our Attorney General, Alberto Gonzales, made use of this absurd euphemism too many times to count in his testimony before the Senate Oversight Committee investigating his firing of eight prosecutors. Finally, he was even too absurd for the president.

I must say more here about my mother, Anne Jesselson Targ—an attractive, irrepressible press agent and reporter for the *Chicago Herald American* in 1933. That was the year my parents met, and were married ten days later. She was tall and very slim, with striking large luminous brown eyes. The dark-eyed energetic reporter and the handsome bookseller, both twenty-six, made a romantic couple in contemporary photos.

My parents, Anne and William Targ, in 1933 at my father's first book shop on Clark Street in Chicago.

They were married at Chicago's City Hall, and although each had a brother and a sister, none of them were in attendance at the marriage ceremony. My parents were far more intelligent and accomplished than their sibs and were not very close to them. My mother was the oldest of three, and my father was in the middle. Judgment was the order of the day, and as a result I rarely saw any of my aunts or uncles. My mother's brother Alfred joined the U.S. Marines, with the Japanese attack on Pearl Harbor. After the war he settled in Norfolk, Virginia, where he married a decidedly non-Jewish Virginia belle named Shirley and was never heard from again. After Alfred died, I learned from a brief meeting with his niece Jennifer that he had been active in his newly adopted church and had created a successful boat-building business there. We got together when I was working with NASA in Hampton, Virginia.

My father's brother Irving was a pharmacist who owned a drugstore on Chicago's West Side. He would always generously make me a cherry Coke as I sat at the marble soda fountain whenever we visited his shop. His son Harry became a writer, teacher, and effective Chicago agitator for liberal and labor-related causes. Harry's wife Marlene Targ Brill is a successful writer of children's books and kindly helped me collect family information for this book. So, the Targs seem to have the writing gene.

But things were not so easy for my mother, even from the start. Her mother Tilly had become a Christian Scientist and was very intelligently concerned about the quality of food she was finding on the shelves of the grocery store. I remember her in the early 1940s arguing that white bread and oleomargarine weren't actually food. At that time she introduced me to the nutrition broadcaster Carlton Fredricks. On the Christian Scientist side, many Jews are very fearful of anything that begins with "Christian." (It took me years to learn not to cringe when my nice Unity Church minister would talk about Christ. Finally, everything became okay for me one Ash Wednesday, when he told us about "the desert meditations of Rabbi Jesus.")

As a result of his mother's wishes—she resented my mother—my father would go alone to Friday night *Shabbos* (Sabbath) dinners at his mother Esther's house, leaving his new bride home crying and wondering what she had gotten into. She was rightfully resentful of this abandonment even a decade later—which is how I heard about it. Though both Anne's parents were Jewish, my orthodox grandma Esther Targ thought of her as a Shiksa, which is a highly pejorative term for a non-Jewish woman—in spite of the fact that many Jews allege that it's simply a neutral and descriptive term. But it is a term connoting "other"—not one of us. My mother did not receive a wedding gift from the elder Targs until her tenth anniversary, because they didn't want to waste a beautiful set of sterling silver on a marriage that might not last! As they say in more liberal Jewish families, "There's no ox like an orthodox." As a result of all this confused feeling, I was circumcised by the very elderly orthodox rabbi of my grandparents and came very close to bleeding to death. This made for further hard feelings on the part of my mother, who had wanted an actual doctor, rather than a *mohel,* to do the job. A surgeon had to be called to sew me up. No one knew then that I have a blood coagulation defect. (I had a second very close brush with death when my tonsils were inexpertly removed when I was five. I recall our family doctor telling my mother that "It's like trying to sew up scrambled eggs," as I was hemorrhaging in the hospital room. He even gave me his little switchblade knife to play with, since he thought I was about to bleed to death anyway. This kindled a lifelong interest in these nifty illegal items.)

Part of my mother's problem with acceptance by the Targ family was that my maternal grandfather Ben Jesselson's parents came from Germany, and Tilly's came from England. Tilly's father was a barrister named Isaac Woolf, with a thin face and piercing dark eyes—definitely not from the *shtetl* (ghetto). At the poignant moment of the circumcision, my clueless mother famously confused two very similar-sounding Yiddish words, one of which means congratulations, while the other, directed toward her mother-in-law, unfortunately means "the evil eye be upon you!" In the world of ESP, we would call that "psi missing"—using your psychic ability to find the worst possible thing to say. Adding in her desire for a family Christmas tree, my mother's fate was sealed.

Mother frequently told me that she was also very anxious about my father's relationship with two wealthy Chicago society women who bought large numbers of rare and valuable books from him and greatly helped to support his little book store. For some unknown reason, he often had to be gone in the evening to personally deliver the books to their downtown apartments. Although I was only eight at the time, I sensed that this had something to do with romance, whatever that was—something about his being out rather than at home. We will never know if my mother's concern had any basis—at least I won't. My mother was quite relieved when we finally left Chicago for our new home in Cleveland. Although this would also have its problems.

One of my earliest memories is standing on my mother's lap as a two-year-old and looking directly into her limpid and unconditionally loving dark eyes. I distinctly remember her telling me that I would soon be too big to do this anymore. I mention my mother again in these passages because the afore-described Sally Rand now reappears to beautifully illustrate Asimov's point about truth. Sally was a high school classmate of my mother's. As a struggling dancer, she told my mom that she would do anything to finally get a break. And Anne said, "I can help you do that." So she arranged for the former Helen Gould to permanently become the more sprightly Sally Rand. And Sally agreed to my mother's plan for her to appear as Lady Godiva at the forthcoming Art Students League Ball at the Edgewater Beach Hotel. Naturally, Lady Godiva (like her tenth-century namesake) would make her appearance by riding down Michigan Boulevard wearing only a long blond wig on a rented white horse—right into the ballroom, or as far as she could get. Of course, as planned, Sally was arrested. Her intrepid press agent—my mother—blithely told all the papers that Sally would be opening the next day as a fan dancer at *The Streets of Paris* at the Chicago World's Fair, known as the Century of Progress.

The following day, I am told that there were ten thousand people waiting in line at *The Streets of Paris*. Sally was sprung from jail, and her career was made. *Nothing has to be true, it just has to seem true.* The whole event was created out of my mother's desire, energy, and intentionality. That was my mother at her best. Unfortunately this great imagination and energy became stifled after her marriage. She was obviously way ahead of her time and became a victim of society's limited expectations for women.

Sally Rand, famous U.S. fan dancer in the 1930s and '40s, as my mother manifested her at the Chicago World's Fair. (Sally Rand publicity photo reprinted with permission of El Campanil Theatre, Antioch, Calif.)

Lady Godiva was the wife of the Earl of Mercia (968–1057), shown here in an 1897 painting by John Collier, protesting the poverty of her husband's serfs.

In the process of moving from Chicago to Cleveland, we somehow became very financially indebted to my father's new company, World Publishing. (I owe my soul to the Company store.) My father dealt with this by giving my mother only two dollars a day for groceries. So, then she had to walk to the store every day with her little shopping cart. But she was always diligent about putting on her makeup first thing in the morning. I remember she would say, "I can't go out to meet people until I've put my face on." I suppose many women of that time used the same expression. (Now, of course most women are freed from the necessity, as well as the odd locution.) In this new city, she felt isolated, lonely, and depressed—and as I came to realize, was nauseated every morning. This continued when we moved to New York three years later. So this humorous, pithy, highly literate woman, always trailing the flowery fragrance of Arpege, was now trapped at home with her reporter's Remington portable typewriter in our little apartment on Eighth Street, because my father, now a New York editor, wouldn't let his wife be seen to work for money. Having been poor in the Polish ghetto on Chicago's West Side, he didn't want to appear poor now that he was editor-in-chief, and later vice president, of a major publishing company.

Of course, they were both trapped. He—by his conditioning and ideas of form—distancing himself from his weak and ineffectual tailor father and his powerful and successful mother, just as my own mother was trapped by his constraints upon her. One doesn't rise from the ghetto to become editor-in-chief by accident. My father had a very strong will and what we call today well-focused intentionality. For example, on his sixtieth birthday, he decided to give up smoking, which had been a significant part of his life since the age of eleven. He was always surrounded by a cloud of smoke, from cigarettes, imported Cuban cigars, or his Meerschaum pipes. Then one day he gave it up—threw out the leather-covered humidor and gave away his beautiful carved pipes—and that was it for the rest of his life.

William Targ, 1975

However, my mother had a far-ranging correspondence, even including Tennessee Williams, and did some freelance publicity for craftsmen in the Village. But she could be paid only in jewelry or handbags. As her depression worsened, she was hospitalized in 1955 at Rockland State Hospital in Orangeburg, New York, and intermittently received shock treatments. Eventually the now famous Dr. Nathan Kline gave her Thorazine—which did her in. Electroshock treatment (ECT) was widely used in the 1950s as an experimental treatment to make depressed and anxious housewives behave more docilely. At this same time Kline was working for Sid Gottlieb and teaching the CIA how to use

ECT in their infamous MK-ULTRA program (the code name for a CIA mind-control research program that began in 1950) to experimentally remove the memories of willing and unwilling subjects. More about Dr. Gottlieb later.

Mother became more and more listless. Finally my once tee-totalling mother reached out to end her pain with a tumbler of my father's best scotch. She died five days later, February 1965, at fifty-seven, of kidney failure (from alcohol and Thorazine) at St. Vincent's Hospital in her beloved Greenwich Village. My father didn't really believe in psychiatry, and for some reason in his memoir, *Indecent Pleasures*, said that my mother's "enemy was schizophrenia." This is utterly untrue—she was brilliant, funny, and *depressed*—trapped without the tools to make a life for herself. She was definitely not delusional. Her very best friend, Lucy Freeman, the author of *Fight against Fear, Killers of the Mind*, and many other books, was of much more help to her than her psychiatrists—especially Dr. Kline.

It's a great loss to my children that they never got to know their smart and loving grandmother. I think of my mother as standing in a long line of intelligent, emotional, and terribly desperate housewives who are married to men who have other, more important things on their mind. Anna Karenina, Emma Bovary, and my mother all ended their lives because they were unable to find any sustenance inside or outside the relationship in which they were trapped. These tragic deaths show the terrible danger of what *A Course in Miracles* calls "special relationships," in which you rely on your partner to define and complete you. And it emphasizes the importance of being part of some kind of sustaining *spiritual community*. An investment club will not meet this requirement. The *Course* is a teaching that was scribed or channeled by Prof. Helen Schuckman, a clinical psychology professor at Columbia-Presbyterian Hospital in New York. It is a teaching that has inspired millions of people worldwide and can be thought of as the *Vedanta* as taught by Jesus. It teaches us to "Look not for love, but rather look for the barriers we have created against the experience of love"—which is who we are.

Anne Jesselson Targ, 1950

As I reflect on my experience of this particular time in my life, I have to confess that almost every man or woman I know who grew up in the 1940s shares with me a distant father and a depressed mother. It's as though we all had the same parents. When my mother died, I returned to New York from my home in California to be with my father. It was then that I sadly realized for the first time that although my father had many hundreds of famous acquaintances he had no close friends. He was famously congenial, but evidently not very empathetic. At least, that's how I see it now. I have no wish to portray my father in an unfavorable light. I see him as trapped in his story, just as most people are. When you come to believe that *who you are* is "head of the firm," you're screwed, in my opinion.

CHAPTER THREE

The Smartest Guys in the Room

Unfortunately, I was not one of them, but I didn't know it at the time. The room we're in is a working-class living room in a Bronx apartment house. We are four college students who have been friends for years. And on most Saturday nights, three of us keep company with the fourth who babysits to earn his lunch money. Of the four, I regret to say I was a relatively undistinguished college student. I studied physics, math, psychology, and philosophy at Queens College, in New York. The others were students at Columbia and City College. I didn't have many friends at Queens because I still didn't recognize people very well, unless they had hair that was bright red, or long and blond, or at least long. That worked for me, as it apparently does for most face-blind people.

But I also didn't recognize written foreign language words, a liability which caused me to almost be thrown out of college. I simply couldn't learn either French, or especially German, even after retaking the classes. Finally I convinced the Dean of Students to let me substitute psychology for the language requirement, and take that as an additional minor subject along with physics and math. My grades were good enough to later get me into Columbia University to study graduate physics. Columbia would prove to be one of my really bad life choices. The subject was right, but it was a bad choice of schools for several reasons, including my poor physics preparation at Queens. For example, in college we were never taught vector calculus, which is critically important to graduate physics. I don't know what they could have been thinking to leave that out of the curriculum.

In spite of these problems, as well as shyness, poor vision, no girlfriend, etc., I was rarely depressed. I was thrilled and energized with the excitement of learning. New York is so stimulating that if you have a little money and reasonably good mental and physical health there is always something to do. If you want to study ESP there is the American Society of Psychical Research. If you are interested in modern films there is Cinema 16, showing *avant-garde* films every week. I eventually had many good friends in New York, and later when I arrived friendless in London, I soon found a circle of friends, just by showing up and talking to people—even though I would show up a little shy and confused. I imagine that energy and an insatiable broad curiosity are pathways to good mental health. Focusing in on one's problems, like squaring the circle, will not win you many friends or get you out of your apartment. I do not claim my lack of depression as evidence of my good character; I consider it, rather, as a genetic gift—like being tall. I have had more than my share of depressing things occur in my life. But from observing my own friends, family, and acquaintances—both happy and depressed—I have formed the conviction that people are born that way, with or without a tendency for depression.

One lovely poetic girlfriend, Marcia, had been depressed and in therapy since childhood—in spite of being an excellent student at Brooklyn College and brought up as a beloved child in a nice, supportive Jewish home in Brooklyn. She and I would often walk along the broad Coney Island boardwalk, which was not far from her home. The wintertime was especially romantic. I remember one crisp night we had the whole park to ourselves. All the concessions were closed, and the unobstructed brilliant moon sparkled on the ocean waves and the ice-crusted boardwalk. And it lit up the sandy beach, making it look surprisingly like snow. It was a good time for cuddling since she was always cold, and I was rarely so. (I do get cold of course, but I am usually the last one.) The next day we went to a Pete Seeger concert at Cooper Union in the Village, where he sang to us that "Kisses Are Sweeter than Wine." I thought he had the right idea, but as usual Marcia was noncommittal. She was a bit like having Virginia Woolf for a girl-friend. Today depression is no longer seen as a kind of character defect, but rather a mixture of genetic predisposition and life's stresses. For example, scientists think a deficiency in serotonin, a neurotransmitter, can cause the sleep problems and anxiety associated with depression. Likewise, a decreased amount of norepinephrine, which regulates alertness and arousal, can contribute to fatigue and depressed moods. Scientists today believe that exogenous circumstances have little to do with whether a person will or will not be depressed. In my life experience, I am convinced that the amount of money—or beauty—a person has is only weakly related to their suicidal feelings—from the richest to the poorest. Either can feel hopeless and despondent.

Meanwhile, the smartest guys in any room were my best friends Harry, Gary, and Menasha. I played chess and bridge with these pals. They introduced me to the heady world of General Semantics and the Logical Positivists of the Vienna Circle: A. J. Ayer's *Language, Truth, and Logic* made a huge impression on me, as did the logical genius Ludwig Wittgenstein's *Tractatus Logico-Philosophicus*. We studied it like the Bible, starting with, "The world is all that is the case," and ending with, "Whereof one cannot speak, thereof one must be silent." So too were we in the thrall of the inventor of General Semantics, Alfred Korzybski, who wrote *Science and Sanity*—"Don't confuse the map with the territory." (He emphasized that we should be aware of the dynamic, changeable nature of things, though their labels or names remain the same.) It was all about questioning reality and so much more. All these great writers wanted to know what, if anything, was real, and how could we know it. It was empowering to learn convincingly from Ayer that "existence is not an attribute," and it is therefore senseless—hopeless even—to consider whether God *exists,* or not. However, infinite love and infinite vengeance are not properties that interest Logical Positivists, because neither can be demonstrated nor falsified. These authors all consider such ideas as "non-sense" data. Of course, logical positivists are not atheists either. If millions of people are having profound transcendent experiences of the Divine that change their lives, it would be absurd to argue that there are no such experiences.

The ringleader of Logical Positivism was Moritz Schlick, who was a philosophy professor at the University of Vienna and the founder of the famous Vienna Circle, which was the fount of this movement. Ludwig Wittgenstein and Kurt Gödel were revered members of the weekly café gathering. Schlick was a pioneering advocate of the idea that any proposition must be verifiable, if it is to be considered meaningful, rather than nonsense. One consequence of this is that "free will" is a non-starter, since it can be neither verified nor falsified. With the rise of Nazism in Germany and Austria, many of the Vienna Circle's members left for America and the United Kingdom. Schlick, however, stayed on at the University of Vienna. On June 22, 1936, Schlick was ascending the steps of the university for a class when he was confronted by a former student who found this teaching extremely disturbing. The student drew a pistol and shot Schlick in the chest. He died very soon afterward. The student was tried and sentenced, but he became a *cause célèbre* for the growing anti-Jewish sentiments in the city. (That Schlick was not Jewish tended to be overlooked.) The student was paroled shortly afterward and became a member of the Austrian Nazi Party. Vienna was a city, like Athens, that took its philosophy very seriously.

Korzybski also taught the importance of what he called "time binding," which is the unique ability that humans have to pass information from generation to generation. As individuals become more awakened to our destiny as a species, the *evolution of consciousness* can be continued and increased. For example, John the Baptist awakened Jesus to his true nature as *One* with the Divine. Ramana Maharshi awakened the great *advaita* teacher Sri H. W. Poonja to awareness of his own powerful, loving self. His student, and my teacher, Gangaji, has awakened thousands to their own flow of loving awareness by generously sharing and demonstrating her loving nature—her love beam—which often sends open-hearted people to the floor, overcome with tears and laughter on finally discovering who they really are.

But in New York, our crowd had not caught on to any of this yet. Our favorite place to seek truth was the Stage Delicatessen on Seventh Avenue, sitting in the corner window over fat corned beef sandwiches. Today, I still choose the corner window, when I can get it. (After all, the Stage is now a publicly held company!) When we would pull open the doors on a frosty winter evening, we would be greeted with the symphonic and intoxicating smells of pastrami, caramelized onions, and chopped liver blowing onto the street from the overheated restaurant.

The issue that concerned us there, as three budding physicists and a mathematician, was to try and make sense of a world that clearly demonstrated quantum mechanics, relativity, and ESP. We were all well acquainted with the evidence. One of the things that troubled us was that if there is such good data for mind-to-mind telepathic connections, for example, why don't we see more of it? That was our main metaphysical concern. Of course, one of the reasons we don't see more ESP in our society is because it is forbidden. If it weren't for the Stage Delicatessen, there probably wouldn't have been a remote viewing program at SRI twenty years later!

On the mundane side, Menasha preferred chopped liver, tomato, and onion with his corned beef, while my favorite was a tongue sandwich with coleslaw and Russian dressing on the sandwich. What Harry ate is lost to the mists of time—but whenever he wasn't babysitting he was my regular duplicate bridge partner. We were very successful in these master-point tournaments and quite telepathic together, occasionally causing an opponent to call the tournament director to complain about "psychic bidding," when we would bid cards we didn't have, to prevent our opponents from reaching their proper contract. Some people have no sense of humor.

In real life Harry was Harrison Roth, round-faced with blue eyes, a ready smile, and thinning hair even at twenty. He is today credited with the popularization of option trading on the New York Stock Exchange. His widowed mother was desperately poor, but nonetheless Harry was a whiz at math. I remember his charming and unassuming mother regularly offering us tea and "salt-free Saltines." For years, we spent our Saturday nights playing chess and cards, working on the riddles of the universe, and babysitting his neighbor's kids, at a time when any normal college student was exploring the mysteries of women.

Menasha, Gary, and I wanted to be physicists, Harry the mathematician wanted to be rich. So, three of us went to graduate school, and Harry went to Wall Street where the money is. In later years Harry liked to tell how at twenty he got his start on Wall Street. He went to lower Manhattan from his home in the Bronx, walked into a small securities firm, and asked what a kid who liked math might do for a living. The rest is, as they say, history. "Since 1985 to Harry's death, every new trader on the floor of the Chicago Board of Options Exchange had taken a class taught by Mr. Roth," according to an exchange vice-president quoted in Harry's 1997 obituary.

I didn't have thoughts about being rich, but I definitely didn't want to be poor either. I had a taste of what that might feel like when we lived in Cleveland. We didn't miss any meals, but money was a constant worry—especially for my mother, who was always the largest figure in my life. Although I was a good student, I was aware, even as a child, that I was severely limited in what I could do to support myself as an adult—so I better pay attention in class. I knew I was a hothouse plant, who would never see well enough to do any of the low-skilled jobs like being a grocery store checker, taxi driver, or a carpenter in the building trades. I'd also never be a shortstop. So, poverty was always an issue for me, in the back of my mind. That's probably why I was a young Socialist—or perhaps everyone is a young Socialist. I certainly never imagined myself flight-testing hardware in my fire-proof flight suit on a NASA airplane.

It also has made me a conservative investor as an adult. I have always been aware that half the U.S. population (150 million people) have IQs below 100 by definition. These are the people who receive the minimum wage, which was just raised seventy cents, after a decade of no raise at all. Next year they may get another seventy cents, to $7.00 per hour if they are lucky. This is structural poverty—what eighteenth century economist David Ricardo meant by the "iron law of wages," where labor is a commodity traded and valued like coal and potatoes. He argued that without some sort of wage controls (or unions), wages under capitalism will *always* tend to fall to subsistence (poverty) levels—especially with an influx of unskilled foreign labor. Contrary to the best-selling book *The Secret,* I do not believe that impoverished people have *attracted* their poverty.

Menasha Tausner was a kind, gentle, and brilliant giant. I am 6 foot 5 inches, and he occupied much more space than I did.

Once when we all entered a movie theater together, someone behind us called out, "When are the midgets coming?" (That's why we love New York.) Menasha received his PhD from Columbia in four years and became a physics professor at Tufts University. After a few years, he tired of teaching physics and returned to Columbia to obtain a law degree. He practiced public interest law for the state of New Jersey, where he had good opportunities to use his near-photographic memory for everything he read.

He oversaw the investigation of the Three Mile Island disaster for New Jersey, and also the Bell Telephone Laboratories, where he was able to correct their equations on the blackboard as he walked down the corridors—quite surprising for a lawyer. Also, we loved to play "science fiction *Twenty Questions,*" in which the subject could be any thing, person, or creature that ever appeared in a science fiction story. Our assumption was that if you read it, you will remember it. It was in such a game that I encountered "G. Washington Slappey," whose only appearance was as a name on a Martian monument to the last survivors of a failed settlement—in Robert Heinlein's *The Black Pits of Luna,* from the depths of the McCarthy era in the 1950s.

At one time, I was dating the first cousin of Menasha's wife Mimi. My new dear friend Teri was a very humorous East Coast leftie, just my age. (Teri's other cousin was Henny Youngman, master of the one-liner, so it was probably in her genes. "Why do Jewish divorces cost so much? Because they're worth it.") We had many adventures together exploring the West Coast. One that was not amusing was when we were kayaking around the San Juan Islands north of Washington's Puget Sound. Our tiny craft was caught in the swift and churning outgoing tide off Friday Harbor. I literally tore the skin off my hand paddling us back to shore as the sun was setting and the wind was picking up. I don't think she ever realized the very real danger of our being swept out to sea.

Several years ago, Teri and I visited Menasha and Mimi at their home in Teaneck, New Jersey, just before my plane was to take me back to California. On the way to the airport, Teri and I couldn't say enough about what a remarkable, fortunate, loving couple those two were after all these years—so intelligent and still so happy. But by the time I was back at my desk in Palo Alto, there was a phone message from Teri, telling me that Menasha had had a heart attack and died while running on his doctor-prescribed treadmill. Sorry to say, I was physically and mentally unable to return to New York for the funeral.

My pal Gary, Gerald Feinberg, received his PhD from Columbia, in an unprecedented three years, working with T. D. Lee. He became chairman of the physics department at Columbia and coined the term *tachyon* for a theoretical particle that travels faster than the speed of light—to date, it has yet to be detected.

Perhaps, if I had had less brilliant friends, I would have gone somewhere less demanding than Columbia for graduate school, and probably graduated. However, I was in good company, since my friend and later boss Gordon Gould also left Columbia early to pursue his invention of the laser. Charles Townes got the Nobel Prize for that, but Gordon got the hugely valuable patent on the laser, with decisive help from an experiment I did while working for him in a laboratory on Long Island.

At Columbia, my professors frequently assigned no textbooks. They made up the classes out of their heads. Nobelist T. D. Lee was a special offender. He not only had no textbook, but his accented English was very difficult to understand, and I of course couldn't see his scribbled blackboard. Nor could I, in the large lecture theater, promenade back and forth to take notes as I did in the lower grades. After one particularly opaque lecture, Prof. Lee asked, "Are there any questions?" People tittered—of course there were. A young woman student raised her hand and asked something about Green's Functions, a complicated mathematical approximation that Lee had used to solve the problem. Lee wrinkled up his nose and spat out, "That is not a question. Are there any real questions?" There weren't any more, as you might guess. But my friend Menasha had no such problem. He took copious notes for Lee's theoretical physics class directly on "blue line" ditto masters, which were printed in the physics department office right after the class, so that we all could have some idea of what was going on.

At Columbia, I was a research assistant, receiving $300 per month and tuition. That was enough to pay the rent for my little bed-sitting room on 113th Street and an occasional dinner at the Russian Tea Room. My professor, C. S. Wu, was a brilliant woman who should have shared the Nobel prize with Lee and Yang for demonstrating the surprising nonconservation of parity in beta-particle atomic disintegration events. (Don't ask.) In spite of having carried out the very difficult and complex laboratory demonstration, she was not included. (This was very similar to the way experimentalist Rosalind Franklin at Cambridge University was excluded from the Nobel prize of Watson and Crick, after she designed the experimental research and provided all the essential and confirming DNA x-ray data to prove their theory.)

At the time I had a cheerful redheaded girlfriend named Libby, who had a beautiful garden apartment just off Christopher Street in the Village. She was a graduate student, studying painting at the Art Students League in Midtown. All this comfort was supported by her Upper Eastside doctor father. Equal to her passion for art was her love for the guppies that she raised in a large glass tank in her living room. One Friday night, she turned me down for a date because she was preparing for the annual guppy show that would take place the next day at the New York Armory. She couldn't go out with me because, she said, she had to take her sleeping bag to the Armory to sleep with her guppies to protect them from unscrupulous guppy raiders who would steal the pregnant guppies from her display tank. The reason I am relating this silly story is that all through my life since then, I have been aware that we all live in our own little guppy worlds—whether it is the guppy world of publishing, lasers, airplane safety, or ESP. I have just come home from a Las Vegas meeting of IRVA (International Remote Viewing Association)—one hundred and fifty intense people whose passion is learning to understand remote viewing and use it as an aid in stock market investment and sports betting. You have never seen a more passionate little guppy world than that—though some seem to be making quite a lot of money. (For more information, see: irva.org.) The members of IRVA, many of whom are retired Army Intelligence officers, are the new subversives, who are working tirelessly to overturn the present paradigm. Perhaps somebody will make a movie called *Guppy World.*

But my most important teacher at Columbia was not a physicist. She was a draftswoman with an office under the eves of Pupin Hall, the physics building where I worked and studied. Mollie Walker Butler was a mysterious "older" woman with straight dark hair. She was almost thirty, and very slim and trim and pale in the dark blue jumper she always wore. For some reason she saw the latent mystic in this skinny twenty-year-old graduate physics student. She tried to get me to see *prana* (energy) in the sunbeams in her loft. She also took me to the New York Theosophical Society to learn about its founder, the mysterious and prolific Madam Helena Patrovna Blavatsky, and the teachings of *Vedanta.* We also heard an early lecture on the alleged (and still hotly debated) *Reincarnation of Bridey Murphy,* the apparent rebirth of a nineteenth-century Irish woman. Thinking of Mollie,

I agree with Tolstoy, who says in *A Confession* that "Nothing forms a young man as an intimacy with a woman of good breeding," especially an *older* woman.

The president of the Theosophical Society was then Dora Kunz, a well-known psychic healer who was the creator of the Therapeutic Touch movement, which has tens of thousands of nurse practitioners today. Dora and I became friends, and I did some ESP experiments with her. She would locate small magnets that I hid around the office, where she said she could see their fields as a direct sense sensation of color. I also did a magic trick in which I re-materialized a playing card that I had allowed her to "freely select" and then burn up in an ashtray. Then (apparently), the very same card reappeared in Blavatsky's *Secret Doctrine* on the top shelf of the library. This was my cautionary tale for her little research group—which I found highly gullible—illustrating that they should always be careful and skeptical with visiting miracle workers. I was young, and this was one of my first and rare investigations out "in the field."

Because of my poor vision, I much prefer to carry out experiments in the laboratory, under my own control. In my experience with poltergeist cases and the like, ghost-busting in someone else's home or office is usually disappointingly inconclusive and very time-consuming—like watching Uri Geller bending teaspoons at a dinner party, which I have done. I happen to think that some small part of supposedly paranormal spoon-bending is real, based on my personal experience with a sturdy aluminum rod. But it is extremely difficult to tell if such a thing is genuine by casual observation, unless they roll up the *bowl* of the spoon— which I have now seen done—not just the handle.

(I worked with Uri Geller for six weeks at SRI in 1973. We found him to be very gifted psychically—general mental telepathy and clairvoyance—spoon-bending notwithstanding. Hal Puthoff and I published the findings in *Nature*. More on Hal later.)

Mollie also taught me kundalini meditation while I was at Columbia. I practiced this diligently for a year before significantly scaring myself with an out-of-control explosion of energy racing up my spine—a hundred times more powerful than any orgasm. I wasn't prepared for this kind of success. I think of this as "the white hot poker up the ass trick"—very dangerous without an experienced teacher.

The revered Indian yogi, Gopi Krishna, describes his own disastrous premature experience in his autobiography, *The Awakening of Kundalini.* It left him hospitalized and mentally ill with buzzing sounds and flashing lights in his head *for years,* until he finally integrated the experience—a very scary tale. I wish I had read it before, rather than after, my own adventure in the fire—another unforgettable glimpse into the unseen world.

My friend Mollie was also the first to introduce me to Buddhism, which I have since studied, if not practiced, for most of my life. In those early days, I didn't get much past the Four Noble Truths. But they ran in my mind in background, as PC users would say, and re-emerged last year in my book *The End of Suffering.* Here's my twenty-first-century take on these ancient truths.

The First Noble Truth is indisputable: We experience pain and suffering because we are aware of the *finite, fragile, impermanent* nature of our lives. Buddhism is a philosophy of taking responsibility for one's mind. If we cannot take charge of our own churning thoughts, how can we take control of our lives in the physical world? Buddhism proposes mind taming, followed by mind training. As Sylvia Boorstein says, "Pain is unavoidable, but suffering is optional." The suffering comes from the story we attach to the pain—the blaming and futurizing about it. Boorstein, the author of *Funny, You Don't Look Buddhist,* is an observant Jew, as well as an inspiring and heartful Buddhist teacher with whom I have sat many times.

A Course in Miracles teaches a similarly hopeful idea: *I give all the meaning there is, to everything I experience.* This is how Victor Frankl was able to find meaning and spirituality in a concentration camp. He found it through focusing on his desire to be helpful to others, even under the most unimaginable cruelties.

Apart from concentration camps, suffering is largely subjective. If you really want to suffer, try personalizing everything that happens. When some bozo crowds you on the pavement, you can always wonder, "Why is he doing that to me?" That always works. Consider the following: One of the worst punishments inflicted on prisoners is solitary confinement. At the same time, some people (like me) from Northern California pay money for a similar experience but call it a silent meditation retreat. Besides being voluntary, one major difference is that the meditator knows what to do with his or her mind to create a gift and an opportunity out of the solitude, rather than a punishment.

In 1971, a famous prison experiment was carried out by the well-known shyness researcher, psychologist Philip Zimbardo, at Stanford University. Zimbardo was also one of the many Stanford University oversight guardians of our remote viewing research at SRI. In the basement of Jordan Hall, ten student "prisoners" and ten student "guards" played *prison* for six days, until the thing got entirely out of hand. My reason for mentioning this experiment—investigating how nice college student guards turn into sadists, and prisoners turn into zombies (learned helplessness)—is that the only prisoner who didn't decompensate (crack up) in solitary confinement was the *one Buddhist student.* This eighteen-year-old young man knew how to manage his mind and considered "the hole" to be a relief from the chaos of prison life. He also led a hunger strike, significantly undermining the authority of the guards. This is all described in Zimbardo's horrifying and fascinating book, *The Lucifer Effect,* which is obviously a prelude to Abu Ghraib. The lesson of the Stanford prison experiment is that situations matter, and that "bad barrels create bad apples."

Meditation allows us to observe our mind and root out unhelpful behavior. If I am feeling peaceful, and then have a fit when someone burns my toast, that dissatisfaction preceded the event—I brought it with me into the restaurant. *A Course in Miracles* charmingly teaches, *Let not little interferers pull you into littleness.*

The Second Noble Truth addresses the suffering caused by *craving and attachment.* It describes how a life lived at the materialistic end of our map of experience can lead to desperation. This craving for stuff, money, and accomplishments profoundly interferes with our passionate enjoyment of where we are now, in the present. A core Buddhist precept teaches that *making distinctions* leads to both error and suffering. Imprecision inevitably follows when you judge and divide *this* from *that.* Buddha taught this concept from direct observation, and now quantum theory has formulated it into the fundamental Heisenberg Uncertainty Principle, which shows that you cannot know both the position and the velocity of an elementary particle with unlimited accuracy. Furthermore, Neils Bohr has shown the Complementarity Principle, which describes the fundamental non-separable nature of waves and particles. And many mathematicians consider Kurt Gödel's Incompleteness Theorem, proving that there always will be some mathematical theorems whose truth or falsity cannot be decided, to be the most important discovery in all of mathematics. All of these factors demonstrate the inherent limitations of our knowledge. We should always remain discerning and courageous in the face of injustice, but *judgment* gets us into trouble — especially the egoical judgment of others. The Buddhists have always taught that such manifestations of separation are an illusion.

It all goes back to meaning. We can all remember standing with someone in front of a closet full of clothes, as he or she cried, "I don't have a thing to wear." And for them it was true. None of the clothes were new or appealing. They had been drained of meaning, through familiarity, and therefore *were* nothing.

One final insight into the suffering of attachment comes from the Tenth Commandment of the Bible. "Thou shalt not covet" is the only Commandment that doesn't pertain to deeds. It just deals with thoughts! It's possible that coveting and greed are the most corrosive of all human tendencies, leading to the most anguish and damage to society. And our daily dose of radio and television advertising is one of the greatest sources of this pain. Without doubt, advertising's goal is to create so much desperate coveting that we seek relief by buying and accumulating objects. That's the bad news. Sometimes I have that feeling, and I turn to my computer, saying to myself, "I shop therefore I am." That usually stops me. Spiritual teacher Andrew Cohen writes: "Enlightenment is the thrill of not wanting anything." This important one-sentence teaching from Cohen embodies an important truth. Enlightenment, peace, and freedom come not from the agreement or concession to not want or need anything. They come from the thrill and exhilaration of *knowing* that you don't need anything anymore, because we already have everything—the love and everything else we think we are looking for. (This assumes, of course, that you are not a prisoner in Guantanamo, or starving in the Sudanese desert.) Jesus taught that "The kingdom of God is within you"—not up in the sky or out there somewhere. That teaching is the entire content of the profoundly nondual Thomas Gospel. In verse 22, Jesus tells us that "you will enter the kingdom of heaven, when you know that two equals one, inner is the same as outer, and male is the same as female." But advertising makes us crazy as it spins the facts and the news. The big multimillion dollar lawsuit of the day is "Equal vs. Splenda," to determine which of these two non-sugar chemical sugar substitutes can be said to be "more like sugar"—trying to make distinctions where none exist.

The Third Noble Truth, that *suffering is in fact unnecessary,* is the terrific good news. As Sylvia Boorstein says, "Peace of mind and a contented heart are not dependent on external circumstances." When we take control of our free-running minds, we have the opportunity to *exchange suffering for gratitude:* I may not have solved my life's problems yet, but I can wake up in the morning and decide to focus my attention on gratitude for life, and my connection to all mankind and the Infinite Consciousness of the universe (or I can resume my kvetching).

An inspiring story of one man who was able to do this is told by the French writer Jacques Lusseyran in his breathtaking autobiography, *And There Was Light.* Lusseyran demonstrated that *what you decide to focus your attention on* is what you get. After losing his sight in an accident at age eight, he relied on his inner resources and the help of devoted friends to complete high school and gain acceptance into university, just as World War II was on the horizon. During the Nazi occupation of Paris, Lusseyran recognized that *information* was the essential ingredient to aid the Resistance and maintain the people's morale. With his friends, he formed an underground newspaper right under the eyes of the Gestapo. He alone was chosen to interview each potential member of the growing Resistance band, because of his unique gift for intuitively determining who could be trusted. Their underground operation continued for two years before they were betrayed by the one person about whom the blind Lusseyran had expressed doubt.

In the concentration camp, Lusseyran occupied himself by finding food for the sickest prisoners. Despite his blindness, starvation, and brutal treatment, he also helped build a secret radio receiver and became an inspiration to his fellow prisoners. At the end of the war he was rescued by the Allies and lived to become a full professor of history at the University of Hawaii. In his book, he declares two truths that his remarkable life has revealed: "The first of these is that joy does not come from outside, for whatever happens to us, it is within. The second truth is that light does not come to us from without. Light is in us, even if we have no eyes." Once again, the third Noble Truth reminds us that anything we see and experience has only the meaning that we give it.

The Fourth Noble Truth *lays out paths* we can follow to find the centered and balanced mental stance that will allow us to take charge of our minds. I describe some of these paths more fully in chapter 13 of this book. Although it is possible to read about these truths, it is vastly preferable to internalize them from contact with an inspired teacher.

These roads to happiness and contentment are described here very briefly in Buddhist terms as the Eightfold Path:

- *Right View:* Understanding that impermanence is the source of suffering;

- *Right Intention, or aspiration:* Compassion and goodwill, and a commitment to self-realization;

- *Right Speech:* No gossip or deceit;

- *Right Action:* Live the Golden Rule and abstain from sexual misconduct;

- *Right Livelihood:* Peaceful helpful work. Don't sell drugs, alcohol, or weapons;

- *Right Effort:* Positive attitude, joy, and wholesomeness;

- *Right Concentration:* Meditation and spaciousness, also single-pointed focus of attention; and

- *Right Mindfulness:* Emptiness, and not hooked by the passions (or anything else).

They are all interconnected, like everything else. But I believe that aspiration is the essential first step on the path. We are also reminded, especially by the great Tibetan teacher Chögyam Trungpa Rinpoche, to watch out for "idiot compassion," where we allow ourselves to be taken advantage of in our effort to be helpful and end up enabling someone's addictions or other craziness. Compassion requires discernment, just like everything else.

The peace we all wish to experience is achieved through the practice of mindfulness. The only way we know to alleviate our pain and our longing for love—to be *in* love—is by stopping our fearful mental chatter and taking control of our mind. Mystical traditions teach that the quiet mind is the most available path for anyone seeking to live in love, or to experience a relationship with God, which I think is the same thing. My conclusion, after many years of searching, is that, if what you are looking for is happiness, then you should *give up the search* for love—and instead, *be love.* *A Course in Miracles* (ACIM) teaches, "Look not for love. Look rather for the barriers that you, yourself, have created against the experience of love."

I am very fortunate to have had many abiding and deeply loving and nonsexual connections with women both younger and older. As a young person, I had deeply longed for a sister—preferably an older sister. Since that wasn't possible, as a child I slowly created an alter ego named Michelle, who became my sisterly companion. She loved the smell of freshly washed hair and the texture and sensuous and exciting feel of silk, and especially satin, wherever she found it. By the time we left Chicago, at age eight,

I had lost interest in secretly wearing my mother's clothes. And my father had given me two pair of eight-ounce padded boxing gloves, so that I could learn the manly art. Michelle was, luckily for me, never attracted to boys. But she and I deeply loved certain women. Looking back on these friendships, I think these women sensed and felt safe in responding, and making a strong heart-to-heart loving connection with the Michelle in me.

I have great empathy and some understanding for Dr. Renée Richards who, as a man, had been a navy captain, a physician, and a professional tennis player named Dick. Renée writes in her second autobiography, *No Way Renée,* of a similar, but much more insistent alter ego, "Renée," who *demanded,* and was finally given, release from Dick, in the form of a sex change operation. A century earlier, after the publication of *Madame Bovary,* its author Gustave Flaubert was brought to trial for writing a so-called licentious fiction. The Parisian judge asked him who was his passionate heroine based upon. Flaubert's now famous reply was, "C'est moi." He was exonerated, and many of his male readers are surprised to find themselves strongly identifying with his romantic heroine, Madame Bovary, rather than with her lovers. (Though, in this novel of sex and shopping, it was unbearable debt to her dressmaker that caused her to take her life, not her romances.)

Renée's path was not my path. But even so, my childhood friend Michelle has not entirely forsaken me. She has reappeared recently as a beautiful soft little black cat, with smooth silky fur and golden topaz eyes, whom Patty and I have rescued and given a wonderful home. Onyx is happy to snuggle with me when I am reading and inexplicably rouses herself from time to time to push my book away, to kiss my nose—truly a little bundle of love with an expressive tail, often in the shape of a question mark. She is uninterested in television (smart cat), but will watch art history DVDs with us by the hour, sitting attentively at the foot of our bed. In intimate moments like this, we think of her as *Fluffy*. The heart-to-heart love that people feel for their pets, and the selfless love that pets show unmistakably for their people, is another illustration that love is our true nature. And that the controlling, possessive love that is so common is a terrible distortion. In the meantime, we are trying very hard not to become crazy cat people. We are deeply into "Cat Psychology," and very impressed with how Onyx can sit by the hour quietly contemplating her options: chasing squirrels, exploring the neighborhood, eating, sleeping, or snuggling.

I am sad to say that my three best and brightest male friends, and Mollie too, all passed from the physical plane in their mid-sixties, leaving only me to tell our story. *No time to lose!* It's amazing how thinking about the death of my good friends focuses my attention on getting the job done and brings feelings of loneliness, missed opportunities, and sadness for words unsaid. Our

The author and his "editor"   *Onyx the cat, a.k.a. Fluffy*

little group had great warmth, but we lacked the skill or awareness to show or express this affection, as a similar group of more
demonstrative, young, huggy women might. However, I should
add that within five years of our sci-fi days, my pals and I all
wised up and discovered that girls knew much more about certain things than we did.

CHAPTER FOUR

Free at Last

All day I think about it, then at night I say it.
Where did I come from,
and what am I supposed to be doing?
I have no idea.
My soul is from elsewhere, I'm sure of that,
and I intend to end up there.

—Rumi

After bailing out of Columbia without a degree, I secured a job in microwave engineering at the Sperry Gyroscope Company in Great Neck, New York. The job had nothing at all to do with the atomic physics of my assistantship, or anything else I'd learned in graduate school. But the very last person of the five who interviewed me liked me and thought I would be good company on his drive from the Upper West Side to the plant on Long Island. So, I was basically hired for my gift of gab, rather than any scientific prowess. Since as a child I didn't read, I was an inveterate radio listener, back when people actually had something to say on the radio—like Henry Morgan, Long John Nevel, the great, inspired Gene Shepard, Barry Gray, Clifton Fadiman, and *The Shadow*—"who knows what evil lurks in the heart of men." As an only child, I deeply loved the intimate companionship of my shortwave Hallicrafters bedside radio and acquired a rich vocabulary although I didn't know how to spell many of the words—a continuing problem, probably connected to face blindness or my poor vision. The advent of automatic computer spell-checking was one of the great empowering events in my life—especially my life as a writer.

The Sperry lab director, Morris Ettenberg, was a multitalented PhD physicist who played the flute and taught Midrash (Hebrew Talmud interpretation) at the Jewish Theological Seminary. He decided a young, Jewish, logical positivist, ESP-nut physicist would be perfect company on the long drive from the Upper West Side—and he might even get some work out of me. With the job in hand, in May of 1956, I set sail on the *New Amsterdam* for England on vacation and in search of real psychics—and perhaps even a girlfriend. On the voyage I had a wonderful five days of eating, bridge, ping-pong, and more eating. I was already an Anglophile, having fallen in love with Katherine Mansfield's crisp, diamond-polished short stories and her alluring "ginger haired" seductresses. (And now I am married to one.)

The first expression of my new freedom, just before going to England, was a bike ride to see the newly opened Shakespeare Theater in Stratford, Connecticut. I rode my trusty bike from Greenwich Village, the length of Manhattan, and right up the beautiful Boston Post Road, eighty miles to Stratford, in one long day's riding. I would stop periodically for a bottle of Dairy Rich chocolate milk to keep me going past the giant oak trees, the big old brick factory buildings, and the occasional white farm house set back from the road in a farm field. I had my sleeping bag, machete, bathing suit, and Holy Bible all packed on my bicycle's luggage rack. In addition to seeing plays, I wanted to take this ten-day time-out to read the whole Bible, of which I was almost entirely ignorant.

It was pouring rain when I arrived in Stratford. The last many miles of my trip, I had to wear a rubberized poncho. I rolled into the first gas station and asked where I could stay. The attendant, of course, had no idea, but he did give me the useful information to be careful, because two campers had been robbed and murdered that afternoon in the nearby forest, and the killer was still at large! That info, together with the rain, cooled my camping plans. As I rode into town, I turned off the Post Road and headed for the Housatonic River on which the town is situated. Almost to the river, I saw a large white clapboard house that was obviously being remodeled, or renovated. I could see this from the piles of lumber in the front yard. I tried the front door, and it swung open. The house was empty except for building material—just like the opening scene in *The Rocky Horror Picture Show*. Still thinking about the murderer on the loose, I pulled my bike inside and began to explore. I decided that this could be my new temporary home. I took my bike with all its stuff on board and pulled it up the wooden stairs and made myself at home on the second floor. It had been a long day. I unrolled my sleeping bag on the floor, and with my Bible and machete by my side I went to sleep. But in the middle of the night, between the thunder claps, I distinctly heard someone, or something, rumbling around downstairs in the dark house. Could it be a rat, or a cat, or perhaps the murderer? Should I lie quietly in my sleeping bag, or should I bang smartly on the floor with the handle of my machete? I chose the quiet approach. Everything returned to normal, and I went back to sleep.

It rained like hell the whole time I was in Stratford. Nearby Waterbury was buried under water, and an apartment house fell over there. The first play I saw was *The Tempest* (no kidding). I rode into the parking lot of the theater with water running up to my hubcaps. The other memorable play I saw was *Hamlet*. What a thrill for a young man on the loose for the first time in his life.

Because of my reading of the Wittgenstein and Ayer, I was very taken with Hamlet's idea: "There is nothing either good or bad, but thinking makes it so" (Act II, Scene 2). Of course, John Milton understood that as well, when he said in *Paradise Lost,* "The mind is its own place, and in itself can make a heaven of hell, a hell of heaven."

I stayed in Stratford for a week, saw a lot of plays, and read my big-print Bible (World Publishing's leather covered Old Folks edition from my father) from cover to cover. I didn't feel like the long ride home, so I took the Bridgeport Ferry back to Manhattan's Wall Street dock and rode home on the cobblestones of Broadway from the Battery to the Village, ready for England, two weeks hence.

The most exciting thing I learned when I got to England was that I didn't need a driving license to drive a motorbike—only a big red "L" Learner's permit, and no eye exam. What a concept! So, I bought my first motor vehicle, a 50cc French Mobilette moped. It wasn't much to talk about, but I loved to ride it from London to Cambridge, and later from Cambridge to visit my new Theosophical friends in picturesque Falmouth-by-the-Sea in Cornwall, and back to London. I found digs in Russell Square over an Indian restaurant and had many dreams permeated with curry. I probably even smelled of curry. I was fortunate to make friends at the London Theosophical Society—which is still very big in England. I was invited to the Theosophical camp retreat in Camberly, in Kent. Although I didn't know it then, a skinny American physicist on a motorbike was pretty exotic in an England still recovering from the war.

At the rustic summer camp with little wall-tents, I fell in love with the adorable and humorous daughter of the most famous psychic in England, Phoebe Bendit, who also happened to be the head of the Society. Her daughter Deidre had pink cheeks and dark curly hair—to my eyes I had found a lovely little English sprite. She and I toured Bath, Wells, Cheddar Gorge, Avebury Circle, and much of Southern England in her Austin roadster—quite scandalizing the Society.

One of our more romantic getaways was a visit to Ann Hathaway's thatched-roof cottage and the home of William Shakespeare at picturesque Stratford-upon-Avon. As we walked hand-in-hand through the expansive flower garden full of summer blossoms at Ann's cottage, I spied a little clutch of canoes at the water's edge. They were tended by the elderly gardener who rented them for a shilling to sightseers for a paddle among the weeping willows and buttercups that dotted the shoreline. As an experienced waterfront counselor, I felt no risk in this bucolic little outing. As I paddled out into the river, I felt very happy to just float along with my little sweetie and drift with the current. After a while, I suddenly noticed a large white sign with crudely painted red letters. I paddled toward it across the river, but it was difficult to read. Finally I could make it out—"Beware The Weir." *What the hell's a weir?* I thought. Could it be a kind of Shakespearian wolf? As the swift current caught our little canoe, I found out that in Merry Old England, a weir is a manmade dam across a river, used to raise its height. With furious paddling I was able to avoid the twenty-foot drop made by the smoothly flowing river to the rocks below. Once more it's Magoo to the rescue.

Deidre and I might even have married, but she was much too advanced for me, psychically. I was interested in ESP, but I hadn't experienced very much. She on the other hand had grown up in the bosom of the Theosophical society with her intensely clairvoyant mother. From my twenty-two-year-old physicist's point of view, Deidre, although a high school teacher, was way-out! Among other things, she saw fairies in the flower garden, just as Theosophists Annie Besant and Charles Leadbeater had described. I already knew of their famous book, *Occult Chemistry,* in which Leadbeater had accurately described the three isotopes of hydrogen in 1895, years before their scientific discovery.

In spite of my love for Deidre, the deal breaker was when we went to see Arthur Miller's *Crucible* in Bristol. This was just after the McCarthy period in America, and I thought Miller was God. When my date tried to explain to me that Miller notwithstanding, some of the people killed in the Salem witch trials might *actually have been witches,* I began to look forward to my trip back to Cambridge. If I had been able to talk to my little sprite about my feelings for her, and my fear of the irrational, we probably would have had a different outcome. I now realize that such "witches" may in fact have been budding freelance psychics that the Church wanted to exterminate and replace with Saints, who were conveniently within the bosom of the Church—and dead. From my days studying and reading about the history of magic, I have long been sensitive to the subject of witches. For example, I know that deep in the psyche of each of us still lingers the smell of burning flesh from a million women and men burned by the church as witches, right up to the eighteenth century. Today, I am counting on my brass Life Membership card from the A.C.L.U. to protect me from the enforcers when they come calling.

Also, face-to-face conversations about relationships have always been a challenge for me because I am not at all sensitive to the supposed cues of body language, unless the person is actively boohooing.

At Cambridge, I had been allowed to experiment with blind African fish called *gymnarchus.* These fish interested me because they hunted and navigated entirely by sensing the electric field generated by waving their electrified tail and sensing the field with their head. I found I could collect them like iron filings, by holding a powerful magnetron magnet in my hand near their glass aquarium. Of course, fish are much easier to talk about than relationships. But one of the things I have learned (that took the

"What do you want, Denise? I'm not a mind reader."

longest time) is that in the end, *relationships are much more important than accomplishments.*

I also was able to spend fascinating time at Cambridge with two researchers, Profs. Brindley and Campbell at Kings College, who were investigating the direct perception of visual phosphenes (hallucinations) as a result of having one's head near a pulsing magnetic field. (I was reminded of Dora Kunz's ability to locate the little magnets I hid around her office.) All together I was treated with great hospitality and friendship at Cambridge. For example, they invited me to sit with them at High Table at Kings College for the week I was there. I recall they were much impressed that this young American had learned to dexterously cut his food with his right hand and eat it off the back of his fork held in the left—as they did. It never occurred to them that I was left-handed, and I didn't enlighten them. I just told them I have always been a fast learner.

One of my most treasured memories of Cambridge is of afternoons, sitting at sunset with friends on the lush green grass by the River Cam, watching iridescent white swans taking off and landing, splashing along on the river and running on the grass, as though practicing for a summer excursion. Whenever someone asks me to think of a time when I have been truly happy, I think of that perfect golden time. One of my good friends from New York, Arnold Faden, was a fellow at Kings College. He had just finished a year of psychoanalyzing himself, and we had a wonderful week sitting in these inspiring surroundings, discussing how we know what we know. What are the limits to knowledge, no less self-knowledge? Arnold went on to become a distinguished professor of economics at the University of Iowa. He knew, even in the 1950s, that automation equals unemployment for the unskilled. Together with unlimited immigration, we see that in the current tragedy of our struggling young.

I loved England, but I must admit I didn't see many psychic happenings there. Once, when I visited the Marylebone Spiritualist Association in London, the entranced medium said that she saw me as an American scientist surrounded with wires and apparatus. I was not impressed, since at twenty-two in my khaki slacks, curly hair, and thick glasses, I was a cultural stereotype of an American scientist. Still, in my first trip abroad, I had only wonderful experiences in the four months I spent in England and France.

Lucky for me, my tall, blue-eyed wife Patricia, my life dharma buddy, is also an Anglophile, so we often spend very happy times in London, shopping at Fortnum and Mason for chocolate-covered ginger, visiting little tea shops on the Embankment, and looking at Pre-Raphaelite paintings in the galleries. In a happy synchronicity, Patty and I met at Unity Church in Palo Alto, the same night that Marc Allen, the president of New World Library, was giving an evening talk on his new book *Visionary Business.* Patty was there to hear an inspiring lecture. I was there to interest Marc in publishing *Miracles of Mind,* which I had just finished co-writing with my friend and spiritual healer, Jane Katra. Patty noticed me, sitting by myself in the big, almost empty church, and came by to chat. Beautiful, tall Patty standing with me was no doubt very helpful in convincing Marc to look at my manuscript. Patty and I made a wonderful heart-to-heart connection, and we were married five years later by my long-time friend Joan Halifax Roshi. Joan is an anthropologist, medical researcher, and now Zen priest and abbot of the Upaya Zen Center in the hills outside of Santa Fe. Patty and I were married on the winter solstice in the Center's spacious and peaceful sanctuary, gleaming with candles and polished wood. We were doubly blessed to be part of an unexpected Santa Fe snowstorm with large fluffy flakes, falling like diamonds and covering everything with glittering white crystals. After that lucky night at Unity, Marc published my book, and two others, *The Heart of the Mind,* also with Jane Katra, and *Limitless Mind,* by myself, in memory of my daughter, Elisabeth. So, it was a very good time in church—I sold my book and met my future wife all in one memorable evening.

It took a few years for Patty and me to finally get together, but finally on our first date we rode our bikes to the nearby Baylands to watch the sunset over the mountains. And since Valentine's Day was coming up, one of my most imaginative and open-hearted friends, Gail Hayssen, known as "Psychic Auntie Gail" to her clients, thought that a good icebreaker would be for Patty and me to attend a weekend tantra workshop for couples in Sebastopol near her home. That was memorable—we still laugh about it. Between our first meeting in church and our first date, we had occasionally chatted after church on Sundays, and we saw each other frequently at the *Course in Miracles* study group meetings that I facilitated weekly at my home. We often had dinner with our miracle-minded friends, or sat across the coffee table from one another in my living room like the two characters in the "What do you want, Denise?" cartoon. I have now been meeting weekly with this group for more than fifteen years. It's what the Buddhists would call my *sangha* (spiritual community). At that time, I was separated from my wife Joan, but we remained married until her death in 1998. Patty and I were married in 2003.

After our first couple of dates in 2002, Patty and I checked out serious things, like whether we liked each other's music. She tried me out on Miles Davis's *Bitches Brew,* which I thought was transcendent. And she surprised me with her appreciation for late Beethoven quartets. With all that settled, we moved into the center of the ring and danced around my living room to Nora Jones's romantic album *Come with Me,* and decided to get married on the spot. When you're sixty you can do that. And if you ever want to

Patty and Russell in New York for our honeymoon in December 2003

find us, we are usually at the California seaside—on the beach, in a hot tub, on a ferry, or walking on the boardwalk, enjoying the life-sustaining salt air. In this photo we are at the New Jersey shore with Manhattan in the background.

CHAPTER FIVE

Search for a Psychic Switch

At Sperry in 1956, I learned how to design and build high-powered microwave tubes, called traveling-wave tubes. They were so powerful and interconnected with an electron beam flashing the length of the tube through a long helix at nearly the speed of light, that they seemed almost alive. I used one of them to try to make a psychic switch—in which I would slow down the electron beam to almost walking speed, and then find someone to try to deflect the beam to the left or the right. I had built this tube in such a way that I could automatically make all the measurements. Sperry's government customer never knew of my psychic modifications. It appeared to me from a few day's data that one or two of my subjects (Sperry engineers) could actually move the beam. This experiment is written up and published in Edgar Mitchell's 1974 book, *Psychic Exploration.*

Sperry was an old-style engineering plant, three-quarters of a mile long and a quarter of a mile wide—eighty acres under one roof. It was paved with cobblestones, and shop stewards on large three-wheeled bikes raced up and down the roadways between the workbenches distributing red shop rags, supplies, and mail. Graduate school had not prepared me for this chaos. I tried to promote my very excellent older technician named Vinny to the grade of Junior Engineer, which was the level at which he was working. But the shop steward told me not to waste my time trying:

"He'll never make engineer. He's got no fucking class." I expected a union leader to be more compassionate—shows how little I knew. About two weeks later, two naked noontime lovers fell through the plasterboard false ceiling onto the workbenches on the factory floor below. They were, of course, both fired. Though quite memorable, I felt that didn't have much class either. It reminded me of the joke dealing with a man who came home from his job at the pickle factory at midday, to explain to his wife that he had had an unfortunate encounter with the pickle slicer—and that she was fired also.

My job responsibility was to design and oversee the fabrication of a new type of high-power traveling-wave tube for an over-the-horizon radar system being developed at the Electronics Lab at Wright Patterson Air Force Base, in Ohio. My first patent came out of the design of this device, and I had frequent trips to Dayton to meet and brief the Air Force people on our progress.

I become good friends with my contract monitor and system manager for the project. He was a highly competent, energetic, young black civilian engineer from Mississippi. In the middle of our project, he decided that we should have our next meeting at my lab at Sperry in Great Neck, so that he could have a look at our laboratory. This was his first trip to New York, and he said that he wanted to see something of the city. I, of course, knew it well and was given the assignment of entertaining Larry for the evening.

I arranged a nice walk up Fifth Avenue—a look at the fairyland of brightly lit and colorful ice skaters pirouetting and holding hands in the sunken rink at Rockefeller Plaza, surrounded by sixty-story granite office buildings. And then we had dinner and drinks at the posh Blue Angel night club on Fifty-third Street to see Lenny Bruce, who was already a hot ticket. What could be wrong with that? Just wait! I knew who Lenny Bruce was from his records and thought he was brilliant and original. But alas, I had never actually seen his act. We had a ringside table, which I always try and get, so that I can see what is happening. The steaks were great, and by the time we had a couple of drinks, Bruce finally appeared. That's the end of the good news.

Bruce opened with the *New York Times* in his hand. He was full of comments about how well the Jews had done when they came to New York, not even speaking English. And wondering why the blacks didn't do the same. "For example," he said, "they could start by learning English." I was already thinking that we should leave. But then, as a surprise guest, the beloved civil rights activist and comedian Dick Gregory was called to the stage from the audience, as though Bruce had just noticed him. In their planned sketch, Bruce played the pre-Civil War plantation owner, while Gregory played "Uncle Tom," who on bended knee had come to take Bruce's daughter out on a date. You must remember that this was in the exact middle of the Montgomery, Alabama, bus boycott. The audience held its breath. Time stood still—and then it was over to great applause. Still, this was probably my life's moment of greatest embarrassment.

Larry seemed to take it all in good humor. He told me, "Don't worry, Russ. If it was good for Dick Gregory, it couldn't be too bad." Not surprisingly, I have amnesia for whatever else was said in the actual act. It was something about a celebration of the daughter's birthday. Well I didn't lose my job, and the contract was renewed, but I still view the whole scene as a very close call.

About this time in the late 1950s, a Swedish engineer, Haakon Forwald, demonstrated that he could significantly control the direction of fall of a line of little cubes dropped down a chute onto a roughened table. His very comprehensive report called *Mind, Matter, and Gravitation* was published by Eileen Garrett's Parapsychology Foundation in New York. I knew Mrs. Garrett as a famous medium, a powerful psychic, and the successful president of her foundation. My father had recently published her captivating autobiography, *Many Voices,* describing her intensely psychic girlhood in Ireland. She knew of my ESP interests and asked me to build a copy of Forwald's apparatus for her office on Fifty-seventh Street.

I met with her research director, the distinguished and famously difficult to understand Lithuanian psychologist Karlis Osis, a pioneer in out-of-body research. We had a lovely dinner at the Russian Tea Room across from the Foundation's offices. I am always happy for an excuse to stop by there for blini with sour cream, melted butter, and caviar. He offered me $500, and I was more than delighted to do the work for the Foundation. It occupied countless hours of technician time, as well as my time to make it work and then fold it up into an attractive wooden box. (I have learned that the device lived a very long and useful life in the Parapsychology Foundation, used by both Mrs. Garrett's daughter Babs, and her granddaughter Lisette, who now runs the Foundation.)

After three years of such activity and my work at Sperry, I was suddenly exhausted and hospitalized for two weeks with mononucleosis. Unfortunately, the doctors could not decide whether I just had mono or was going to die of leukemia. This would have to be settled by a two-day blood test. But since I was in Beth Israel Hospital, they couldn't begin a non-emergency test that would extend into the Jewish Sabbath (Friday evening). Similarly they couldn't do it over the weekend, because Monday was Rosh Hashanah (the Jewish New Year). So, I had to sit in fear and uncertainty for five extra days while the hospital celebrated their holidays. This is when I used my bedside telephone to have my first contact with the AAAA (The American Association for the Advancement of Atheism), an organization similar in many ways to the American Humanist Society. I didn't join, but they were sympathetic to my problem. Today I might have called the

Libertarians, who are on the same wavelength, but are less doctrinaire about it.

While I was in the hospital, several friends from Columbia recruited me to leave Sperry to work with Gordon Gould, in an effort to build the first laser, for which Gordon had just received a large government grant. I accepted and went to work for Technical Research Group (TRG) in Syosset, Long Island—even further out than Sperry. I would have to get up at six o'clock, to give me time to take the subway to Penn Station and catch the 8:05 for an hour's trip to Syosset. I did that for the next three years.

The other notable event of 1958 for me was that I married my first wife Joan Fischer, daughter of Regina, a brilliant, left-leaning physician and linguist. I met Joan because she was a Brooklyn College classmate of my then-girlfriend, Marcia, the aforementioned poetic and languid English major, to whom I gave my beloved *Collected Stories of Katherine Mansfield.* Marcia became a Mansfield devotee just like me and eventually went off to do research in New Zealand, to earn her PhD examining the author's life. Joan and I had three dates before she aced her nursing credential examination (highest in the state) and went off to Chile for a year to visit her father Gerhardt, who had lived there since the start of WWII.

She had not seen him since 1939, when she was two and her mother came home to the U.S. from France. Her father could go only to Chile (because he was a German and a communist who fought in Spain with the Loyalists, in an unsuccessful attempt to keep the fascist General Franco from toppling the legitimate Spanish government). In this war, the Germans (and the Italians) demonstrated for the first time, in 1937, the devastation and wholesale murder that could be rained down on a civilian population by aerial bombing. This slaughter of 1600 people on market day was memorialized in Pablo Picasso's famous painting, *Guernica,* depicting the atrocities committed upon this devastated city. I studied this powerful 11-by-25-foot painting many times at the Museum of Modern Art, as I was growing up in New York. It always made me shiver at the indiscriminate brutality of war it depicted. In February 2003 at the United Nations, a replica of the painting with its screaming mother and dead children had to be draped and covered with a cloth by the U.S. government spin-masters, to hide it from TV cameras, before Colin Powell could make his famous speech to the United Nations—the one in which he lied his ass off about weapons of mass destruction as he explained to the world why the United States was about to invade Iraq. But it was Colin Powell, so we believed him. Things have only gone downhill since that momentous and monstrous histori-cal resonance.

Guernica, *Pablo Picasso, 1937, Museo Nacional Centro de Arte Reina Sofía in Madrid*

Joan was not one of those depressed poets I was attracted to. She was a beautiful, bright, and highly competent woman, even at twenty. After about six months, I wrote Joan a long letter from Europe, proposing that we get married. (I had returned to Europe, still with the idea of marrying Deirdre. But again, painfully decided not to.) This was back in 1957 when people still knew how to write letters. Joan and her physicist father Gerhardt

Fischer discussed the idea for several weeks and decided that I looked like a good prospect. He had been a pioneer in the development of the EEG (brain waves) in Germany, before he and Regina left for the USSR in 1933, to keep a step ahead of the Nazis. (The same year Albert Einstein left.) Regina, on the other hand, was opposed to our marriage. She wanted to know why her beautiful and talented daughter chose a blind man to marry. My parents were also not thrilled.

Nonetheless, we were married the following year—after a missed communication thwarted our intention to be married in Belgrade. The *New York Herald Tribune* reported that Joan had gone to Belgrade to marry Svetozar Gligorić, a handsome Czech newspaper reporter and grandmaster chess player—just another screwed-up newspaper story. He was actually just accompanying the attractive twenty-year-old to his home city so she could marry *me!* At the time of our marriage, I was deeply engrossed in the mid-Manhattan salon of the Russian-born novelist and libertarian philosopher Ayn Rand, which was held in her luxurious apartment. Alan Greenspan was also a regular—and cranky—attendee, already clad in his ubiquitous pinstriped suit. In a letter to the editor of the *New York Times* about her just-published, mammoth novel of capitalism, he wrote, "*Atlas Shrugged* is a celebration of life and happiness. Justice is unrelenting. Creative individuals of undeviating purpose and rationality achieve joy and fulfillment. Parasites who persistently avoid either purpose or reason perish as they should." Rand and I quarreled over physics. As an "objectivist" she felt that she could not accept Einstein's theory of general relativity! (If you're an objectivist, nothing is relative.) Since physicists don't consider this a matter of belief, it became what is called an irreconcilable difference, of which Rand tolerated none.

As markets crashed around us in the Fall of 2008, our financial guru Alan Greenspan stood before Congress and said, "I have made a mistake. . . . I have found a flaw in my fundamental ideology. Markets don't correct themselves. Those of us who have looked to the self-interest of lending institutions to protect shareholders' equity, myself included, are in a state of shocked disbelief!" Ayn Rand, his mentor, was wrong about the desirability of totally free markets.

At Ms. Rand's we were also taught to love and appreciate Tchaikovsky in all his shapes and forms. And the young women all learned to smoke cigarettes in long holders like their teacher. We had two other teachers besides Rand. There was the tall, charismatic psychologist Nathaniel Branden, and his beautiful slim, blonde wife, Barbara. Nathaniel was an outstanding teacher, but we were all in love with Barbara. Meanwhile he, according to his autobiography, *My Years with Ayn Rand,* was off having a secret love affair with our objectivist leader, while her husband dozed quietly in the corner of our large meeting room. Nathaniel tells us that he eventually figured out that this was not exactly rational behavior and separated himself from our little clan, going on to be an important teacher in the self-esteem movement, which Rand had pioneered. But such is the kingdom of libertarian heaven. Sexual relationships between gurus and students are so common as to need no further comment here. The student may get the transmission directly from the teacher, but it destroys the credibility of the teacher for everyone else and often wrecks the *sangha.*

Although I worked on Long Island, Joan and I lived in a large apartment at 115th Street and Broadway in New York, overlooking the city, from the green quad of Columbia University at our doorstep, all the way to the East River. We frequently had musical gatherings in our living room, organized by my lifelong friend Bob von Gutfeld. Bob was an IBM physicist, a very talented cellist, and had been a classmate at Queens College. However, he had the wit to leave Columbia and get his PhD at

NYU. He is, alas, my only surviving male friend from that era in New York.

Bob had the six-room apartment right under ours. And next to him in this fabulous building was the world-famous magician John Mulholland. He would invite us in for drinks and astonish us with his peerless sleight-of-hand tricks. I was even more amazed to learn, after moving to California, that John had worked for the CIA's notorious MK-ULTRA mind control program, teaching agents how to slip LSD into drinks and load drugs into cigarettes. Years later, I would find myself being interviewed by Sid Gottlieb, the same spymaster he was working for. John's exploits and contributions to spy craft are described in detail in "The Sphinx and the Spy: The Clandestine World of John Mulholland," a piece by Michael Edwards in *Genii: The Conjuror's Magazine,* April 2001.

Joan and I also lived directly across from Arlene and Alan Alda. I had gone to college with Arlene, who was an accomplished clarinetist and often participated in our at-home musicals. Alan was just at the beginning of his acting career. I would often tell him about my latest physics or ESP projects, and he would listen with interest and ask extremely insightful questions. I have often thought but never said, "You know Alan, you're really very smart for an actor." Over the years, Arlene has become a highly regarded professional photographer, and Alan now hosts *Scientific American Frontiers* on television.

In the early 1960s, Alan did daily improvised press conferences at the Compass Playhouse in Hyannis, just a few miles from the Kennedy's Hyannis Port retreat on Cape Cod. Each morning President John Kennedy would have a press conference on his front porch, and in the evening Alan would have one for the same press corps in the theater. He had to thoroughly read the papers to prepare himself to answer questions on any subject—being both knowledgeable and funny. Joan and I attended several times.

In his daily shows, Alan was amazingly funny and brilliant. A reporter asked him (this is 1962), "Will the U.S. beat the Russians to landing a man on the moon?" Alan said, "I can't be sure that we will be the first to put a man on the moon, but I can promise you that we will be the first to put a man on the sun."

One time, after Alan's performance, Joan and I rode our bicycles the length of Cape Cod, from Providence to Provincetown—about eighty miles—to celebrate Joan's freedom from our daughter's babyhood and our daughter Elisabeth's first birthday. Elizabeth was left with a neighbor, and we got to rent a large two-person sailing surfboard (a Trident) to get out into the ocean off

Photo of Alan Alda and Russell backstage at Art *in 1998*

the Cape. We once got in irons (dead in the water) in the path of the Nantucket ferry, and we thought it was going to be curtains, but they barely avoided us. Our reward was the continual discovery of delicious, succulent fried clams and fresh oysters on the half shell at every pier we visited.

In 1998, in the play *Art,* Alan played an expatriate American doctor in Paris who buys a completely white painting to add to his art collection. His buddy asks him, "Could you please tell me why you paid $80,000 for that pure white piece of shit?" I don't remember what Alan replied, but I do know that we are the ones who give all the meaning there is, to every white piece of shit we encounter. I only realized recently that that's what the whole play was about.

For example, at the present moment there are three completely white paintings hanging at the New York Museum of Modern Art (MOMA). One is called *Presence* and has some barely discernable grey dots forming a band. A second white masterpiece is called *Attendant* and is completely unblemished, except for its aluminum hanger. The third is simply a shiny white square painted directly on the wall! The three are part of an exhibition called appropriately "What is painting?" But I love the MOMA, nonetheless.

CHAPTER SIX

Failure of Imagination—
Racing for the First Laser

I was invited to join the TRG (Technical Research Group) team, not because of my intellectual gifts, but because of my Sperry experience with ultra high vacuum and electrical discharges in gasses. I landed the job based on my first luncheon interview with Dick Daily and Gordon Gould. They had ordered martinis. Because of my very low tolerance for alcohol, I had an orange juice. I know that many people enjoy alcohol. They go from verbose, to jocose, to bellicose, to morose, to lachrymose, and finally to comatose. I go directly to the latter. My winning comment to Dick, the lab director, was that his martini "looks pretty weak." He said, "What do you mean it *looks* weak?" I told him that it appeared to have an index of refraction very close to water. I was correct and I got the job.

There were many highly intelligent men and women at TRG, all working to build the world's first laser. Ironically Gordon, by far the most knowledgeable of us all, was sequestered in his own wing of the building and could not visit the labs, because he was supposed to have been a Communist or possibly was married to one years before. It was a bizarre situation. The man who knew more about lasers than anyone in the world could meet us only in the library.

The rest of the facility was classified Secret, and Gordon's voluminous proposal to Advanced Projects Research Agency

(ARPA) was also classified Secret and could not be read by the man who wrote it. His proposal describing many different types and applications of lasers had won a $2 million contract for the tiny company. It was clear that Gordon had mentally internalized the electronic energy level structure of almost all the atomic species that could be used to make a laser. This made him an invaluable timesaving resource. But there was a literal chain-link fence across the plant separating the brains from the workers!

Remember this was the Cold War. I would have probably been in the cage with him if the government knew that as a thirteen-year-old on Eighth Street I had been listening to Radio Moscow and its Moscow Mailbag on the nine-meter band on my short-wave radio. The following year, 1948, I was approached by my local "Marxist Study Group," located in a little brownstone on West Tenth Street. But they were much too fanatical for me. They had to mindlessly consult *The Daily Worker* to figure out whether it was a good idea to blockade West Berlin. I was able to determine that was a bad idea all by myself. What we could agree on was our passionate opposition to strike-breaking in the industrial North, and that the violent centuries-long segregation of Negroes in the South was inhuman and a disgrace to the country. We all celebrated the death of the dreadful, foul-mouthed racist, Senator Bilbo from Mississippi.

In those days Pete Seeger was omnipresent at concerts and hootenannies in the Village loft buildings. This was before he and his immensely popular group, the Weavers, were blacklisted under McCarthy for their often biting left-wing protest songs. One of my great musical memories was sitting on the stage behind the Weavers (Pete Seeger, Ronnie Gilbert, Lee Hays, Fred Hellerman) at their standing-room-only 1955 reunion at Carnegie Hall. From the point of view of my personal history, that was my last date with my Queens College sweetheart, who went on to marry harpsichordist Paul Maynard.

A few years later my brand new wife Joan and I were at Carnegie Hall to see Pete Seeger, who just that night introduced the music world to Joan Baez. He came out on stage holding the hand of this shy, thin, barefoot girl with streaming, long dark hair, whom he had just discovered in a Cambridge coffee house. She was nineteen years old, with a thrilling clear soprano voice, and not yet a radical. I am pretty confident that she opened with, "Where Have You Been, Lord Randall, My Son?" But she soon moved to more relevant music. Recently, at Esalen, she confirmed this for me.

This Cold War isolation of Gould at TRG reminded me at the time of the HERBLOCK cartoon in the *New York Times* showing the great physicist J. Robert Oppenheimer and a giant pile of atomic secrets on one side of a brick wall and a bunch of men in white coats scratching their heads on the other side. This was a few days after the U.S. government took away Oppenheimer's security clearance to "protect the country"— from him.

My inspiration at TRG was Morty Schiff, a masters-level physicist with whom I worked for three years standing in a darkened lab, trying to build a laser out of mercury and krypton gas. We sent light from a krypton discharge tube—basically a long glass tube filled with krypton that we excited with a radio-frequency coil. We carefully directed light from this lamp down the length of a two-meter discharge tube filled with krypton and mercury vapor. The idea was for the excited mercury to put energy into the exactly matching upper energy levels of krypton, which is the requirement for a laser. This so-called *collision of the second kind* allowed us to make an amplifier, but not a laser. This approach works like a charm for the ubiquitous helium-neon laser, because of its inherently higher gain (amplification). Years later, our publication of this laser amplifier was decisive in helping Gould win a multimillion dollar patent away from Bell Telephone Labs.

Meanwhile, my TRG lab buddy Morty, with his thick glasses, slim build, long brown hair, and curly brown beard would go every second week into the most horrendous parts of Mississippi to take part in the increasingly dangerous Freedom Rides. I'm sorry that I never told him how much I admired his courage.

My other colleague and office mate was Gerry Grosof, a good friend from Columbia and years before in Greenwich Village—when we had a little group of friends who got together monthly to gossip, talk politics, and eat—very little making out. We called ourselves, in the late forties, the Village Intercultural Group (VICG) and met at the old brownstone home of my best friend, the very literary John Jacob Simon on East Fourth Street, right next door to the still-standing "Old Merchant's House," whose basement was a stop on the underground railroad in Civil War times.

John's four-story brownstone now appears about ready for demolition. I get to see both of these historic buildings regularly when I visit Ingo Swann at his loft building and studio on the same corner (Bowery and Fourth Street) in the East Village. At least one hapless member of the VICG listed this ephemeral organization on his Brookhaven National Laboratory personal security questionnaire—it delayed his Q-clearance for the Atomic Energy Commission (AEC) by half a year. Ours may have been the only organization that he ever belonged to. We were all pretty serious-minded pre-college students. I remember that the VICG folded when John went off to Bard.

That's when Gerry surprised us all by marrying the smartest girl in town, Miriam Shapiro, still under twenty. She grew up to become chair of the Math Department at Yeshiva University. Her father was Meyer Shapiro, the renowned art historian at Columbia, and I remember that he generously answered my questions about the intentions of the Impressionists and never minded that I was ignorant about art, as long as I was curious. He surprised me by explaining that Impressionism was *not* a particular technique or style, but rather a state of mind. It allowed the artists more freedom of expression in various ways than did classical painting of the official Salon held annually in Paris.

In spite of our efforts, we did not build the first laser at TRG, and neither did the 800-pound gorilla, Bell Labs, who had Charles Townes and Arthur Schawlow (very well-known professors from Columbia and Stanford) working for them. They eventually won a Nobel prize for their discovery of the microwave maser (maser stands for microwave amplification by stimulated emission of radiation. It's just like a laser but with microwaves), and work related to the laser. These two towering intellects had all the facilities of Bell Telephone Laboratories, along with a coveted two-meter Jarrell Ash spectrometer, to analyze the optical spectral properties of possible laser crystals. At TRG we had only a half-meter instrument (one-quarter the wavelength resolution). But as so often happens, the leading experts were limited in their view of what is possible.

A few months before the first demonstration of the ruby laser, Shawlow and Townes published a paper in the *Physical Review,* describing how their detailed spectrographic studies proved that the highly touted crystal ruby would never be a laser. Ted Maiman at Hughes Research Laboratory in Malibu, California, had a different idea. He demonstrated the world's first laser (a ruby) on May 16, 1960. But Maiman was working in an aircraft laboratory, and his calculations encouraged him to put much more energy into the rod than Shawlow and Townes ever imagined.

His success was not exotic. It came from using a commercial photographer's spiral flash lamp to powerfully pump (excite) the ground state of ruby—something the masters said could not be done. That was what we call a failure of imagination. My algorithm has always been that when the *acknowledged expert* says that something *can* be done, he is almost always right. When such an expert says that something can't be done, he is frequently simply out of touch.

After three years in the stimulating atmosphere of TRG, my wife Joan and I decided we wanted to take baby Elisabeth out of the grime and soot of upper Broadway where we lived. We could actually see the soot settling on her bare little legs, as we would carry her on our walks down Broadway, where we would frequently meet our friends for Chinese dinner or at the West End Bar. I had already received two job offers from budding laser labs in Palo Alto. So, we packed up and moved to sunny California, where our child could safely play in the backyard in the shadow of Stanford University. Little could we have known that our little daughter would spend ten years at that institution, getting a BS in biology, a masters degree as a translator in Slavic Languages, and eventually an MD.

CHAPTER SEVEN

Building an ESP Machine

Working with Burt McMurtry at Sylvania Electric and the very brilliant Steve Harris from Stanford, I helped start what in its time was the largest laser lab on the West Coast. I was twenty-eight years old, but I had three years of hands-on experience in laser research at a time when lasers were only one year old.

Shortly after coming to beautiful Palo Alto, I attended a lecture at Stanford on ESP research given by a distinguished philosophy and religion professor, Jeffrey Smith. After his talk in a large lecture room, he received some very hostile questions, which the gentle philosopher was having trouble answering. Being fresh from the streets of New York, and quite familiar with the material, I stood up and swiftly dealt with the troublemakers and other uninformed skeptics by citing data from published experiments. I had learned well the New York survival rule, "Don't let them shit all over you. Open your mouth!"

I then introduced myself to Prof. Smith, and we decided on the spot to create a parapsychology research group, which we called PRG. We formed this with two other distinguished researchers, my dear friends Charles Tart, the great researcher into altered states of consciousness at University of California, and Arthur Hastings, dean of the Institute of Transpersonal Psychology right here in Palo Alto—with whom I am still working forty years later. PRG flourished for twenty-five years, while the Sylvania laser lab lasted only a decade.

I actually did some very useful work for Sylvania in addition to helping set up the lab and getting contracts from the government. I had an idea for a uniquely powerful carbon-dioxide laser. At that time—and probably still today—a CO_2 laser is limited to an output of about 100 watts per meter of discharge tube length. This limitation occurs because you can't put any more than about 1,000 watts of electrical energy into a one-meter discharge without heating it up and extinguishing the laser action. Lasers need to be kept cool. My idea, with another colleague, good friend, and Stanford PhD Bill Tiffany, was to air-condition the laser.

By thinking out of the box—or out of the tube in this case—we had the idea to have the laser beam go from left to right as usual. But we arranged to have the electrical discharge go from top to bottom, while we would additionally blow the gas from front to back and around in a circle through an actual automobile radiator to cool it! I had to go to Buffalo and buy one right off the floor of Buffalo Forge. That worked excellently—after a year of engineering. We finally tamed the discharge, which always wanted to become a lightening bolt instead of a uniform glow. But in the end we got 1,000 watts of infrared light out of a laser the size of a file cabinet, rather than one that would normally be ten meters long. We were issued a U.S. patent, and the laser rights were sold to nearby Spectra Physics Company for several million dollars.

The inventors, of course, didn't get any of that money, since the company owned the patent. The theory is that they pay us our salary, even when we don't patent anything, so they get to keep the booty when we do. So, all I got was a severe ultraviolet burn on my cornea while a publicity photo was being taken of me looking at the laser while it was burning a hole in a fire brick. I was of course wearing infrared protective goggles, but the white-hot brick was like a little piece of the sun, strongly emitting in the UV. It produced 100 million watts per-square-cm in its focus—enough power to cut up a fire brick, a steel bar, or a two-by-four in a couple of seconds. Psychologist Tart liked the idea of light cutting up fire bricks.

Spectra Physics put the laser into production, as the Gas Transport Laser, and eventually, after I left the company, the very inventive Mike Sasnett and the Sylvania team got 5,000 watts of light energy out of it, to heat-treat locomotive cylinders for General Electric. It was so successful that the government wanted to classify it Secret as part of the Star Wars program (as a project code-named Eighth Card). But Sylvania said absolutely not, since it was developed entirely on their money. Twenty years later, when I was working at Lockheed, I helped build a much larger Airborne Laser system to be installed in a 747, with a complex plan for shooting down enemy missiles, or perhaps even satellites. I left aerospace and Lockheed in 1997, before this mammoth system was tested. I was disappointed at missing the first phase of the testing, which was basically shooting at fifty-five-gallon oil drums five miles away in the desert—definitely a guy kind of program.

CALIFORNIA DREAMING

Returning to my other parallel life—my work with PRG continued. I was the first president of the Parapsychology Research Group, and my daughter, Elisabeth Targ, who became a research psychiatrist successfully investigating distant healing, was the last. Famous ESP researchers visited us from all over the world. Even J. B. Rhine from Duke University made a pilgrimage to California to see us. An important project that Charley Tart and I thought of and built independently was an ESP teaching machine. This portable computer-driven gadget would ask the user to choose which one of four pictures *would be* chosen by the machine. It would then give them immediate feedback, so they could learn what it felt like when they were in contact with the part of themselves, or their awareness, that was psychic. Many people learned to improve their psychic scores with these machines, and the machine became the basis of my first NASA contract, when Hal Puthoff and I co-founded the remote viewing program at Stanford Research Institute in 1972. I even had built a coin-operated version of the machine in 1968, to go into

Elisabeth Targ operating the first commercial ESP testing machine, 1971
(Reprinted by permission of the San Francisco Chronicle.*)*

two local pizza parlors, including the flagship Round Table Pizza in Palo Alto.

The machine, called *ESP Test,* was very profitable—pulling in tons of quarters. It was built for me by a young engineer, Nolan Bushnell, just before he founded the billion-dollar game company Atari. We took it to the Chicago Arcade Game show, but I was told that the Mafia bosses who control game placement "didn't know what an *esp* was." So, we were unable to get national distribution.

The Sylvania lab was six miles from our spacious, one-story modern California house—an Eichler—very innovative for its time. Every room has a large sliding glass door to an outside garden or patio—quite a change from 115th Street and Broadway. Silicon Valley had scores of brilliant people doing all kinds of paradigm-changing research. What this oasis did not have was any public transportation. From my college days, I was an indefatigable bicycle rider. Most of the time I was a graduate student I rode my bike from Greenwich Village all the way up Broadway to Columbia University, some seven chaotic miles of pitted city streets. Riding to Sylvania wasn't a problem for me, but the San Francisco Bay Area has natural air conditioning all summer long. Every afternoon the cool marine breeze comes in through the Golden Gate and blows south along the Peninsula—sucked in by the 100-degree low-pressure of the interior valley. My daily homeward ride was due north, against the wind. I had the idea that if I attached a suitably small gasoline engine to my bicycle, I might be able to get a license for it.

I found a tiny 50cc French engine called a Mosquito that could power my bike by rubbing against the tire. I pedaled this contraption to the Department of Motor Vehicles and asked if I needed a license for it, which of course I did. Since I couldn't come close to passing the eye exam, I proposed that I bring them a letter from my ophthalmologist at Kaiser Hospital, saying that in his opinion I could ride safely. The DMV agent thought that was a possibility for such a small engine.

My doctor at Kaiser understood that, although I couldn't read the eye chart, my distance vision, though limited by resolution, was much more useful to me than for a person who sees things out of focus. We agreed on a letter that said, "There have been no changes of any sort in Mr. Targ's vision over the five years he has been my patient that would make it more dangerous for him to drive than at any time in the past. It is my opinion that he should be allowed to drive a motorized bicycle, so long as he can do so safely." Incredible but true, this vacuous letter got me a permit to drive a motorized bicycle. (As the saying goes, *Nothing has to be true* . . . Just watch out for the nose of the camel.)

After a year, I upgraded this piece of junk for a very cool Italian Ciao—still a moped but much more comfortable, and with better brakes and lights. By the time I quit motorcycling thirty-five years later, I was driving a 250cc, freeway-legal Honda Nighthawk.

Alex, Joan, Russell, Nicholas, and Elisabeth in Palo Alto, 1979

This was the first decade of my marriage. I was focused on Joan and my three children, Elisabeth, Alex, and Nicholas, and my new exposure to home ownership: cutting the grass and repairing the sprinklers—still one of my least favorite tasks. California in the '60s was a peaceful and expansive place to be— lasers, Pink Floyd's "Inter-Stellar Overdrive" and plenty of dope, big redwood hot tubs in sunny Palo Alto, with San Francisco Bay a few blocks to the east, and the beautiful blue Pacific Ocean just over the western hills. As Tolstoy famously reminds us, "All happy families are alike. . . ."

Esalen, Time Dilation, and Professional Wrestling

Sitting naked in hot water in 1972 at the beautiful Esalen Institute in Big Sur, overlooking the rocks and waves of the limitless Pacific Ocean, was freeing and life-changing for me. It opened me up sensually in many different dimensions and put me on a new trajectory of self-exploration in the areas of my body, my mind, and my spirit, as it has done for countless other Esalen visitors. It made me aware that sexual energy is just as real as electromagnetic energy, as Ingo Swann describes in his book *Psychic Sexuality*.

I have now been teaching at Esalen for more than thirty years. I also teach regularly at the Omega Institute in Rhinebeck, New York, and at the Science and Consciousness Conference in Santa Fe. For all this lecturing, I have to carefully organize my material, because I don't use any notes for my presentations—they would be too difficult for me to read comfortably. So far, my memory has not failed during any of these hour-and-a-half or two-hour talks. I have asked my dear wife Patty to be sure to pull me off the stage, and tell me to give it up, before I appear befuddled and forget what I am doing. So far the memory drugs bacopa and phos-phatidylserine (PS-100) seem to do the trick.

Also in the early 1970s I had my first experience with mar-ijuana, which was another sensory awakening—this one more ear-opening than eye-opening. As many people have reported, the drug gives the experience of time slowing down. As a music lover, the exciting experience for me was the sudden appreciation of the *spaces between the notes.* In Haydn quartets, for example in the Sun Quartets (Opus 20), the music appears as a tapestry, much more complex than I would expect from four musicians. This works for Pink Floyd also. I especially remember their extraordinarily spacious number called "Inter-Stellar Overdrive." It all begins to sound orchestral. I assume that this new apprecia-tion of the fine structure is the result of an increase in the speed of my own mental processing. The only way for subjective time to slow down is probably by sampling it faster. I imagine that must be the reason that marijuana is associated with jazz musi-cians. Not necessarily a sign of loose living and bad character, it allows them to hear what's actually going on.

One night, some friends and I were listening to the Floyd album under a cloud of mind-altering smoke, when one scientist friend had to leave and go to work the night shift at Lockheed's "Blue Cube" Satellite Test Center (tracking spacecraft for the Air Force). He arrived to find a note on his chair telling him to be sure to check the satellite's "under-voltage override." He called us in a reasonably clear-headed state to ask if that wasn't the name of the Pink Floyd track we were just listening to. We told him that the beat was right, but the words were slightly different.

One bit of drama that crept periodically into our lives came from my desire to share with my boys all the finer things of my own youth. That included, of course, a chance to sit near ringside at a professional wrestling match. In the 1950s, wrestling was one of the staples of television, and I covered it as a photographer for my high school newspaper. (The blind photographer was the harbinger of the blind biker.) In San Francisco in the 1970s, wrestling was a regular event at the Cow Palace. One memorable Saturday night I took my boys, ten-year-old Nicky and twelve-year-old Alex (Sandy), to a match, along with my good friend Jerry Hiken. Jerry, a successful New York actor, had just appeared in Chekhov's *The Cherry Orchard* on Broadway.

Jerry and his wife Barbara had moved to Palo Alto so he could teach drama and set up an MFA program at Stanford, and get off the Broadway treadmill. Jerry's ten-year-old son Noah was with us, and close enough to see the spit flying out of the mouths of the wrestlers. Noah loved the spectacle, the sound of bodies smashing into the canvas, and the screaming of the fans. He got into the spirit of the thing as only the son of an actor could. "Kill 'em, kill 'em. Hit 'em again!"

The main event was Pat Patterson vs. Moondog Mayne, with Patterson a great San Francisco favorite and a nice-looking good guy. Noah was so enthusiastic, standing on his chair and rooting and screaming for the bad guys, that the large fluffy-bearded man on his left turned to him at intermission and handed him a ten dollar bill. He told Noah, "Hey kid, you're such a great fan. Here's ten bucks. Buy your dad a beer!" It showed me that little Noah knew better how to behave at a wrestling match than I did. Of course, not much of the body slamming is what it appears to be either.

In addition to the blood and guts in the absurdly popular professional wrestling, we should not overlook the powerful but unspoken sexual overlay to all the violence, or simulated violence. I am confident that a significant part of the appeal of this, the NFL, as well as the more violent video games, is to frustrated, repressed, and often sexually thwarted men who are looking for an opportunity to feel at least something in their lives. It is a big stretch to get Joe Six-pack to put down his bottle of beer to contact his inner divinity and learn who he really is, but it can be done. In India there is a very successful program to introduce insight meditation (Vipassana meditation) into the most violent portions of the prison system. The results that I have seen in some films show a complete turnaround of all kinds of violent, crazed men into beautiful, peaceful, and self-aware meditators. The most breathtaking film is called *Doing Time, Doing Vipassana*. If you can just get someone's attention, there is always hope. But the pain level has to be pretty high for a person to begin to discover that the experience of love begins to take place on the inside, not outside.

This whole scene came back to me as I sat in Jerry and Barbara's Palo Alto living room last night, watching the great actor playing Lear to a group of assembled friends. At eighty, Jerry is still a wonderful treasure to the community. He reminded me that it was our mutual friend Alan Alda who told him to look me up when he first came to Palo Alto forty years ago.

CHAPTER EIGHT

My "Pier" Group—
Life in Silicon Valley

The first Government support for our ESP research had its origins in April of 1972, on a wind-swept pier at St. Simon's Island off the North Carolina coast. I had just finished talking to a hundred futurists at a NASA conference on Speculative Technology, about Russian parapsychology research and experiments I had done with my electronic ESP-teaching machine. And I had my computer (integrated circuit) driven machine with me for the conference—all pretty fancy for 1972. I had been kept longer than I had expected at the lecture hall, answering questions about ESP research, while everyone else had gone off to put on sweaters to counter the chilly evening breeze off the Atlantic.

After my talk, I walked down to the water's edge with astronaut Edgar Mitchell, rocket pioneer Werner von Braun, NASA Director James Fletcher, science fiction writer Arthur C. Clarke, and NASA's New-Projects Administrator George Pezdirtz, who had organized the conference. At the time I was looking for a way to leave my job in laser research at Sylvania, where I had worked for the past decade, in order to start an ESP program at nearby SRI—which would have to be independently funded.

As I stood in my short-sleeved shirt on the pier, I tried to remember a kundalini meditation I had learned from Mollie back at Columbia, in order to summon up enough warmth to keep from freezing. I struggled not to shiver—successfully I think—while I explained the concepts of contemporary psi research to the men I knew could determine my entire future as a psychic researcher.

In my experience trying to interest people to support ESP research, I have often found that the top people in most organizations know that psi is real and are willing to admit it. Edgar Mitchell had just carried out some ESP card-guessing experiments from space and had had a spiritually transforming experience viewing the earth while returning from the moon. Werner von Braun told us of his beloved psychic grandmother, who always knew in advance when someone was in trouble and needed help. He was very friendly and supportive to the whole idea of ESP research. (Since then, I have come to realize that everyone will admit to having a psychic grandmother.) I suppressed my knowledge that the great German rocket scientist's biography was called *I Aim at the Stars,* and contemporary stand-up comedian Mort Sahl said on one of his records that it should have been called, "I Aim at the Stars but I Usually Hit London." Fletcher was concerned that the Russians were ahead of us in psychic research, a fear based in part on the recently published book *Psychic Discoveries behind the Iron Curtain.* Only the science fiction writer Clarke expressed skepticism, despite his hugely successful book *Childhood's End*—which was all about psi.

In the end, with Mitchell's great assistance and continuing help from Dr. Pezdirtz at NASA, physicist Hal Puthoff and I were offered a contract by Fletcher to start a research program if we could find a home for it. As I had hoped, that home turned out to be Stanford Research Institute, where Hal was already employed. The four of us met with Charles Anderson, the broad-minded president of SRI, in his spacious office. Mitchell and Pezdirtz played the NASA card, arguing that this was just the right moment to start an ESP research program and offering their financial help. Hal and I promised the very fair-minded Anderson that we would try very hard to keep a low profile, and Anderson said okay. Sometimes "piling-on" has its value.

Two months later Joan and I and our children flew to Iceland to watch Joan's brother Bobby Fischer compete for the chess championship of the world against then-champion Boris Spassky from the USSR. Joan had taught Bobby to play chess when they were children on vacation in an old seaside cottage by the New Jersey shore. Joan was ten and Bobby was five when they serendipitously came across an old scrapbook containing several years of carefully collected chess puzzles from a local paper. Joan taught her little brother the moves with the aid of a one-dollar plastic chess set, and the rest, as they say, is "history."

It had been a tremendous struggle to get notoriously temperamental Bobby to agree to sign up for any financial or official physical arrangements. Finally, with tireless handholding and brilliant negotiation at home and abroad by my attorney Andrew Davis—for which he was of course unpaid—Bobby actually got on a plane to Iceland. After forfeiting a game over playing conditions (a TV tower on the stage), Bobby won the match 12½ to 8½ and became the first and thus far *only* U.S. Chess Champion of the World. The gentlemanly Spassky came to Iceland to celebrate chess. Bobby came to Iceland to crush Spassky.

That's what we call *single-pointed focus of attention*. And the outcome is what one would expect. The Hindu sage Patanjali taught that with this intense focus, you can learn to see into the distance as well as the future. You can even heal the sick and diagnose illness and that teaching corresponds to my own parapsychology research findings through the years, as well as the Russians', though at that time the Russians were mainly interested in distant behavior modification (things like remote strangulation, described in my book *The Mind Race*). The Russians were afraid that Bobby was using some kind of ESP trick to crush Spassky, so they insisted on taking apart his special leather chair. But, when asked about ESP and mental conditioning, Bobby said in an interview before the match, "I don't believe in psychology. I just believe in good moves."

One bright night while we were still in Iceland with Bobby (it was July), we all went bowling at the U.S. Army base. Of course I can't see bowling pins very well, but I throw the ball really hard, and it often hits something. The next day, newspapers published a story about how Bobby had rudely thrown food at a waiter in the hotel restaurant that evening. He wasn't even in the hotel! But newspapers have never been kind to Bobby. In fact, whenever I have been personally involved in a news story—whether about lasers, ESP, or Bobby—the story has been significantly bogus or distorted, offering more opportunities to question reality.

BEING PREPARED

Joan and I and our three children, Alex, Nicholas, and Elisabeth, often went hiking and camping in the Sierras, the beautiful mountains just three hours drive east from our home. In spite of my poor vision, I had been an enthusiastic Boy Scout as a kid, and now we made a habit of going camping with our good friends and neighbors Steve and Fran Harris. Steve was a very young Stanford professor in the Electrical Engineering Department—probably one of the youngest. He went on to become much honored and celebrated for his many discoveries and inventions in nonlinear optics and optical materials. He and I had worked closely together during my early days of laser research at Sylvania. Unlike Magoo, Steve was a very experienced and competent camper and woodsman. So, Joan and I were very happy to have him for a guide on our many adventures.

When Joan and I had first come to Sylvania for an interview, the highly intelligent and energetic department head Burt McMurtry had introduced us to Steve and Fran, knowing that it was likely we would become friends. Although Burt was a football player from Rice University in Houston, he was astute enough to know that two young East Coast Jewish laser physicists would probably like each other. Steve and Fran were basically the bait to get us to come to California—to show us that the area was at least somewhat civilized and familiar.

On our first spring outing, Steve arranged for the four of us to go white-water canoeing on the Russian River near Santa Rosa, California. I actually knew how to do this. Because of my Scout camping experience, I had taken Red Cross lifesaving courses and was even an assistant lifeguard for two summers at a children's camp in the Adirondacks—which is to say, I was a strong swimmer and knew how to paddle my canoe.

After being introduced to our canoe and life jackets, we put in at Alexander Bridge and headed for the ocean. In late April, the Russian is an exquisite, fast-moving river, sparkly blue and green, and a hundred feet wide with spring flowers on both banks rising high above the gorge. We put the "girls" in the bow of the canoe, where they could assemble our chicken sandwiches for lunch when the time came. For me, that is never soon enough. Steve wisely put himself in the stern to steer the canoe, since he was both experienced and could see the rocks. I was kneeling in the middle to provide power and follow instructions.

As soon as we pushed off from the shore, the swift current took hold of our little craft and sucked us into the middle of the river, where we were surprised to find ourselves flying past the beautiful flowers like a bat out of hell. We had this lovely scene to ourselves for a good reason—every knowledgeable person in the area knows that the Russian River is treacherous in the early spring run-off. As I looked back over my shoulder, I noticed that Steve was sitting on the rear seat, which I had always been taught was a bad idea. But, he was a PhD, and it was his party.

All went well on this beautiful thrill ride, until the river began to narrow and rocks began to appear. I actually had to put down my chicken sandwich to give my full attention to paddling in this fast-developing situation. Steve skillfully guided us past the thundering white-water rapids and around the looming boulders and whirlpools threatening to smash our little canoe. Finally, after quite an exhausting half hour, we came into quiet open water and things were beautiful and peaceful again. Then in the distance, we heard a voice—far away. Someone was calling, "Hey kids. I'm in the water." It was Steve, who had been pitched over backwards out of his seat at the last boulder. There was no way to stop the canoe in fast-moving water. But within a minute or two, we passed beneath some overhanging tree branches. I stood up to my full height, perhaps even on tiptoes, and stretched to grab a branch high overhead, while hooking my feet under one of the struts. That did the trick—we stopped. And within a few minutes, Steve came floating down to us. If I had jumped for a branch, the canoe would have passed underneath me, and left me hanging from the branch in even worse shape than Steve. After another glorious hour in the sunshine, we finished our sandwiches and put into Healdsburg. From there, the canoe outfitters took us back upriver to our car. Welcome to California!

So now, fifteen years have passed, and we're on the road again with Steve and Fran and our three kids and two of theirs. This time we are headed for the Sierra Nevada mountains for what will turn out to be our last family outing because Elisabeth is almost sixteen and is headed for college in the fall. She will have other interests more attractive than camping with her parents and little brothers. We drive over the mountains, past Lee Vining to an Eastern Sierra entrance known as the Devil's Post Pile. It comprises dozens of acres of mysterious hexagonal columnar basalt pillars up to sixty feet long, hence the name. It is thought to have been formed by a slow-cooling lava flow half a million years ago. Eleven-year-old Nicholas had the sniffles the week before this ten-day backpacking adventure. So, we took him to the doctor for a checkup and blessings for the journey. "No infection, a little congestion—don't worry, Mother." Those were the days when you called him "Doctor," and he called you "Mother."

We leave Palo Alto in the early morning, and it is past noon when we begin the climb to our first destination, which is Shadow Lake. This circular hike is exceptionally beautiful and is one that we have done several times before. As we climb higher and higher into the mountains, we encounter a series of exquisite mountain lakes—Garnet Lake, Ruby Lake, and Emerald Lake, fed year-round by the mountain snowpack. There are usually very few other hikers here, because we enter the mountains from the back door, so to speak—from the sparsely populated eastern side.

As we start the long climb out of Shadow Lake, our pathfinder Steve calls everyone to a halt because he sees a sizable rattlesnake sunning himself (or herself) right across our trail. What to do? Steve says we have to kill the snake—can't leave a rattlesnake on the trail. He grabbed a large rock from the side of the trail, aimed it squarely on the sleeping snake's head, but missed. Quickly seeing another similar-sized rock, he carefully aimed, and again missed. How is this possible? And the snake never moved. Finally, being a sturdy fellow, Steve grabs a truly huge boulder. He positions this last super bomb directly over the snake's middle. And you guessed it, the snake is now well barricaded in a sturdy rock house, and Steve loses his footing in the loose gravel and falls ass-foremost onto the snake and the rock pile. Steve is bleeding. Did the snake get him, or is it just a nasty fall? And how do you put a tourniquet on a snake-bitten behind? All these things rushed through my mind, though I don't know what the others were thinking. Thank God, the snake is now gone, and it is up to nurse Joan to make the diagnosis. "Take off your pants and I'll have a look." All it requires is some antiseptic ointment and a Band-Aid, and off we go.

We are all carrying sizable backpacks—food, tents, bedding, and brandy for the ten days ahead of us—and we are all good eaters. On our past jaunts we have had both rain and snow. It is quite shocking to emerge from our big dome tent and find it covered with two inches of snow, looking for all the world like an igloo, up at 12,000 feet. But on this trip we don't make it that far. About an hour into the long hot climb out of Shadow Lake, Nicholas begins to have a coughing fit. Could it be the dust? We have forgotten Nicky's sniffles. Is he out of shape? No. Eleven-year-olds don't get out of shape. By four o'clock, Nicky is complaining that he is having a hard time breathing. We are only at 8,500 feet, so lack of oxygen shouldn't be a problem yet. Steve and I divide up Nicky's stuff, and we begin to look for a camping place as we come to our destination, which is Garnet Lake. By six o'clock, Nicholas is noticeably wheezing, and Joan the nurse is getting concerned. This is her baby after all—five foot eight, but still her baby. We pitch our tents by the lake and make dinner over our propane stoves. By eight o'clock it's getting cold and dark, and Nicholas is in considerable distress. It is obvious to everybody that he can't breathe, but it's much too dark to think of going down. Joan begins to boil water in our largest cooking pot, inside our tent, creating a croup tent as they would do in the hospital for a person with emphysema. Nicholas feels a little better breathing the warm, moist steam. But, the truth is that he is suffocating, in spite of steam, and the fact that we are at only 8,500 feet is irrelevant.

Joan tries to give him a decongestant pill to ease his distress, but he can't swallow anything. Nicholas wants to know if he is going to die. His chest is rattling, and he is gasping for each breath. We assure him that he is tough, and we will get him to a doctor first thing in the morning. He says, "But I can't breathe!" This is the most heart-wrenching possible moment for a parent, sitting in a cold dark tent with your beautiful dying child.

Then Joan has a bright idea. Rummaging around in the bottom of her first aid kit she finds anti-emetic Phenergan suppositories that she packed at the last minute for no known reason. She stuffs this into Nicky's bottom, meeting very little resistance at this point. And within an hour he is able to swallow two Sudafed decongestant pills. After a surprisingly short time he begins to breathe a little easier.

At the first light of dawn, we break camp and begin our run down the mountain. Steve and I are holding Nicky under his arms as we now crash through the underbrush with our unwieldy packs, to take a shortcut back to the car and civilization. We all reach our car by eight and are rolling into the little ski town of Mammoth by nine. In the emergency room we hear the words "mountain pulmonary edema" for the first time. Nicholas survives unscathed, except perhaps for the eleven-year-old's trauma of facing his death in the wilderness. We learn that the reduced air pressure in the mountains can suck the fluid out of a congested person's lungs and drown him. It's like pneumonia, only worse because it's a mechanical problem, and antibiotics are useless. The doctors in Mammoth are very familiar with the problem. They have several every year—often with a fatal outcome. Within one week of our return to Palo Alto, we read in the local paper of a Stanford math professor who died of mountain pulmonary edema while climbing Mount Hood in Oregon.

Nicholas went East to a private school, and Elisabeth went off to college, to be followed in two years by Alex. Elisabeth was a somewhat immature college student entering Pomona College at sixteen. But, she was ready for a life of the mind, and we felt that the rest of her would catch up as she participated in this new and exciting life. I had a similar experience entering college at sixteen and quickly made friends. I was not nearly as smart as Elisabeth, and I was handicapped besides. But, because of this head start in her education, Elisabeth was able to complete her important and pioneering work in distant healing, before her tragic death at forty. My recommendation is that you should let your gifted and energetic kids run as fast as they can. Who are we to hold anyone back?

My two sons now both live in the San Francisco Bay Area. Alex, whom I still call Sandy, is a physician and anesthesiologist and lives with his Taiwan-born wife Phine, also a doctor, just across the park from my wife Patty and me in Palo Alto. They have three little girls, Sasha, Sonia, and Sylvia. Alex, always an inventive tinkerer, has created a very imaginative and successful business for himself. He is rare journeyman anesthesiologist, with his anesthesia machine in the back of his SUV. He is doing exclusively freelance mobile pediatric anesthesiology. Alex had wanted to be a physicist when he was at Stanford. But, I discouraged him, saying that from my experience as a physicist, scientists today are wage slaves, working at the pleasure of the bosses and corporate heads, or even worse, academic department heads. So, I proposed that he become a doctor, work for himself, and explore biophysics if he still wanted to. I don't know if he remembers any such conversation, but, that seems to be what he has done. In my youth I was a stereotype ectomorph, tall, skinny, and happy to read a book. Alex, on the other hand, was always a mesomorph, a solid athlete type, in addition to being a scholar. Among the Targs, there are no pudgy endomorphs—based on the three somatotypes of William Sheldon, which they taught us in

"Psychology of Personality" fifty short years ago. Again, I don't mean to imply that this has anything to do with character. Alex was an oarsman in college, and just a few years ago at age forty, he took part in a triathlon in which he swam from Alcatraz Island across San Francisco Bay, rode his bike seventeen miles, and then ran five miles to end up at the Marina Green, where we were all waiting for him in amazement and admiration.

One of Alex's other remarkable accomplishments is that he may be the only person to have turned down Harvard University on three separate occasions. He applied to Harvard as an undergraduate, but chose Boston University because of its six-year freshman-to-MD program. He left Boston University after a year because he felt the courses were too weak, though he loved being an oarsman with them on the Charles River. He again turned down the Crimson as a sophomore transfer student, to go to Stanford where his loving sister was already a junior. Finally he turned down Harvard's acceptance to its MD-PhD program because he realized that he would owe them a quarter of a million when he was done, while University of California (UCSF) would give him an MD with no debt at all.

Nicholas and his wife Elise have just moved to California, after a decade as attorneys in Washington, D.C. She still works as a senior counsel for the Justice Department, dealing with environmental issues—mainly prosecuting the bad guys. When they were in Washington, Nicholas was working for the Environmental Protection Agency. He helped to greatly expand their Department of Environmental Justice, to determine who the bad guys are. He was interested in investigating questions—like why are incinerators and other stinky polluting projects always sited in poor or black neighborhoods. No doubt, his interest in land use came from the years he spent with his parents traipsing over undeveloped property to determine if it would be suitable for our mythical intentional community. He and Elise, and their three-year-old baby Bobby, live in the beautiful eucalyptus-forested Presidio of San Francisco, within the shadow of the Golden Gate Bridge. I consider this to be his reward for the many years he worked for the Department of the Interior. Nicholas has now become a partner with an environmental law firm in San Francisco. He is the most likely one to return to his mother's dream of an organic farm at our Peninsula property—Hayfields. Nicholas carries the tall Targ genes; at 6′8″ he tops his father by three inches. But, fortunately he has an exceptionally equanimous disposition, reminding me very much of my best friend from New York—my large peaceful physicist-lawyer buddy, Menasha.

Alex (on his tip-toes) and Nicholas, 2006

My daughter Elisabeth was a lifelong explorer and seeker after truth. Her luminosity and visionary thinking were evident to all who knew her and are apparent in her TV interviews. As a child, Elisabeth was encouraged to be polite, intelligent, and *psychic*—she was able to describe, for example, what was inside her birthday presents before she opened them.

Elisabeth died at age forty, in 2002, of a glioblastoma brain tumor—exactly the disease she was studying as a candidate for distant healing. At the memorial service for her at California Pacific Medical Center, where she worked as a psychiatrist and head of Alternative and Complementary Medicine until her passing, the Center director described her as "probably the smartest person I ever met." Her widely praised research in distant healing at that hospital showed that prayerful healers across the United States could affect the health and well-being of seriously ill AIDS patients in San Francisco. In the *Western Journal of Medicine,* she demonstrated that patients receiving healing prayers felt more mentally positive about themselves, had many fewer

Elisabeth Targ, 2000

opportunistic illnesses, significantly fewer trips to the hospital, and spent many fewer days in the hospital than the control group for whom no prayers were said. This result occurred in spite of the fact that neither the patients nor the doctors knew which patients were receiving the prayers—a "double blind" experiment. This gave meaningful real-life evidence for our nonlocal mind-to-mind connections and encouraged NIH to support similar research at other laboratories.

Elisabeth had participated in many ESP studies with me since childhood. As a ten-year-old, she was an early participant in the ESP teaching machine experiments that showed one can learn what it feels like when you successfully use your psychic abilities. The machine would randomly select one of four possible internal states. The user would then press one of the four buttons on the front of the machine to indicate *her* choice of what the machine had selected. The correct one of four colored lights would then be illuminated. A score of six out of twenty-four was expected by chance. Encouragement messages were: *A Good Beginning* for six out of twenty-five; *ESP Ability Present* for eight; *Outstanding* for ten; and *Psychic, Medium, Oracle!* for twelve. Some people could learn to increase their score by practice, even though the machine was making its choices randomly. Elisabeth was one of the most successful from the outset, often scoring in the highest category. This is now a free iPhone app called ESP Trainer.

My wife Joan died in 1998, in her sixtieth year and just two months short of our fortieth wedding anniversary. She had been in a six-year legal battle to create a small organic vegetable garden on our beautiful fifty-acre hillside property—dubbed Hayfields—in Portola Valley, California. A vengeful neighbor vowed to "break the financial back" of Joan's garden with continuing lawsuits, which were diligently followed by all the local newspapers. Ironically on the day that Joan received the judge's final and unconditional approval for every aspect of her garden, she had a cerebral hemorrhage and passed from this earth. She was a passionate organic gardener, a nurse, a Montessori teacher, a visionary, and a great pioneer in introducing computers into Silicon Valley classrooms at all grades. We have a large tree planted in her memory, in the middle of her beautiful garden. (Four years later, we sadly planted a similar tree nearby in memory of Elisabeth.)

This lovely four-acre wood-fenced garden was the outgrowth of an eighteen-year search for a little piece of land. Just before moving to California, we had been considering starting an intentional community. That was just about a year into our marriage. After two years of living on Upper Broadway, we began to think how nice it would be to live in the country. We were both infatuated with the American tradition of intentional communities, such as the Shakers, the Quakers, the Amish, and the Oneida community of Upstate New York. Our first outing was with our good friend Gary Feinberg, who had a car and knew how to drive—Joan didn't at the time. Along with baby Elisabeth, we investigated all sorts of nearby farmland. I especially recall eighty beautiful acres and a farmhouse in Hudson, New York, on the river and about an hour from our home. But, instead of buying that, we moved to California.

After another decade of crawling through the underbrush all over the San Francisco Peninsula looking for land to develop, we finally found fifty acres in the Portola Valley foothills, 800 feet above Stanford University. It had breathtaking views across San Francisco Bay, but alas it had no water available. It was owned by a real estate company, and even they couldn't figure out what to do with it. But standing on the hilltop, Joan could see a large water storage tank. Who, we asked, owned that? It was the California Water Company, a quarter of a mile away. The next day we went to town hall and discovered that a retired dentist owned the thirty-acre intervening property. Six months later, in 1976, we had mortgaged our Palo Alto home, found a likeminded visionary partner, Nancy Kiesling, and bought the two properties, comprising eighty acres for $160,000. The question is, why couldn't the big realty firm have figured out that their beautiful hillside property could get water from the tank in plain sight? Especially since the dentist who owned the connecting property was the cousin of the realty firm's president. In this case, it is literally an issue of expanding awareness in order to see the next hilltop.

What they might have realized was that it would take four years from the time we bought the property until we were able to sell the first lot. The Town of Portola Valley liked to think of our newly purchased property as a town park, though of course they didn't own it. As a result we met resistance to each phase of our subdivision. All this occurred in the time of Jimmy Carter, when interest rates were approaching 20 percent. The result was that we had to sell our first lot at a bargain price to avoid going broke

Joan, with her plans for the Hayfields subdivision
(Photo courtesy of the San Francisco Chronicle*)*

and losing our homes. Joan then became a full-time land developer. She quit teaching at the local middle school where she ran the center she had created for gifted and talented children. (The center is long gone—no more encouragement for the gifted.) We had to learn how to do percolation tests for drainage, how to bring in water across the quarter mile of active landslides, and how to site houses so that they too wouldn't slide down the hill.

It took us many years to realize that some of the people who were delaying us were simply waiting for their customary bribes. But, we were too inexperienced to know it at the time. However, we became experts in pier and grade-beam foundations. The result was nine beautiful houses in the development that we called the Hayfields. But it was not the intentional community of our dreams. It simply cost so much money to do all the phases of development, that the friends who had wanted to live with us could no longer afford the price. We sold eight of the houses to various buyers, and kept one. I lived there until 1992, when I left because of personal tensions in the family and the dangers of riding my motorcycle to work each day through the hills in the rain and the dark—and also a health emergency that I will describe shortly. The previous year, I had a serious accident in which a pickup truck ran a stop sign and hit the front of my cycle at full speed. The bike was destroyed, while I sustained only a broken wrist, which kept me in the hospital for a week as they pinned me back together. I looked formidable for the next six weeks, with two large pins like turkey skewers sticking out of my cast. Today they wouldn't have let me on an airplane. It was a time when I was doing a lot of traveling for Lockheed, between San Francisco, NASA-Langley in Virginia, and our laser contractor in Palm Beach.

I still own the beautiful hilltop house that Joan and I built. Perhaps one of our children or grandchildren will eventually live there. It was a very intense and challenging ten years from 1976 when we bought the property until 1986 when we finally moved into our house. But, it was this continuing focus of attention, mainly on Joan's part, that eventually allowed us to achieve financial independence. My four decades of work as a wage slave in aerospace would never have accomplished this. We did what America wants you to do—borrow lots of money and build

The house that Joan and I built in the Hayfields, looking out across San Francisco Bay

something. But, I can tell you that building a nine-home subdivision from scratch, on undeveloped land, is not recommended for the faint of heart. If we had known that interest rates were going to 20 percent in the middle of the project, we wouldn't have undertaken it.

To end this chapter, it must be said that Joan was a woman of extraordinary intelligence and limitless resourcefulness. She demonstrated those abilities in everything she did, whether overseeing a multimillion dollar real estate development, or saving the life of her child on a Sierra mountainside. The rest of us just have to be the best we can, with what we've got.

CHAPTER NINE

The Real X-Files—
Two Decades of Psychic Spying

It's now more than thirty years since Hal Puthoff and I began the remote viewing program at SRI. At this writing there are almost a million Google! pages devoted to "remote viewing," so it's no longer exactly a secret. Remote viewing is an ability we all have to a greater or lesser degree, that lets us describe and experience activities or events blocked from ordinary perception by distance or time. It is absolutely clear from the data that we seriously misperceive the nature of the space and time in which we live. That's what I mean by the need to question our reality. From my teaching experience around the world, I have seen that many people can learn to quiet their minds and describe what is happening in a distant room, or in a distant city. The distance does not matter—we have done experiments up to 10,000 miles, and Ingo Swann has described previously unknown rings around the planet Jupiter. Similarly we have learned that it is *no more difficult* to psychically describe a future event than to describe one that is hidden from view but has already occurred.

Phenomena like remote viewing that are independent of space and time are called *nonlocal*. Physicist Henry Stapp of the University of California has said that "the discovery of nonlocality may be the most important discovery in all of science." I agree with that assessment. Hal Puthoff and I have published our R.V. findings in the world's most prestigious journals, *Nature,*

Proceedings of the Institute of Electrical and Electronics Engineers (IEEE), *Proceedings of the American Association for the Advancement of Science (AAAS),* among others. Most recently Prof. Elizabeth Rauscher and I presented data at an AAAS conference, dealing with retro-causality (how the future affects the past). But it was our SRI applications of remote viewing for the government that kept our program funded for twenty-three years.

Nonlocality and entanglement were first described by Erwin Schrödinger, who perfected quantum mechanics with the development of the elegant quantum wave equation that bears his name. That equation allows problems to be solved using straightforward math instead of the unwieldy matrix algebra that Heisenberg had pursued. Schrödinger developed it in the snow-covered Alps over Christmas vacation with his then-current girlfriend. He and his *schatzi* returned to Vienna ten days later with the completed wave equations, though the name of his muse is lost in the mists of the mountains. In 1927, Nobelist Schrödinger pointed out that quantum theory predicts that elementary particles or photons of light created in a single event or instant *will remain twins over their lifetime.* In other words, if one of a pair of entangled photons is put through a variable polarizer in Geneva, its twin's polarization measured in the city of Basel will be correlated with it, if they were born together. Schrödinger famously said that this "entanglement" was not *one* of the differences between quantum theory and classical theory, but *the* difference between the two worldviews—locality and nonlocality. This entanglement between the twin particles is called *nonlocal* because the connection is *instantaneous and independent of spatial separation.*

Ingo Swann is a highly talented and successful visionary artist in New York, and a great natural psychic who taught us at SRI how to understand nonlocality. (He is also a hell of a nice guy, and a very entertaining friend.) Ingo actually taught Hal and me remote viewing, and we taught the Army, and the Army taught the world. Pat Price, another natural psychic, was a recently retired police commissioner of Burbank, California, who had incorporated his prodigious ESP ability into his police work. The report of Ingo and Pat's amazing abilities has been described in several of my previous books. For the two years he was with us at SRI, Pat was our good friend and constant companion. He was an amiable and charming Irishman, a man among men, and adored by the women. He is the only person I have ever known who functioned continuously day in and day out as an obvious psychic being. He regaled us at lunch, over his Coke and cherry pie, with upcoming political and world events, days or weeks in the future. Swann also had this ability, but he was a more private person at that time.

Pat Price died in 1975 at the age of fifty-seven. His death in Las Vegas, on his way to see us, has remained a mystery. We don't know if it was the CIA—with whom we had been working—who got him for funneling classified remote viewing data to the Scientology Guardian's office, or the Russians, or just a bad heart. But, I do know that he said goodbye to many of his friends before he left to see us. And he purchased a $1 million term life insurance policy, which he put into the hands of his wife Ann just before he got on the plane. So, it seems obvious that he knew something was up. Two years later Admiral Stanfield Turner, then director of the CIA, told reporters about his encounter with an unidentified man who sounds suspiciously like Price:

> WASHINGTON - The CIA financed a program in 1975 to develop a new kind of agent who could truly be called a "spook," Director Stanfield Turner has disclosed.
>
> The CIA chief said that the agency had found a man who could "see" what was going on anywhere in the world through his psychic powers.

Turner said that CIA scientists would show the man a picture of a place and he would then describe any activity going on there at that time.

The tight-lipped CIA chief wouldn't reveal how accurate the spook was, but said that the agency dropped the project in 1975.

"He died," Turner said, "and we haven't heard from him since." (*Chicago Tribune,* Saturday, August 13, 1977)

At SRI, we frequently had visitors from the military intelligence community who wanted to "see something psychic." If we were successful, they might renew our program for another year. Such visitors came from all branches of the government, right up to the Under Secretary of Defense, Walter LaBerge, and we were very happy to see them. Because our program was supported mainly by the CIA and DIA, we tried to keep a low profile. So, no one was pleased when LaBerge announced that he was coming to see us by helicopter, which required the clearing of the SRI parking lot to accommodate his not-very-discreet arrival. When he walked into our secure remote viewing room, he looked around and asked who we were going to have for a psychic today. He was quite shocked when I told him that *he* was the psychic. Our experience had been that if a Washington visitor does the remote viewing himself, he then goes back to his office with his own (usually successful) experience, rather than a story about something weird he saw in the lab.

Hal and LaBerge's major traveled to a randomly selected site, which turned out to be the Allied Arts Center a few miles away. It has a circular brick plaza, in the Spanish Mission style. After the usual cool-down period, I asked LaBerge to "describe his mental pictures with regard to where the travelers had gone." I, of course, didn't have any idea of the answer, so I was totally noncommittal as he carefully drew an oval brick plaza with buildings, walkways, and a gushing fountain in the center. When the travelers came back, we took LaBerge there with Hal and his major for feedback. LaBerge was quite surprised and pleased by the correspondence between his drawing and the target site. He repeatedly asked his adjutant to verify that this was really the place they went to. With this, our contract was renewed, and we gained a very important and strong supporter in the Defense Department, which led to our many contracts with Army Intelligence Command (INSCOM). The plaza is shown below from an oil painting by Patty Targ. This was the first and only time Allied Arts had appeared as a target, out of a pool of sixty possible targets.

Allied Arts Plaza: Remote viewing target accurately described at SRI by Under Secretary of Defense Walter LaBerge

In 1976 Hal and I published a detailed description of our remote viewing findings in the highly prestigious *Proceedings of the IEEE (Institute of Electrical and Electronics Engineers)*. We also wrote a book called *Mind Reach,* which was very successful in the

United States and translated into nine foreign languages. The book even attracted the attention of Gene Roddenberry, the creator of *Star Trek*. The TV series was in production, and Gene was just starting work on the first *Star Trek* movie. He optioned our book for a new movie about government spying with ESP. The screenplay was written, but Gene had a nervous breakdown and our film never got made. But we did get to visit the set on a fabulous soundstage in Los Angeles where my little son Nicholas had a chance to sit in Captain Kirk's chair on the bridge of the *Enterprise,* and we all walked on the rocky home planet of the dreaded Klingons. Apart from a $10,000 option fee, our only residual was my immortality as the favorite Klingon delicacy known as "heart of Targ"—yum. Cooking instructions can be found in *The Star Trek Cookbook,* by Ethan Phillips. I considered our book to represent a real scientific breakthrough. And I wanted to get one of America's preeminent scientists to endorse it and write a preface. I searched and found just one degree of separation between myself and Margaret Mead, director of the New York Museum of Natural History. I knew that she had been one of the principal movers responsible for the acceptance of the Parapsychology Association into the AAAS. I called her at the Museum, and she agreed to look at the book. A week later she called and said she would write our preface, if we would delete our chapter dealing with U.S. forces opposed to psychic research. She said "You and Harold are well-paid and free to publish your work. You are in no danger of being burned or thrown out of your comfortable laboratory. I think you should cut all the complaining out of your very interesting book." We did just as she suggested, and she wrote us a very thoughtful and positive preface.

OUT-OF-BODY EXPERIENCES

Remote viewing is a safe and very exhilarating activity that you can learn and practice at home with no fear of a bad or frightening experience. All you need is a friend to bring you little objects in a paper bag. Meanwhile you practice visualizing, as you learn to separate the fleeting psychic signal from the mental noise of memory, imagination, and analysis—which Ingo Swann calls analytical overlay. I describe this learning process in detail in my book, *Limitless Mind*. Ever since the publication of Robert Monroe's book, *Journeys Out of the Body* (1973), people have been asking me about the relationship between remote viewing and out-of-body experiences (OBEs). Here is a brief summary:

In a remote viewing experience you quiet your mind and describe the surprising images that appear in your awareness—on your mental screen—in response to the question of the day, such as, "I have a target, or a hidden object that needs a description." You can describe and experience color, shape, form, or weight of the object, or the overall architectural appearance of a target location. You can even go inside a distant building. But that's where it begins to merge with out-of-body territory.

Basically there is a *continuum* from remote viewing to a full out-of-body experience, with no discrete break between one and the other. In an out-of-body experience you generally start with a simple remote viewing, and then bring along with you your emotionality, sensitivity, and sexuality—to whatever degree you are comfortable. Unlike remote viewing, you definitely have the opportunity to scare yourself in an OBE because of the significant emotional commitment. In an OBE, you have mobility of your point of view at the distant target. You also can have significant emotional interaction with a person at the target. (Bob Monroe describes such an interaction as leading up to his eventual marriage to the woman he was psychically visiting in an OBE journey.)

I had such an experience in the big wooden OBE box at The Monroe Institute in Virginia. Fred (Skip) Atwater, research director of the Institute and teacher of the Army Intelligence remote viewing program at Fort Meade, led me through the typical long, quiet, initial OBE cool-down. Meanwhile, their patented Hemi-Sync musical selections were playing in my earphones and wishing me bon voyage. I found myself in the living room of a good friend who is a singer-songwriter in Nashville, where I had been working with her to produce CDs of her wonderful original music. I saw her clearly—dressed in a yellow sweater and brown skirt, gathering up a briefcase and handbag, getting ready to leave her apartment. It was a totally lifelike and quite surprising visit. I later confirmed all the details and time with her by telephone. OBEs are much more realistic, lifelike, and cinematic than the more diaphanous flickering in-and-out of most remote viewing experiences. The OBE has a much higher (more detailed) data rate and is much more involving. Nevertheless, as a remote viewer becomes more experienced, the R.V. perception also becomes increasingly stable.

I find that OBEs have a similar feeling to lucid dreams, where you find that you are awake in a dream. Once you learn to have and recognize lucid dreams, you will never be overtaken by a nightmare, because you will be able to be an active participant. Dr. Stephen LaBerge received his PhD from Stanford University for his investigation into lucid dreaming and has been teaching the subject for the past twenty years.

Patty and I took part in a ten-day "Dream Vacation" on the big island of Hawaii with LaBerge, where we learned to have lucid dreams. After a week of practice, I had an exhilarating flying dream in which I successfully flew out of my room and over the dark craggy bay and sparkly moonlit ocean next to the North Coast retreat center where we were staying. I also fulfilled my objective for the trip, which was to learn to control my occasional frightening nightmares, which I have not had since his workshop. However, it is important to remember that a lucid dream is not an OBE. What you see in the dream does not necessarily (or usually) exist.

The great Dzogchen Buddhist teacher, Namkai Narbu, teaches that gaining control of your dreams prepares you for your journey through the *bardos*—during the period between lives where you have to deal with peaceful and rather terrifying wrathful deities. In my view Dzogchen Buddhism is unquestionably the fast track to freedom, truth, and self-liberation.

I must say, we did not teach any of this at SRI. We didn't want anyone to have a bad experience and complain to the management—or the government—that we had separated their consciousness from their body and they were unable to put themselves back together again.

People also report powerful and quite realistic sexual experiences, including transgender ones. (You might have the surprising experience of the physical sensation of being a lover of *either* gender.) These may or may not be physical. (Which is to say, a remote sexual experience may manifest as an energetic encounter, like a remote kundalini experience, but associated with another distant person.) Swann calls this "sexuality clairvoyance." For any of these interactions to make sense, it is best between consenting adults. Swann describes this "sexual vibe as a combination of clairvoyance and telesthesia . . . involving a transfer of sensations." Otherwise it would be a kind of psychic rape. Swann's book, *Psychic Sexuality,* is all about sex on the astral plane. And a volume for the truly adventurous is *The Confessions of Aleister Crowley,* where he writes about his experiences with astral journeys. But, don't say I didn't warn you! The classic teaching manual on the subject is *The Projection of the Astral Body,* by Sylvan Muldoon and Hereward Carrington. I recommend this 1929 monograph by a scientist and a psychic traveler to get an earlier perspective and good instruction on how to start your OBE career. I can personally attest to most of the above experiences, under totally satisfactory *double blind* conditions. Since mental telepathy is well known to function quite independently of distance, none of these opportunities should be at all surprising.

MacKinlay Kantor, Pulitzer Prize–winning author of a Civil War tale called *Andersonville,* wrote an OBE novel called *Don't Touch Me.* I knew Kantor from when my father published *Andersonville* and his next book about the daily life of American Indians, called *Spirit Lake.* From conversations with him at parties, I learned of *Don't Touch Me* and came to believe that it is not entirely fiction, but at least partly based on his personal experiences in the war. In it he chronicles his trans-pacific lovemaking with his passionate sweetheart who was living in the States while he was stationed with the U.S. Army in Korea. In the novel, she loved her boyfriend Wolf, but the time difference made the long-distance relationship very problematic for her. Everything else he has written is very authentic, why not this first-person narrative? There are very powerful psychic forces acting to pull separated lovers together. Although, these don't seem to necessarily exist for lovers who live in the same house and are continually bumping into each other in the kitchen.

Dreams of the Future

Out-of-body experiences can be viewed as our awareness moving into the distance. In precognitive dreams we can move into the future. These future-telling dreams are probably the most common psychic event to appear in the life of the average person. They often give us a glimpse of events that we will experience the next day or in the near future. In fact, I believe that the precognitive dream may be *caused by* the experience that we have at that later time (retrocausality). I had a dream of a toy train running on little tracks all the way around the upper walls of my living room, close to the vaulted ceiling. I thought it was such a strange dream that I told Patty about it upon awakening. That morning I looked at the front page of the *New York Times* on my computer screen. The large photo on the front page was the Chicago elevated train as it circles the downtown Loop. The story was about the need to repair the hundred-year-old system that millions of people use every week. I would say that the previous night's dream of an *elevated* train in my living room was caused by my experience of seeing the train in the paper (on my screen) the following morning. *This is an example of the future affecting the past.* There is an enormous body of evidence for this kind of occurrence.

To know that a dream is precognitive, you must recognize that it is not caused by the previous day's mental residue, by your wishes, or anxieties. Precognitive dreams have an unusual clarity and often contain bizarre or unfamiliar material. Dream experts like to speak of their preternatural clarity. These are also not wish-fulfillment or anxiety dreams. For example, if you are unprepared for an exam and dream about failing it, we would not consider that to be precognition, but ordinary cause and effect. On the other hand, if you have taken hundreds of plane flights over many years and then have a frightening dream about a crash, you might want to rethink your travel plans.

During the SRI remote viewing program, our CIA contract monitor saved his own life by delaying his flight out of Detroit by a day, after he had a particularly frightening dream about being in a plane crash. He later got to witness the actuality of the crash firsthand, because his partner *did* take the flight and perished before his eyes at the airport in a ball of fire. I had the opportunity to examine this particular crash very thoroughly when I left ESP research at SRI for windshear research at Lockheed. There were so many factors leading up to this crash that it was almost inevitable. The plane was filled to capacity with passengers. It was a very hot day, thus reducing lift, and the flight was moved to a shorter runway. In addition, the pilot was occupied making a date with an on-board stewardess for their layover (as it were) in Las Vegas and had turned off the annoying "flaps not deployed" buzzer as they taxied between runways. The buzzer would have told him that he had not deployed the flaps for takeoff. In addition, there was an unknown windshear on the runway, which is why I was examining the flight. Talk about ill-starred. Pat Price would say it was "shining like a beacon in psychic space." It was shocking to read the transcript of the cockpit recorder years later and realize that the hopeful and ignorant lovers chatting away would be dead in forty-five seconds.

It is also interesting to note that the aircraft that flew into the Twin Towers on 9/11 were unusually empty. I specifically checked to find that all the hijacked planes were carrying only half, or less, of the usual number of passengers. Perhaps one unusually empty plane could be explained away, but all four? Similarly, W. E. Cox (at J. B. Rhine's Duke University laboratory) found in the 1950s that railroad trains that crashed or derailed on the East Coast had significantly fewer passengers on the day they crashed than the same trains on other days—even taking weather into account. These data show that people can indeed use their intuition to save their lives.

We would say that the frightening crash that actually occurs can be the stimulus or cause of a dream the previous night. This is called *retrocausality,* and it may be the basis of most precognition. I just attended a conference organized by physics professor Daniel Sheehan at the University of San Diego dealing with retrocausality. The very thoughtful proceedings, *Frontiers of Time,* were published by the American Institute of Physics (2006).

OPERATIONAL REMOTE VIEWING

At almost every turn in my career I have encountered naysayers who attribute our psychic successes to luck. But the fact is that day after day, year after year, people in our laboratory were able to accurately and reliably describe what was happening thousands of miles away, and sometimes in the future. It is clear to me that it is *conventional reality* that needs questioning.

Project Scanate

In 1973, we began our very first CIA test of the possible usefulness of remote viewing. The classified Scanate (scanning by coordinates) program began with a bang. An agent at the CIA sent Hal the coordinates—latitude and longitude—of something on the East Coast that we were supposed to psychically describe. We had begun doing remote viewing by such coordinates at Ingo's request. He'd said that it was a "trivialization of my ability to ask me to look into envelopes [to describe pictures]. If I want to see what's in an envelope, I'll damn well open it!" Most of Ingo's pronouncements ended with an exclamation mark. Hal and I would never have thought to use something as arbitrary as geographical coordinates to demarcate targets. But, Ingo said it would be simple and direct. And it proved to be so. Using their psychic powers, the psychic artist Ingo Swann and the psychic policeman Pat Price looked into what turned out to be a National Security Agency (NSA) super-secret crypto-radar listening site in Virginia. I still tremble with amazement as I type the words. Pat named the site and *read code words* from the files, leading to a NSA and CIA investigation—not a trivial event.

Working with Hal at SRI, Ingo described and drew a map of the facility, with a circular driveway, a large circular building, and numerous underground bunkers. Price, however, called in from his home in Los Angeles, even before he was formally working with us—as a demonstration of ability. As he began his narrative, he said he was psychically flying in to the site at 1,500 feet and described many elements similar to Ingo's. But Price went on to say that "it looks like an old missile site, big roll-up steel doors cut into the hillside, well concealed with large 100-foot rooms underground . . . some kind of command center." He even correctly read off several "code word" classified labels on a folder on a desk and on a filing cabinet: CUEBALL, 8-BALL, RACKUP, etc., including the NSA name of the facility, which was HAYFORK or HAYSTACK. We, of course, had no idea if any of this was correct. So Hal just mailed the combined data in to the analyst who had provided the coordinates. (These data were all released to me under Freedom of Information when the program was declassified in 1995—otherwise I'd have to kill you after revealing the info.) My son Nicholas, working as a lawyer in D.C., was extremely helpful to me in the eighteen-month process of getting through the right channels to get past the stonewalling bureaucrats.

When you are doing such psychic research for NSA or CIA, you learn to take your miracle, put it into a manila folder, wrap it up with scientific ribbons, and call it data. *Here is where we get to question reality.* The coordinates were actually for the analyst's vacation cottage in the Eastern Virginia hills. But, it turned out that the Secret NSA facility was just over the hill about a quarter mile away. The agent verified Ingo's and Pat's description with an NSA analyst, who was furious at the idea that the CIA was targeting California psychics on a Crypto Secret NSA site. The next week we met our CIA friend and a very angry guy from the NSA. He wanted to know why Ingo and Pat had targeted his site, if the coordinates were actually for the cottage. Pat explained that, from his years of psychic police work, "The more you try to hide something, the more it shines like a beacon in psychic space."

Soviet Weapons Factory

In the fall of 1974, one of our contract monitors came to SRI with a new task for us. This was a do-or-die demonstration-of-ability trial for John McMahon, director of intelligence at the CIA, whom Hal and I had briefed the previous month. Hal and I approached the agency director with our shared gift of self-confidence that comes from being only children, accustomed to getting our way. If it weren't for Wittgenstein, I would never have had the *chutzpa* to argue to the director, who was trained as a lawyer, that ESP is the way of the world. And although we don't understand how it works, we are still confident that "the world is all that is the case." That is, ESP is not magic. We surprisingly obtained McMahon's agreement to our proposal that if we could successfully describe his operationally important site, he would support our work, and he would not need any further proposals from us. (If you want to get, you have to ask.)

Before we could start our program, we had to go the basement of the CIA building to have an interview with Dr. Sidney Gottlieb, the notorious director of the CIA's MK-ULTRA program. Although Gottlieb's degree was in chemistry, his interest was in poison and mind control. He ran a twenty-year U.S. program of brainwashing, to discover to what extent the Agency could erase a person's memories, develop a truth serum, or create a "Manchurian Candidate" who would unconsciously commit murder in response to a command. His principle means were repeated electroshock, LSD overdose, and sensory isolation.

We met this small, amiable man from the Bronx in his spacious, book-lined office. He could have been anyone's friendly old uncle Sid. He did not look like America's own "Angel of Death," playing the part of Dr. Josef Mengele, the Nazi S.S. physician who conducted horrific concentration experiments on Jewish prisoners. Gottlieb thought our program was very interesting and recommended to the upper management that we move ahead with it. He offered that it would be particularly interesting to find out if LSD would make people more psychic—it doesn't appear to. Once a person is high on acid, he or she is no longer interested in ESP experiments.

Not all researchers agree with this. My good friend Dr. Andrija Puharich had a decade-long research activity at his Round Table Foundation in Maine in the 1950s. By scouring the woods all summer in Maine and Massachusetts, Andrija discovered a local source of *amanita muscaria* mushrooms. With his extensive medical and parapsychological knowledge, Andrija was ready to test the psychic effects of this highly toxic mushroom on human beings. Interestingly enough, none of the "normal" subjects—and thirty-five were studied—experienced any noteworthy psychic effects. This was quite different from the great psychic Harry Stone, who by then was employed as a laboratory subject in Maine.

Andrija's aim in the clairvoyance test with Harry was to find out if he could "see" through covered plastic boxes to match two sets of ten hidden photographs with one another. He quickly blindfolded Harry and placed before him the covered matching abacus test (MAT). Within a matter of seconds, Harry completed the entire test. He literally threw the two sets of picture blocks together—ten above and ten below. When Andrija took the cover away from the blocks, he was amazed to find that Harry had scored ten correct matches out of ten—a score whose significance is one in ten factorial—better than one in a million. During a previous series of tests, Harry had obtained just a chance score. My own experience with drugs and psi includes correctly naming three playing cards in a row, number and suit, with my first experience of the drug MDMA (Ecstasy) as a psi enhancement many years ago, when it was still legal. Marijuana just created a superabundance of colorful images, hugely diminishing my signal-to-noise ratio. Generally, marijuana just makes you *feel* psychic (or insightful).

Price and Swann had already demonstrated that they could describe distant locations that a co-experimenter was visiting. We had just begun a series of new and more difficult experiments to describe distant sites, in which the remote viewers were given only the site's geographical latitude and longitude. Our contract monitor, a physicist from the CIA, had brought us the coordinates for what he described as a "Soviet site of great interest to the analysts." They wanted any information we could give them, and they were eager to find out if we could describe a target ten thousand miles away, with only coordinates to work from.

Armed with a slip of paper bearing the coordinates, Pat Price and I climbed to the second floor of SRI's Radio Physics building and locked ourselves into the small electrically shielded room that we used for our experiments. I joked with Price that this trial was just like our many successful off-site experiments around Palo Alto, only further away. As always, I began our little ritual of starting the tape recorder, giving the time and date, and describing who we were and what we were doing. I then read Price the coordinates.

Again, as was Pat's custom, he polished his spectacles, leaned back in his chair, and closed his eyes. He was silent for about a minute, and then he started to laugh. He said, "What I see reminds me of the old joke that starts with a guy in his penthouse looking up at the Third Avenue elevated train." Pat then began his description: "I am lying on my back on the roof of a two- or three-story brick building. It's a sunny day. The sun feels good. There's the most amazing thing. There's a giant gantry crane moving back and forth over my head. . . . As I drift up in the air and look down, it seems to be riding on a track with one rail on each side of the building. I've never seen anything like that." Pat then made a little sketch of the layout of the buildings, and the crane, which he labeled as a gantry. Later on, he again drew the crane as we show it in the previously secret illustration, shown on page 142.

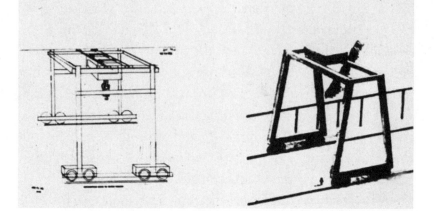

Above left is Pat Price's drawing of his psychic impressions of a gantry crane at the secret Soviet research and development site at Semipalatinsk, showing remarkable similarity to a later CIA drawing based on satellite photography shown at right. Note, for example, that both cranes have eight wheels.

After several days we completed the remote viewing. We were astonished when we were told that the site was the super-secret Soviet atomic bomb laboratory at Semipalatinsk, where it turned out they were also testing particle-beam weapons to shoot down U.S. satellites that were taking these photos.

The accuracy of Price's drawing is the sort of thing that I, as a physicist, would never have believed if I had not seen it for myself. The drawing in the next illustration was made by the CIA from satellite photography of the Semipalatinsk facility. Price went on to draw many other items at the site, including the cluster of compressed gas cylinders shown in the satellite photo.

One of the most interesting things Price saw was not in the CIA drawing at all, because it was inside the building that he was psychically lying on top of and unknown to anyone in our government at the time. In this 1974 experiment, he described a large interior room where people were "assembling a giant *sixty-foot-*

CIA artist tracing of a satellite photograph of the Semipalatinsk target site. Such tracings were made by the CIA to conceal the accuracy of our satellite photography at that time.

diameter metal sphere." He said that it was being assembled from "thick metal gores," like sections of an orange peel, which he carefully drew. But, they were having trouble welding it all together because the pieces were warping. Price said that they were looking for a lower-temperature welding material. We didn't get any feedback on this for more than three years. Then we discovered how accurate Price's viewings had been when the sphere-fabricating activity at Semipalatinsk was eventually described in *Aviation Week* magazine.

SOVIETS PUSH FOR BEAM WEAPON . . .

The U.S. used high-resolution photographic reconnaissance satellites to watch Soviet technicians dig through solid granite formations. In a nearby building, huge extremely thick steel gores were manufactured. These steel segments were parts of a large sphere estimated to be about 18 meters (57.8 feet) in diameter. U.S. officials believe that the spheres are needed to capture and store energy from nuclear driven explosives or pulse power generators. Initially, some U.S. physicists believed that there was no method the Soviets could use to weld together the steel gores (sic) of the spheres to provide a vessel strong enough to withstand pressures likely to occur in a nuclear explosive fission process, especially when the steel to be welded was extremely thick. (*Aviation Week,* May 2, 1977)

Although we were happy to receive this confirmation, we were saddened that, unfortunately, Pat Price had died two years earlier. So, from the point of view of the experiment, he made his perception of the sixty-foot spheres and "gores" without any feedback at all. Price's detailed drawing of the sections of the large sphere he psychically saw shows that his remarkable perception was *a direct experience of the site.* He was not reading the mind of the sponsor, because no one in the United States knew of the spheres. Nor could Pat have been precognitively looking at his feedback from the future, because he died before the details of the sphere he saw were independently confirmed.

We would consider Price to be in the ranks of the psychic superstars, and it was a privilege to have been involved in the series of transcendent experiments we carried out with him. I have been longing to talk about them for more than twenty years. But until recently the secret was so tightly held that I could discuss it with no one outside of our very small group of SRI researchers and CIA sponsors. I feel extremely fortunate to be able to describe these extraordinary events in my lifetime, and to pay homage to Pat Price's abilities.

This 1974 experiment was such a stunning success that we were personally forced to undergo a formal Congressional investigation by the House Committee on Intelligence Oversight to determine if there had been a breach in National Security. Hal and I went to Washington for the interrogation. We were supported by our contract monitors—physicist, Ken Kress; physician, Kit Green, Branch Chief for LSD (Life Science Division) at CIA; Jack Verona, Deputy Director for Research at Defense Intelligence Agency; and Senator Claiborne Pell and Representative Charles Rose, who had an ongoing interest in our work. Of course, no breach was found, and our research into psychic functioning was supported by the government for another twenty years. The House Committee told us to "press on." We were taken to lunch in the White House dining room in the basement of the residence. With its polished, wood-paneled walls and

A 1974 photo showing the co-founders of the SRI program: Hal Puthoff and me, Russell Targ, together with CIA contract monitor Kit Green, and psychic police commissioner Pat Price

gleaming silver coffee decanters, it provided a wonderful celebration for us after our inquisition by a skeptical House committee in an overheated committee room. For lunch, they were serving roast pork, collard greens, and black-eyed peas, all contributed by a senator from Mississippi who had just slaughtered one of his hogs—no kidding.

On pages 145-147, I show photographs of some of the original research team at SRI. Hal and I founded the program in 1972. Dr. Kit Green was our hugely supportive CIA contract monitor. The above photo was taken at an East Bay glider airport, where we all flew for forty-five minutes to test Price's remote viewing from a glider. We were towed aloft to twenty-five hundred feet by a small plane and then released over San Francisco Bay. The test was very successful, and we were all surprised to discover how extremely noisy airborne gliders can be—nothing like the peaceful sail in the sky that I expected.

So, I would say that Ingo Swann created remote viewing as we know it, and Stephan Schwartz was the inventor of "associative remote viewing," which we later used to successfully forecast the changes in the silver futures market.

Data from our formal and controlled SRI investigations were highly statistically significant (thousands of times greater than

Russell Targ, Ingo Swann, Stephan Schwartz, and Hal Puthoff at International Remote Viewing Conference 2002, celebrating the thirtieth anniversary of remote viewing at SRI

chance expectation) for each series of trials and have been widely published. I wrote about the twenty years of remote viewing research conducted for the CIA and the Moscow to San Francisco experiment in my coauthored book with Jane Katra, *Miracles of Mind*. But it took a Freedom of Information request and eleven years to get the CIA to release this material. On August 14, 2005, I received the declassified package, still stamped "No Automatic Downgrade." Shortly after that the whole program was declassified and Robert Gates, now Secretary of

Photographer Hella Hammid began working at SRI as a control subject because she had never done anything psychic before. It turned out that she was an outstanding remote viewer and was with our team from 1973 to 1982

Defense but then a CIA director, announced on the TV program *Night Line* that the CIA had indeed supported the SRI program since 1972, but he declared that nothing useful ever came out of it. I wondered at the time why the interviewer, Ted Koppel, didn't ask him why he supported such a stupid program for twenty-three years if indeed "nothing useful ever came out of it."

People often ask me about Hal, Ingo, and Pat and their membership in the Scientology organization. What can I say? Ingo and Pat both felt that they learned certain useful techniques from Scientology that enhanced their already significant psi ability. To the best of my knowledge, Hal and Ingo left the organization in the 1980s. But, equally proficient remote viewers Hella Hammid, Gary Langford, Keith Harary, Joe McMoneagle, and Mel Riley had no such association with Scientology. Nor did I. So, it is not necessary to give away all your money, or eat porridge at the feet of a guru, to develop your ESP. Whatever one thinks of Scientology, it in no way interfered with Hal's brilliant, creative, and penetrating intellect—nor Ingo's either.

Even a Scientist Can Do It

During one experimental series at SRI, I was working with Pat Price. One day he did not arrive for the scheduled trial. So, in the spirit of "the show must go on," I spontaneously decided to undertake the remote viewing myself. Prior to that, I had been only an interviewer and facilitator for such trials. In this series, we were trying to describe the day-to-day activities of Hal Puthoff as he traveled through Colombia, in South America on a vacation trip. We would not receive any feedback until he returned, and I, therefore, had no clues at all as to what he was doing. I closed my eyes for my first remote viewing trial and immediately had an image of an island airport. The surprisingly

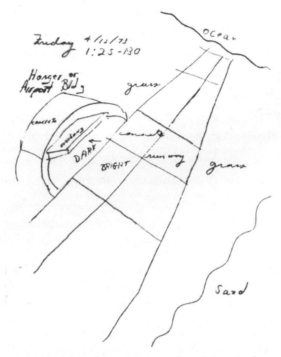

I produced this sketch when I spontaneously took the role of remote viewer in the absence of psychic Pat Price.

This photograph shows the target, which was an airport on an island off San Andreas, Colombia. I correctly saw "ocean at the end of a runway," airport building on the left, and sand and grass on the right.

accurate sketch I drew is shown below. The site was verified by Hal upon his return. What we learned from this trial is that even a scientist can be psychic when the necessity level is high enough!

With practice, most people become increasingly able to separate out the psychic signal from the mental noise of memory, analysis, naming, judgment, and imagination. Targets and target details as small as one millimeter can be sensed. Moreover, again and again we have seen that accuracy and resolution of remote viewing targets are not sensitive to variations in distance.

In 1984, my daughter Elisabeth and I organized a pair of successful remote viewing experiments performed in Moscow under the auspices and control of the USSR Academy of Sciences. Famed Russian healer Djuna Davitashvili was asked to describe where an SRI colleague of mine would be hiding in San Francisco at a specific time. She had to focus her attention six thousand miles to the west and two hours into the future in order to correctly describe his location. Elisabeth interviewed Djuna in Russian, as Djuna drew a picture of trapezoid-shaped buildings and "some sort of cupola," as well as a large animal with glass eyes. In fact, the SRI colleague in California was standing in front of the merry-go-round on Pier 39, and the buildings and merry-go-round animal with glass eyes were evident in the photo of the target site, shown to Djuna later on as feedback. (The only other time a viewer mentioned a "cupola" in a remote viewing session was when the target was also a merry-go-round—this time in Palo Alto, and the remote viewer was one of our CIA contract monitors.)

The great success of the remote viewing protocol comes from the fact that we recognize the mutual importance and interdependence of both intuition and analysis. We invite the viewer to describe his or her unfiltered non-analytic impressions of a distant target, while at the same time we have the interviewer provide analytic attention to assist the viewer in separating out the psychic signal from the mental noise. This evenhanded approach reflects the highly successful bicameral functioning of the human brain, where analysis is said to predominate in one hemisphere, and holistic reasoning goes on in the other.

Since we are encouraging a nondual view in all aspects of life, I believe that we should all experience both the Apollonian and Dionysian aspects of our awareness in the way we live our lives. Since we are given both gifts, we should develop, enjoy, and expand them. I believe this is our evolutionary trajectory—we should follow it. When everyone in society becomes in touch with their psychic and Divine selves, the world will become a different and a better place. That's what the Essenes in the Holy Land at the time of Christ, and the Gnostic Catheri (or Albigensians) in Southern France in the twelfth century, were trying to do before the former were slaughtered by the Romans and the latter massacred in the Catholic Church's crusades. The Church has never liked freelance spirituality. Through the ages, the religious hierarchy has preferred pain and self-mortification to self-transcendence.

The Kidnapping of Patricia Hearst

In the second year of our research program, on the night of Monday, February 4, 1974, a group of American terrorists kidnapped nineteen-year-old newspaper heiress Patricia Hearst from her apartment near the University of California at Berkeley where she was a student. The kidnappers identified themselves as the Symbionese Liberation Army. They were radical anarchists whose slogan was "DEATH TO THE FASCIST INSECT THAT PREYS UPON THE LIFE OF THE PEOPLE." The conservative and wealthy Hearst family was a perfect target for them. While the press was trying to find "Symbia" on the map, the Berkeley police department was trying to locate the daughter of one of the most prominent celebrities in the city of San Francisco—namely the publisher of the *San Francisco Examiner* and president of the nationwide Hearst syndicate of newspapers.

The day after the kidnapping, the police remained entirely clueless. It was such a desperate situation that the Berkeley police department was moved to think about asking for psychic guidance. They called Stanford Research Institute on Tuesday afternoon, and our laboratory director, Bart Cox, asked us if we thought remote viewing could help with the problem. Pat Price, our astonishing psychic policeman, said that he had often done this kind of thing. So, Hal Puthoff, Pat Price, and I all piled into Hal's car and drove to Berkeley to meet with the detectives on the case and visit the scene of the crime—Hearst's little Berkeley apartment where pistol shells were still rolling around on the floor under the bed.

The kidnappers were known to be violent, since two people had been badly beaten and several neighbors had been shot at during the abduction. It was all quite strange and confusing for Hal and me. But Pat felt quite at home in the Berkeley police station. The police had a lot of questions they were planning to ask us. However, Pat stepped forward first and asked the detective who was working with us if he had a "mug book" of local people who were recently out of prison—the usual suspects. Yes, they had just such a book. Pat took the book and laid it flat on a big wooden table so that we could all see the pages. There were four lineup pictures—mug shots—on each page.

Hal and I and the detectives all huddled around Price as he turned the pages, looking carefully at each picture. Then, after about ten pages (forty people) into the book, he put his index finger right on the face of one of the men and said, "He's the leader." The man Price singled out from the mug book was Donald "Cinque" DeFreeze, who had managed to walk out—actually escaped—from California's Soledad prison a year earlier. Within a week, the detectives were able to verify Pat's remarkable hit.

The police, of course, had no idea where to find DeFreeze. So they asked Pat if he could locate where he might be. Pat sat back in the old oak swivel chair, polished his glasses, and closed his eyes. After a moment of silence, he said, pointing, "They went that way. Is that North?" It was. Pat continued, "I see a white station wagon parked by the side of the road. But, they're not in it anymore." The detective asked, "Where can we find the car?" Pat replied, "It's just past a highway overpass, near a restaurant and two large white gas or oil storage tanks." One of the detectives said that he knew where that might be [on the road to Vallejo]. A half an hour later they found the abandoned car just where Pat said it would be. By that time it was midnight and Hal and I were tired and happy to go home to more peaceful surroundings. I think Pat could have stayed all night.

We had several additional opportunities after that to interact with the Berkeley detectives. The most memorable for me was a trip to a potential hide-out location of the SLA. A detective and I were in a patrol car parked on a tree-covered hillside in the Santa Cruz mountains. He asked me if I knew how to handle a gun. I thought this was a surprising request, but I told him that I owned an automatic pistol, actually a classy Walther PPK, and knew how to use it. (At fifty feet, it is not necessary for me to see individual target rings to cluster my shots in the center of the target—isn't that reassuring?) He then handed me his service weapon and said to me, "Cover my back," as he walked around the apparently abandoned house. I covered him with the gun as he cased the building. I am sure he had no idea that he had his back to Mr. Magoo with an automatic. After that incident I realized that I was way beyond my psychical researcher's "job description," and I retired from the field, feeling that my graduate studies at Columbia never prepared me for this.

Even during her brutal confinement by the kidnappers, Patricia had some knowledge of our activities. In her riveting autobiography, *Every Secret Thing,* she writes as follows:

> Paranoia must be contagious, for everyone in the house had caught it. When Cin [Cinque] came to me one day and said that the newspapers were reporting that my father had hired psychics to fathom out where I was being kept by the SLA, I was paralyzed with fear. "Don't think about any psychics now. Don't communicate with them," he told me. "Focus your mind on something else all the time." I did as I was told. I did not want psychics or anyone else to point the FBI in my direction.

I believe strongly that the kidnappers could have been caught while they were still in Northern California if the Berkeley police department, the local sheriff's department, and the FBI had worked together, instead of at cross-purposes. At this writing, the SLA fiasco seems similar to the non-cooperation of the FBI and CIA in the months before 9/11, where there was essentially *no* information shared among the agencies. Each thought that they alone were on the verge of catching the big prize. For the information we were able to provide, the Berkeley police department did send a very nice letter of commendation to SRI, thanking them and us for our work in their behalf.

Chinese Atomic Bomb Test

One of the most remarkable requests we ever received from the CIA was to describe what would be taking place at a particular set of geographical coordinates *three days in the future.* Ingo

Swann was the remote viewer in this operational exercise. After he calmed himself and began to sketch, he called out for someone to find him some colored pencils. I rushed downstairs from the classified vault where we did our remote viewing, to the departmental office where the secretary was able to produce the required pencils. I raced back upstairs to Ingo and watched him set to work drawing a beautiful hemispherical-pyrotechnic display in many different colors. He said that it was some kind of explosion or fireworks display with lots of people and trucks in the distance. The target, unknown to us of course, was a Chinese atom bomb test to be carried out three days hence. The information that Ingo provided indicated to the CIA analyst with us that the test would be carried out and that it would fail. The pyrotechnic display that Ingo had drawn was the result of burning rather than exploding uranium. And the test did indeed fail three days later! Once again, let me remind you that all our data reaffirms the idea that it is no harder to describe a future event than it is to describe one that is contemporaneous. Time and distance do not exist for our nonlocal awareness—whether or not we are comfortable with that state of affairs.

The Downed Soviet Atomic Bomber

In 1979, a Russian TU-22 bomber crashed in northern Africa, and after a week of fruitless searching, one of our contract monitors, Dale Graff, from Air Force Intelligence asked us to help find it. There was great interest in locating the plane before the Russians because the plane, fitted out for reconnaissance, was full of crypto code keys in addition to possible nuclear weapons. If we could find the bomber first, we then would have the keys that would allow us to read their mail—always an extremely exciting prospect for the intelligence community. I worked with

Gary Langford, a highly intelligent SRI physicist and remote viewer. Gary had worked for a time as a photo interpreter both at Lockheed and at SRI. He had outstanding success because he could sometimes describe what was going on *inside* a building that was represented only by a speck on the film. How did you do that, they would ask him? He told them to just chalk it up to experience. I gave Gary a large map of Africa on which he could try to match and record his mental pictures as they emerged. The first thing he saw on his mental screen was a river flowing to the north. Working with his eyes alternately open and closed, he followed the river until it flowed between some rolling hills. After half an hour's work, he drew a circle on the map and said the plane was in between the river and little village shown by a dot. Within two days, the TU-22 was found within the circle that Gary had drawn. Reuters reported that President Jimmy Carter specifically confirmed this at a press conference after a commencement address at Emory University—where he was reportedly holding our classified "Grill Flame" remote viewing folder in his hand, which led to the name of the *Grill Flame* program being changed to *Star Gate*. But, just one of these R.V. successes each year was sufficient to keep our program funding renewed.

They Can't Have a Submarine That Big

By 1979, we at SRI had been working very successfully with CIA and the Army Intelligence Command INSCOM for several years. The Army was beginning to feel that it should have an independent remote viewing cadre under its own control. Hal and I were asked to come to INSCOM headquarters at Fort Meade, Maryland, and interview thirty pre-screened Army Intelligence officers and then choose six to come to SRI to learn how to become remote viewers. We chose the six to work with us. But one officer whom we had rejected, partly due to personality traits, was passionate about his interest in the field due to his association with J. B. Rhine at Duke University in times past. So, we agreed to include him. He turned out to be the only one of the six who did not produce highly significant results at SRI. Over many years, we had learned to look for intelligent, successful, and outgoing viewers, and this man was withdrawn and moody. Of the six, Joe McMoneagle was the star. He was an excellent remote viewer and an excellent artist as well. Twenty-five years later, he is probably the premier remote viewer in the Western world.

Air Force Intelligence had satellite photos showing a lot of activity at a large building in a Soviet port city near the Baltic. Could they be building a huge battleship, or perhaps their first aircraft carrier? This is a perfect job for a remote viewer. By then, Joe, a very experienced remote viewer, did not need to work with an interviewer. What he described in a series of drawings was a massive submarine—more than 500 feet long. This would be three times the size of any existing subs at that time. Not only that, he had the missile-firing tubes in front of the sail (conning tower), unlike any sub at that time. Also, the building in question was a quarter of a mile from the sea. I know for a fact that many Intel analysts laughed at Joe's drawings. However as the months wore on and satellite pictures started to come in, it became clear to everyone concerned that Joe McMoneagle had indeed psychically described the construction of an astonishing 500-foot Soviet Typhoon-class submarine—a full year before it was known to anyone in the West. As for the quarter mile gap, the Soviets quickly dredged and bulldozed a channel for the launch. This caper is described in more detail by Paul H. Smith, in his comprehensive history of the remote viewing project at Fort Meade, where he was a trainer and security officer for seven years. His book is called *Reading the Enemy's Mind*.

The Release of Hostage Richard Queen

The Iran hostage crisis provided a diplomatic crisis that lasted from November 4, 1979—shortly after the Iranian revolution—through January 20, 1981. The situation involved members of the "Muslim Student Followers of the Imam's Line"—university students who were supported by the new Islamic regime. At the time they were holding sixty-three diplomats and three additional U.S. citizens hostage inside the American diplomatic mission in Tehran, Iran.

Around July 9, 1980, a civilian from the Chief of Naval Operations office came to our lab at SRI with an unusual request. He wanted to know if we could psychically tell him anything about the health of the person whose photograph was in the sealed envelope he was holding. One of the men on our team, whom we knew to be a particularly empathetic individual, offered to do this task.

As in many of our operational tasks, I was the interviewer. We knew nothing about the person in the envelope except that it was a man. We went upstairs from our second floor offices to our windowless remote viewing suite on the top floor of the Radio Physics Building. We sat down on opposite sides of the three-by-six-foot worktable in our gray-painted viewing room, located off to the side of our much more comfortable conference room. After a few minutes of cool down, the viewer began by saying that the person in question is in some sort of dim and dingy place . . . He is very thin and about six feet tall, and quite depressed. The viewer went on to describe the person's general weak and debilitated condition. Finally, after a break of a few minutes, he said that the person was actually quite sick and was taking an airplane somewhere: "I am sure he will be on a plane, and soon." As it turned out, that was just what our visitor wanted to know. Two days later, on July 11, 1980, twenty-eight-year-old vice consul Richard I. Queen, who had been captured and held hostage, was released because of a multiple sclerosis diagnosis and flown to Germany for treatment. He died years later on July 14, 2002.

The Iranian captors released several captives at the outset, but fifty-two hostages remained until the conclusion of the crisis. During the hostage crisis, the United States attempted a rescue operation—Operation Eagle Claw. You probably remember that the operation failed and resulted in the deaths of eight American soldiers. Some political scientists argue that the unsuccessful resolution of the crisis was one of the primary reasons for U.S. President Jimmy Carter's loss in the U.S. presidential election of 1980. Many believe that the release was delayed by secret Republican intervention until after the election—the so-called October Surprise. The crisis reached its conclusion with the signing of the Algiers Accords. The following day, on January 20, 1981, the hostages were formally released into U.S. custody after spending 444 days in captivity. The release took place just minutes after Ronald Reagan was officially sworn in as president.

The Kidnapping of General Dozier

Brigadier General James L. Dozier was clubbed and kidnapped from his apartment in Verona, Italy, at approximately 6:00 p.m. on December 17, 1981, by four men posing as plumbers. It was later reported that as many as four additional terrorists provided support with multiple vehicles. Dozier's wife was not kidnapped, but was left bound and chained for six hours in their apartment.

The following day, Captain Skip Atwater, commanding officer of the Fort Meade remote viewers (and now president of The Monroe Institute), grabbed Joe McMoneagle and told him that the

INSCOM group had just been tasked to work on a kidnapping. Over a period of two weeks, Joe described various aspects of the kidnap ordeal. He was asked to target the case with only a photograph of the general to work with. Joe went into the quiet remote viewing room to cool down and almost immediately described the circumstances of the kidnapping, and the blue and white van used as the getaway vehicle. The concern was that, with a full day's delay, the kidnappers could have taken Dozier anywhere in Europe. But within a week, Joe found himself floating over a city he recognized. In his book, *Memoirs of a Psychic Spy,* Joe describes his remote viewing experience:

> I suddenly found myself hovering directly over a fairly large town not far from the coast, and south, southeast of a very large mountain range. I moved closer to the ground and began to pick out roadways and buildings. I followed the roadway and soon found myself near a small central plaza across from some kind of fountain. I picked up smells of a butcher shop . . . I got the image of some kind of very large apartment building and came in on the second floor.

As he re-drew his images he realized that the city was very close to Venice—with which he was familiar. From the location on the map he had drawn, he deduced that the city must be Padua, in northern Italy, not far from where the kidnapping took place. During this same time period, one of the other INSCOM viewers had the impression that "the general was being held inside something, that was inside something else . . . something made of cloth, very much like a tent . . . and that he was secured by a handcuff attached by a long chain to some pipes."

In the end, the Red Brigades held Brigadier General Dozier for a total of forty-two days until January 28, 1982, when a team of NOCS (an Italian anti-terrorist team) successfully rescued him from an apartment in Padua. After his return to the U.S. Army base in Vicenza, he was congratulated via telephone by President Reagan for regaining his freedom.

General Dozier confirmed to INSCOM that he had indeed been confined inside a tent in the apartment; that he was held by a chain attached to the steel bed frame, which was made of pipes; and that Joe had correctly identified the exact building and apartment where he was held. The reason that the remote viewers didn't free him earlier—even though Joe's material had been forwarded to Interpol—was that there were several other freelance psychics who had already handed in bogus data, and the Italian police were no longer interested in dealing with psychically derived information. Even so, in this case, Joe had actually identified the building where the general was confined.

SRI's remote viewing program ran for twenty-three years with continuous $25 million funding from CIA, DIA, NASA, the Navy, Army Intelligence, Air Force Intelligence, and others. We created a parallel program at Fort Meade, Maryland, for Army Intelligence. In our first evaluation, the six army intelligence officers that we trained there received eighteen first-place matches out of thirty-six one-in-six trials, in which they were asked to describe distant locations where someone was hiding. The odds of such a success are less than one in a million. They were conducted in formal double blind trials scrutinized by the army and the SRI oversight board—which was much tougher. (To put this experiment in perspective, it is as though Hal had been kidnapped thirty-six times, and a judge had to read a psychic's transcript to find him each time. And we would have found him the *first* place we looked in half the sessions.) As a scientist, the part of our program that meant the most to me was the controlled laboratory trials that informed us about the nature of remote viewing.

We could publish these findings and discuss them with our colleagues all over the world. But, it was the classified application of remote viewing that paid the bills and kept our program going year after year. And these we couldn't discuss until the program was declassified. From 1972 to 1995 the program was classified SECRET and compartmentalized with Limited Access. That is to say, the program was not only classified, but every single person who was informed about the program had to personally sign a so-called bigot list to acknowledge they had been exposed to the program data. It was called a bigoted program, with limited access—definitely not part of anyone's spiritual path.

NO END OF PHYSICS IN SIGHT

What are we to make of all these amazing data? It is clear that even modern physics does not yet have an explanation for psi phenomena. We often hear that the end of physics is just a few years away—to be described, as Michio Kaku said a few years ago, "with an equation less than one inch long." Scientists have been saying this sort of thing for more than a century. For example, in the late 1800s, Lord Kelvin made the now famous statement that physics was complete, except that "only two small clouds remain on the horizon of the knowledge of physics." The two clouds were: first, the interpretation of the results of the Michelson-Morley experiment (which did not detect any effects of the widely hypothesized *aether*); and second, the failure of then current electromagnetic theory to predict spectral distribution of "black body" radiation. These little clouds led respectively to the discovery of special relativity, quantum mechanics, and furthermore to what we think of today as modern physics.

In 1975, Nobelist Steven Weinberg declared at Lawrence Berkeley Laboratory, "What we want to know is the set of simple principles from which the properties of particles, and *hence everything else,* can be deduced." Then at Cambridge University, in 1980, revered astrophysicist Stephen Hawking told his audience, "I want to discuss the possibility that the goal of theoretical physics might be achieved in the not too distant future: say by the end of the [twentieth] century. By this I mean that we might have a complete, consistent, and unified theory of physical interactions that would describe *all possible observations.*" Not only did this not come close to happening, but I believe it is not very likely in the foreseeable future.

Physicists are still struggling to explain or even comprehend newly discovered *dark matter,* which appears to make up 25 percent of the universe, and *dark energy,* which is 70 percent, leaving only 5 percent to account for what scientists have been observing for the past 4,000 years. It is now evident that the edge of the universe is expanding at a velocity greater than the speed of light. This doesn't strictly violate special relativity, because it is the space itself that is expanding, but it is quite surprising, nonetheless. Physics today has many other surprises for us and is very much further from its end than it was a decade ago. I believe that with the incorporation of additional spatial and temporal dimensions, as are contemplated for string theory, we will be able to describe the nonlocal space-time in which we observe psychic abilities.

Prof. Elizabeth Rauscher and I have created a comprehensive physics model to describe nonlocal awareness. It is published, under the title "The Speed of Thought," In the *Journal of Scientific Exploration,* and is available on my website: www.espresearch.com. We propose that each of the four dimensions of our familiar space-time universe is actually made up of a real and an imaginary part, and that our consciousness has access to this complex space-time manifold.

However, I believe that little progress will be made on these mysteries of physics until the powerful data of nonlocal psi phenomena are included in the mix. For example, the data supporting psychic perception is incomparably stronger than the almost nonexistent data supporting string theory.

I believe that these "end of physics" statements are not only untrue, but logically impossible and misleading. The hubris of brilliant and famous scientists is still with us today. The issue is very important because it shows what terrible trouble we can get into if we are totally lacking in awe, wonder, or spiritual questioning.

Great visionary scientists such as Einstein, Newton, and John Archibald Wheeler had no such lack of wonder. At ninety, Wheeler is still asking, "How come the universe?" In his writing, Einstein said that we "use our intellect to solve difficult problems, but the problems themselves come from another source."

We may well ask: Will there be an end to mathematics? To biology? To history? Will the human mind withdraw from science? Does curiosity ever achieve completion? I think not!

I believe, a thousand years from now, our current views of physics will seem as primitive as the phlogiston theory seems to us today. The phlogiston was an element, or fluid, thought in the eighteenth century to cause combustion or be produced or given off by anything burning. It has long since been discarded along with the aether and Newton's clockwork universe. I'm reminded of physicist John Klimo's remark, "Whenever I hear that something is *ineffable,* I want to eff it." There is no limit to what we can learn. If physics has an end, which I doubt, it is far, far away.

CHAPTER TEN

Delphi Associates— Applying Psychic Abilities

I left the "X-Files" in 1982. The remote viewing program had become more and more applied and classified and I didn't go to graduate school to become a psychic spy for the CIA. From the beginning, the bargain we struck with the devil was that half our effort would be directed toward such applications and tasks as finding kidnapped agents, downed airplanes, etc., and the other half we could apply to research questions such as, how does ESP actually work. That's the agreement we made with John McMahon, who was Director of Intelligence when we started the program with the CIA. But as in the aphorism, "Be careful what you wish for," we had such success in our various spying exploits describing Soviet, Chinese, and Iranian activities that the research part of our effort fell to almost nothing. So I departed the program. Hal Puthoff left two years later. But, it was continued under the leadership of yet another physicist, Dr. Edwin May, who successfully led and expanded the Star Gate program, worth $20 million, until its termination in 1995—after the collapse of the Soviet Union. At that point the CIA, in its wisdom, felt that the United States no longer had any serious enemies requiring remote viewers.

So in 1982, I organized Delphi Associates with two other partners, Keith (Blue) Harary and Anthony White. Tony White was a successful businessman, investor, and husband of Daphne

Crocker White, a clinical psychologist, whose grandfather and great-grandfather, Charles Crocker, were among the California Big Four who built the Central Pacific Railroad, the Transcontinental Railroad, and the Crocker National Bank. Our other partner, Keith, was a very gifted psychic and psychologist who had been with the SRI program for several years as a researcher and remote viewer. Delphi, a company made entirely out of our imagination, had two large psi projects and a number of small ones during its brief, three-year life.

Associative Remote Viewing

For our first Delphi project, our team of psychics and investors wanted to investigate the possibility of using psychic abilities to make money in the marketplace. For this project, we were very fortunate to add to our merry band a spiritually minded and enthusiastic big-time investor, Paul Temple, and a highly intelligent and adventurous stockbroker, John Rende. It is well understood that reading numbers or letters psychically is an exceptionally difficult task, so we knew we couldn't forecast silver commodity prices by asking our psychic to read the symbols on the big board at the Commodity Exchange and forecast future prices a week ahead. Instead, we used a symbolic protocol first described by Stephan Schwartz of the Mobius Society.

In this scheme, we associate a different object with each of the possible states (prices) the market could produce the following week. We wanted to know a week in advance if the commodity called "December Silver" would be "up a little" (less than a quarter); "up a lot" (more than a quarter); "down a little, or unchanged"; or "down a lot." These are four discrete conditions that could be represented by or associated with four objects, for example—a light bulb, a flower, a book, and a stuffed animal. For one week's trial, we would ask our businessman, Tony White—who actually ran the project because of secrecy requirements from Keith and me (viewer and interviewer)—to choose four such strongly differing objects, and associate one of them with each of our four possible market conditions. Only Tony knew the objects. I would then interview the remote viewer, Keith, over the telephone and ask him to describe his impressions of the object we would show him next week. The broker would then buy or sell silver futures contracts, based entirely on what the viewer saw, whether it be a flower, a teddy bear, or whatever. That would be the object associated with what the market did in the next week, which is why it is called "associative" remote viewing. At the end of the week, when silver finally closed, we would give the viewer feedback by showing him the object corresponding to what the market *actually did*—the feedback for the trial. Our nine forecasts in the fall of 1982 were all correct, and we earned $120,000, which we divided with our investor.

Our enterprise was on the front page of *The Wall Street Journal*. Erik Larson wrote the article, "Did Psychic Powers Give Firm a Killing in the Silver Market?" (Oct. 22, 1984). And Tony Edwards made a film about us for PBS's *NOVA* series called "The Case of ESP," which was first aired in England as a ninety-minute program on *BBC Horizon,* and later as a fifty-five-minute program in the U.S. (English viewers apparently have a longer attention span.)

The following year we were not so successful. Our investor wanted to carry out two trials per week, which significantly confused and rushed our protocol—especially the critically important feedback to the viewer. I believe that we also lost our "spiritual focus," in that the first series was at least partially for science, while the second series was definitely out to break the bank—serious greed had entered into our planning. Each of the participants has his own idea about why we could not repeat our initial stunning success.

Since then, healer Jane Katra and I have personally conducted many such experimental series in workshops in which people have described and experienced events that didn't occur until two or three days in the future. One of these, we carried out in the living room of my house with the help of two scientist friends, Dean and Wendy Brown. This series was a formal precognitive experiment to forecast changes in the silver commodity market (up or down) in which we were successful in eleven out of twelve market forecasts. This published result was again through associative remote viewing with small objects to be seen at a later time. We, therefore, have no doubt that the precognitive channel is available to almost anyone.

"The Case of ESP" was frequently shown on PBS from 1984 until 1995, at which time, for some unknown reason, it disappeared from *NOVA*'s files. It is now gone also from the files of WGBH–Boston who produced the film, and from Time-Life who distributed it for sale. This is not a fantasy, since I have several tapes and DVD copies of the program on my desk and portions on my website at www.espresearch.com. Interestingly, 1995 was also the year in which the remote viewing program was officially declassified by the CIA. The disappearance of the film has never been explained. My guess is that the CIA put pressure on *NOVA* to pull the film. Since they alone were the U.S. copyright holder, only they could have accomplished such a complete disappearance.

About five years after he built the ESP teaching machine for me, Nolan Bushnell created the Atari video game company—in 1972. Because of my connections with Atari, Delphi obtained a three-year, $320,000 contract to design and build a new line of ESP video games for them. We built and tested several games that allowed players to use their psychic sense to increase their scores and get in touch with the part of themselves that was psychic. Unfortunately, Atari was run by and for children. Nobody had any experience in marketing, and things only got worse once they were sold to Time/Warner, whose president, Steve Ross, had even less of a conception of what an electronics company should be doing. But the company in its heyday appeared to me to be powered by sex, cocaine—and arrogance. They felt that if a game had an Atari label, it should sell. After buying the rights to make an E.T. video game—based on the highly successful movie—the management gave the game designers only six weeks to create a new concept, write the computer code, and manufacture the game. That's how they eventually ended up burying $20 million of extremely stupid E.T. games in the Nevada desert! I should say that the people we dealt with at Atari, especially our good friend Angelo Pezzani who headed their legal department, were always very respectful and fair with us. We were one of the very few outside contractors who actually got paid as Atari collapsed. It was fun while it lasted. The corporate lobby was all very futuristic with stainless steel and black velvet décor. We especially liked the large, dimly lit video game arcade just off the lobby, where visiting VIPs could play the latest Atari games, and even the games of their competitors, free and to their heart's content.

Although we were supporting ourselves at Delphi, the business required much more cold calling than I was comfortable with—too much begging for money. So, in the fall of 1984, we folded Delphi. Around this interesting period of Cold War citizen diplomacy, I went to the Soviet Union with my daughter Elisabeth, to meet some of the researchers there and give a formal talk to the USSR Academy of Science on remote viewing. The Esalen Institute and Dulcy Murphy were very helpful in making this all happen. Dulcy introduced me to Joseph Golden, the Russian magician and citizen-diplomat who facilitated the trip. Again and again ESP researchers documented that accuracy and resolution of remote viewing targets are not sensitive to variations in distance of up to 6,000 miles, as demonstrated by the two long-distance viewing experiments Elisabeth and I did with Russian healer Djuna Davitashvili. As we visited various scientific establishments, we discovered that nothing in Russia starts without some sort of a drink. At the Radio Technical Institute in Moscow—which had translated our first SRI remote viewing papers from the *Proceedings of the IEEE* into Russian—there was a morning coffee break at ten-thirty. The lovely little tea wagon came tinkling down the hall, visiting each office to inquire whether we would like vodka, cognac, or tea for breakfast! The scientists there often described their work situation to us with the homily, "They pretend to pay us, and we pretend to work." That was at the height of the Cold War. It is likely today everything is less elegant and more austere in this changed world.

On my return home from Russia, I discovered that I had colon cancer. It was detected very early, as they say, and I was scheduled for surgery the first of the following year. The surgery was successful, but it left me with a permanent colostomy. The only reason I mention this operation is because it is of absolutely no consequence to my life. I have read in the medical literature of people who have chosen to die rather than have the surgery. (I guess some people, even at an advanced age, still can't deal with their own shit.) I hope that doesn't show a lack of compassion. What I mean is that the colostomy has not interfered in any way with sports, swimming, traveling, finding girlfriends, or making love. I was grateful that neither the nerves nor my functioning was damaged by the surgery—a result which occurs occasionally. I'm not sure that I can take any credit for my positive outcome— but I'll take it in any case.

CHAPTER ELEVEN

The Weapons Factory— Can This Be Right Livelihood?

By 1985, I decided to return to my roots and find a job in the thriving laser industry. I still had friends doing research from my previous incarnation at TRG and Sylvania. So, I spent a week at the Engineering School library at Stanford and got myself up to date on what had happened in the laser field during my thirteen-year ESP mid-course correction. I read of great improvements in carbon-dioxide lasers, and combined this new information with an idea I had years ago to use lasers to look out in front of an airplane to sense the direction and velocity of the wind, which is otherwise invisible. With Gordon Gould, I had co-authored the very first paper on coherent detection with a laser in 1962. We were pioneers, with others at TRG, in what is called optical heterodyne detection, where you mix a little of the laser beam you are transmitting with the tiny amount of light scattered back from the atmosphere. Since a Lockheed plane had just crashed in Dallas from violent windshear and air turbulence, I had a perfect opportunity to interest Lockheed in such a program. The FAA dispatch on the crash reads, "On Aug. 2, 1985, a Delta Lockheed L-1011 jumbo jet en route to Ft. Lauderdale crashed near the Dallas-Ft. Worth Airport, killing 137."

I applied a month later to the Lockheed Research and Development Laboratory in Palo Alto, with a proposed solution to this problem. The renowned director of Electro-Optical

Sciences at the lab, Dr. Kermit Cuff, gave me a thorough grilling to see if I remembered anything useful about lasers and optics, and offered me a job—if I promised that I would not try to get Lockheed into the ESP business. I told him that if I could get money from the CIA to do ESP research, I should have no trouble getting money from NASA to investigate windshear. And I was indeed successful.

With financial support from NASA, my Lockheed staff and I designed and flight-tested airborne laser systems to detect windshear several kilometers in front of an aircraft. We built both CO_2 gas laser systems and more modern solid-state systems. Although we successfully measured windshear in dry air, we never were able to interest the FAA or the airlines to buy the system, because, as the airlines say, "safety doesn't sell." Meanwhile, I had a chance to fly through the most violent imaginable weather to demonstrate that we could detect a hazard several minutes before it was encountered. I was pretty alarmed when our NASA chief scientist gave us all fireproof Nomex coveralls before our first flight,

Here I am with NASA's 737, ready to test our laser windshear sensor (1994).

together with instructions as to the best way to crawl out of a burning aircraft. All this was on the tarmac at NASA Langley Research Center in Virginia, on the windswept flats next to Chesapeake Bay. The NASA scientists were senior men, and very competent and experienced with wind hazards and flight dynamics. My Lockheed buddy, Paul Forney, and I were the only ones who weren't "good ole boys." Nonetheless, we faithfully went with them to Hooters after work for beer and shrimp, and friendly Virginia lasses in halter tops. (Sorry, no photo available.)

One other teammate who wasn't a good ole boy was a delightful engineer from Georgia, who worked for our laser subcontractor in Palm Beach, Florida. We'll call her Ruthie. She had been a ballet dancer with the Atlanta Ballet for six years before getting her masters degree in physics from Georgia Tech. She was about five-foot-two with a slim dancer's body and curly black hair. She explained to me, "I loved being a human gyroscope, but I didn't like waking up every morning in pain." The first time I saw her, she was wearing a white lab coat—and was chained by the wrist to the top of a large steel table in the optical shop of our West Palm Beach subcontractor. I had never seen such a thing before in my research experience, and wondered if it had something to do with Southern traditions of which I was ignorant—white slavery crossed my mind.

Physicists are trained to solve problems by going immediately to the limiting case. It turned out in reality (as we like to say) the wrist chain was just to keep Ruthie electrically grounded, to protect delicate solid-state components from being damaged by her static electricity. I have since learned that this is quite common practice in production environments. For a New York boy, the South is just one surprise after another.

We spent a lot of time together during the six weeks the lasers were being built and tested in Florida and then later flight tested at NASA Langley. Ruthie was a serious-minded Christian with a gold cross on a chain around her neck to scare off married Jewish engineers. Still, she took me to the famous Dixieland jazz bars in Palm Beach on weekends and to church on Sunday. This was at the time when young William Kennedy Smith, a medical student, had a well-publicized 2 a.m. adventure with a local Palm Beach girl on the Kennedy family's oceanfront estate. It seems the NASA management became quite concerned that I was having an affair with this beautiful, highly intelligent young woman. What they didn't realize was that every evening after work we would slip off together to the beach at sunset to do nothing more scandalous than read her concordance Bible. Still, I enjoyed it all enormously.

One steamy Sunday morning, she took me to an Evangelical church service held in a double-wide trailer all the way out in Key West. The minister introduced us to the congregation of about a hundred as "Mr. and Mrs. Targ," which was quite shocking to us both. Although there was plenty of closeness and affection in our relationship and we greatly enjoyed one another, we were aware of the really serious consequences of bad behavior, for all kinds of obvious reasons. It was a dangerous but exciting game. Also, I was twenty-five years older than she, and about a foot taller. We had had heart-to-heart discussions of my tense and deteriorating situation at home and she knew that I loved her, but I believe that she considered me too odd, too old, and too married.

As I sat in church quietly meditating on these new complications, I began to watch the large, slow-turning fans in the ceiling. I thought to myself like countless others before me, "If God really exists, I would like a sign." After a little while, the fan right in front of me seemed to be slowing down. That got my attention. As I mentally tried to help God stop it, by psychically grabbing two of the blades, the fan turned slower and slower, and finally came to a complete stop. The other three fans continued to merrily turn in the hot humid little church. Nobody but me noticed the miracle, though I did point it out to my Ruthie. This was the most convincing psychokinetic event I had seen up to that time. (Taking part in convincing spoon-bending demonstrations was still a decade away for me.)

Our whole relationship, though quite open-hearted and loving, made Ruthie very nervous. Whenever, in our travels, we would find ourselves at a bed-and-breakfast, she was always shushing me to keep my voice down.

I think she was greatly relieved when our NASA program was completed and I retreated back to California. She now has a PhD in physics, a husband, a baby, and a professorship. God bless her.

Our test plane was the very first Boeing 737 (serial #1). It had been retired and put out to pasture with NASA after thirty years of service with Lufthansa. After a similar plane had its ceiling ripped off by the wind and a stewardess sucked out of the aircraft over the Pacific, our ship had to have all its rivets reset (a so-called C-check). We even got a thrill ride in the famous NASA "vomit comet" to test our new hardware by flying to 35,000 feet and then heading approximately straight down to give us and the equipment the experience of free fall for more than a minute. We all did fine, except for some notebooks that went floating away in the zero-G environment. I understand that NASA gave the great paralyzed physicist Stephen Hawking a ride in this zero-gravity contraption. From the videos, it looked like a really terrible idea.

After the *Challenger* crash, I got the bright idea that we could use our windshear detection system to look straight up to make real-time wind measurements at launch time for the space shuttle. It is a little-known but true fact that the *Challenger* was brought down by two synergistic problems. There was the well-known and recurring defect of the burned-though O-ring in the booster rocket—due to the sub-freezing temperature at launch time—as demonstrated by Richard Feynman at the press conference. But this had happened before. What brought down the shuttle was the simultaneous occurrence of a hundred-knot windshear at 32,000 feet. This horizontal wind blast ripped the shuttle from the giant liquid oxygen tank with its now damaged strut—and that combination of events is what led to the explosion. This is clearly shown in all the photos displaying the horizontal smoke track of the falling booster rocket in the *Report to the President* on the *Challenger* accident. But, NASA found it much more politically comfortable to blame the manufacturer of the booster rocket, Thiokol, than to blame its own meteorologists, who failed to see the windshear with their outdated balloon technology. It was even swept under the rug that the Thiokol scientists agreed with Lockheed technicians at the launch site that *it was too cold to launch*. The disaster was due to a human systems failure. NASA top guns and President Reagan wanted the launch to take place, and it didn't matter what anyone said! The president wanted to talk to the schoolteacher, Christa McAuliffe, in orbit during his State of the Union address. Winshear was also implicated in the *Columbia* shuttle crash.

NASA asked us at Lockheed to guarantee that our proposed system could see to 80,000 feet. This was theoretically possible. But, it would require the laser of a new type, neodymium-yttrium-aluminum-garnet (Nd:YAG), and all the optics to operate perfectly, which of course rarely happens. I, as project engineer, demurred. Our very supportive NASA project monitor said, "Russ, if you want this here contract, you're goin' to have to sharpen your pencil"—a frequent request. (This is what gives rise to contractor overruns.)

So we agreed to NASA's requirements, and were saved (as I have often been similarly saved) this time by the eruption of Mount Pinatubo in the Philippines a few months later. That enormous explosion put so much dust in the atmosphere that our pioneering laser radar system had plenty of particulates in the high atmosphere to scatter back our probing laser light. So, we had another success, this time working with Milton Huffacker's LIDAR company, Coherent Technologies. (And I had just finished writing one of my most successful books, *Miracles of Mind*.) Even though our laser radar reached the altitude, wind accuracy, and speed of measurement goals, *far exceeding* the presently used helium balloons, our hardware never became a permanent fixture at the Cape because of the hundreds of workers in what we thought of as the "balloon Mafia," who were rightfully concerned that they might be displaced. A real-time wind measurement scheme such as ours could have prevented the *Challenger* and *Columbia* disasters, because we could make continuous wind measurements along the actual flight path right up to the time of launch. There is still time.

At that point I had brought four major contracts to Lockheed and seen them all to successful completion. This gave me an opportunity to write ESP books in my spare time, as long as I got all my Lockheed work done. Back in 1985, I was one of the first engineers to have a big 19-inch computer monitor on my desk for writing reports and doing spreadsheets. I had this monster because of my poor vision. But of course today, everyone has one. Lockheed operates by what is called "management by exception." That is, when an engineer has his annual performance review, his manager tells him principally all the different ways in which he has screwed up in the past year. This leaves the engineer grateful to still have a job. The purpose is to keep everyone fearful—and it is used throughout the aerospace industry.

I was already studying (sitting in meditation) with my spiritual teacher Gangaji, so I was not available to be scared by the bullies. I had already internalized the idea that who we are is a flow of loving awareness, and definitely not the story that appears on our business cards. Also I worked happily for a decade at Lockheed with a very intelligent, humorous, and compassionate program manager, Bob Otto, a PhD from NYU. He had attended the highly prestigious and selective Bronx High School of Science, where he told me that he felt he had been accepted as the "token Christian" in an otherwise entirely Jewish student body. (Today it's largely Asian.) In fact, in one of my last performance reviews, my normally cheerful boss told me (just before *he* was fired), "You know, Russ, you don't even look like a Lockheed engineer!" I have never fully understood what he meant. Did I look too happy—too Jewish? But, I took it to mean that it was time to leave, in spite of my success—very few Jews in aerospace.

IMAGE MAKING

Engineers at Lockheed often worked there for decades, for a lifetime—thirty or more years. Frequently, after they retire, they live a shockingly short time—only two or three years. In my calculation, they die significantly sooner than actuarially predicted—by odds of twenty to one. Pretty scary for those of us who worked there. I believe there is an existential reason for the premature death. The worker's business card, or story card, says he is a "Lockheed (or Boeing) engineer." When they leave, these men—and most are men at Lockheed and Boeing—have lost their business cards, security badges, and their identity. Losing their life wasn't far behind. Actuarially, a man who lives to be sixty-five has managed to avoid the perils of war, car crashes, being shot in the face by his hunting partner, and the other events that shorten men's lives. Such a person would normally be expected to live into their eighties. But, when they retire after a lifetime of service, they believe that they are suddenly "nothing." One of my good friends at Lockheed, who was the head of marketing, bought a little house in the country. He told us he wanted to "get out of the pressure cooker while he still had a chance to smell the flowers." He had a fatal heart attack one week after his retirement party. To my mind this shows the very serious penalty one pays for believing his or her story.

This image penalty is illustrated by the tragic story of our beloved Marilyn Monroe. Norma Jean created "Marilyn Monroe," as a supreme comedic accomplishment. Although some moviegoers considered her to be no more than a blonde tart, there were numerous serious-minded critics who viewed her as an accomplished actress. Lee Strasberg of the Actor's Studio and Marilyn's playwright husband Arthur Miller both thought she was one of the great actresses of the century. Jean-Paul Sartre said that she was the greatest actress alive. Her tragedy is that she came to believe that her posters, her made-up persona of "the girl"—her business card—represented who she was, rather than just her story. Another of her many tragedies was that at a time when she was the most profitable and famous star in Hollywood, Fox was paying her only 10 percent of what other actors on the set with her were receiving. Miller writes of his late wife, "the simple fact, terrible and lethal, was that no space whatever existed between herself and the star. *She was 'Marilyn Monroe,' and that's what was killing her.*" Constant waiting for applause is enough to turn a person inside out.

Sartre was a strong early influence in my life. I read his book *Existentialism* shortly after it came out in the late forties. Later I read and loved *Intimacy* and *The Age of Reason*. His appeal to me was one of *freedom and responsibility*—mainly freedom, of course. His romantic *Intimacy* suggested to me that there might be a loving partner out there for me, and that I would find her if I kept looking. In Simone de Beauvoir's *The Mandarins,* her sexy teenage heroine Nadine keeps reminding us that shit happens to everyone, all the time, but we don't have to own it, because it has no intrinsic meaning—we can step over it and keep going. I have always believed that. Many people find Existentialism depressing—at twenty I found it extremely hopeful. Sartre taught that there was no innately "God given" law. We each have to decide what is right for ourselves, *and* be prepared to defend and be responsible for any actions we take based on our ideas and choice of right and wrong. An existentialist can never say, "I had to do something." Because for an existentialist, there is no such thing as compulsion to do anything. Years later, I realized that the reason the existentialists felt that life was absurd and meaningless was that they totally excluded any spiritual aspect to life. If we are automata, I reasoned, then life is indeed absurd. On the other hand, if we take the opportunity to experience our own divine, loving, and spacious nature, and choose to be helpful and reduce the world's suffering, then our life takes on new purpose and meaning. As philosophers, Sartre and Camus became doctrinaire atheists in response to their childhood experiences of narrow-minded repression under French Catholicism. This struggle to get free from the Church is all spelled out in Annie Cohen-Solal's stimulating, readable, and very comprehensive biography of Sartre and his philosophy *(Sartre: A Life)*. For example, she makes quite reasonable his turning down of the Nobel Prize for literature.

THE BOBBY SAGA

In the winter of 1992, Joan went to Europe for an extended visit with Bobby, whom she had seen very little of in the past twenty years, since he'd won the World Chess Championship in Iceland. Bobby had just won a twentieth anniversary rematch of that famous event with Boris Spassky—with a score of ten wins, five losses and fifteen draws—at a seaside resort in Yugoslavia. Because of the regional conflicts in various parts of that country, the first President Bush had declared a trade embargo on Yugoslavia, but Bobby chose to play there anyway. By winning the match, he came away with about $3.5 million. Since the president apparently had no other ideas about what to do regarding the Yugoslav situation, he declared the Chess Champion of the world to be *persona non grata,* and subject to immediate arrest should he appear in the U.S. Bobby wisely decided to go to Budapest and stay with his good friends the Polgar family and their three attractive, chess-playing daughters—grandmaster Judit, along with Zsuzsa and Sofia. Judit became a grandmaster at fifteen, making her the youngest in history—even younger than Bobby. Today at thirty, she is still the strongest woman chess player, having beaten many of her male counterparts. There in Budapest is where Joan met up with Bobby.

Bobby Fischer never returned to the U.S. He lived in Hungary, Germany, and Japan. He was greatly celebrated in Japan, even though that country is not usually thought of as a chess-playing people. But in fact, there is an active chess community, and in August 2004 Bobby became engaged to marry Miyoko Watai, the Japanese women's champion and president of the Japanese Chess Association. He had been happily living with Watai in Japan and traveling with her all over the world for the previous four years, when he was suddenly and unexpectedly arrested on July 14, 2004, at Tokyo/Narita airport while on his way to the Philippines. Japanese immigration told him that he was on a U.S. watch list because his U.S. passport had been cancelled—in spite of the fact that he had renewed it at the U.S. embassy in Switzerland only three months earlier. Since he no longer had a valid U.S. passport, the U.S. government connived with the Koizumi government to imprison Bobby for the crime of being in Japan without a valid passport! Bobby was forced to spend the next eight months of his life in a stinking Japanese jail for absolutely nothing—on this bogus Kafkaesque charge.

During Bobby's imprisonment, I worked with Bobby's fiancée, Watai, and a very hardworking Canadian reporter in Japan, John Bosnitch, to try and get Bobby a German passport, since his father of record, Gerhardt Fischer, was a German citizen at the time of Bobby's birth. Although we made many calls and I miraculously located and sent all the required passports and birth certificates for both Bobby and Gerhardt to the German Bureau of Citizenship, they dragged their feet, and nothing happened. We were told through back channels at the German Consulate in the United States that the powerful German foreign minister, Joshka Fischer—no relation—didn't want to grant Bobby German citizenship because of his outspoken and quite crazy anti-Semitic remarks. In fact, from the perspective of German Blood Law, Bobby *was* a German citizen *ipso facto* because of his father's native-born citizenship. But, it didn't help.

Just as Bobby was about to be turned over to the U.S. marshals to be brought back to the U.S. in chains for a "show" trial and to spend the rest of his life in prison, the Icelandic government decided—through the passionate urging of his many friends in Iceland—to give Bobby full Icelandic citizenship because of the great credit and celebrity he had brought to Iceland during the 1972 World Championship match. We all were thrilled. Watai and his Icelandic friends, who had come to Japan to pick him up, were especially thrilled. But Bobby, as usual, was marching to a different drummer. On his supposed last day in jail in Japan, the guards were serving hard-boiled eggs for breakfast to the low-security inmates, and they gave Bobby an egg. But Bobby wanted *two* eggs, and a scuffle ensued between the diminutive guards and six-foot-three-inch, 220-pound Bobby. That landed him in solitary confinement, instead of on a plane to freedom in Iceland. We all had to beg the Japanese to let the rascal go. On March 25, 2005, after four days of face-saving, he was finally released, and he and Watai successfully left for Iceland, where they were living very quietly on Bobby's winnings from the Yugoslav match until Bobby's untimely death on January 17, 2008. Bobby's situation in Iceland was akin to the chess position called *zugzwang,* where a player is safe in his present position, but will greatly worsen his position wherever he moves. Bobby was safe in Iceland, but he could have been arrested by Interpol at any foreign airport.

Unfortunately, nations often treat their greatest geniuses with contempt and disrespect, as was the case with Alan Turing, who is considered by many mathematicians to be the father of modern computer science. He formalized the concept of the algorithm and of computation itself. My longtime friend Jacques Vallée, a distinguished Internet pioneer, points out in his book *The Heart of the Internet* that today, any practical computer has the equivalent capabilities of his first *Turing machine*. With the *Turing test*, he made a significant contribution to the debate regarding artificial intelligence—whether it will ever be possible to say that a machine is conscious and can think. Can you tell whether you are communicating with a computer or with a person?

During the Second World War, Turing worked at Bletchley Park, Britain's code-breaking center, and was for a time responsible for all German naval cryptanalysis. Through pure visualization, he devised a machine and a number of techniques for breaking German ciphers, including the famous German Enigma machine. His work and his genius were hugely important in allowing England to decisively prevail in naval warfare and win the critical air Battle of Britain—of which Churchill said, "Never have so many owed so much to so few." Turing was one of those precious few. He should have been knighted and had a monument erected to him in Trafalgar Square. Instead, in 1952, Turing was convicted of "acts of gross indecency" after admitting to a sexual relationship with a man in Manchester. He was placed on probation and required to undergo hormone treatments, which resulted in obesity and breast enlargement for the normally very thin Turing. He died in 1954 after eating an apple he had laced with cyanide. Curiously, he was a lifelong fan of *Snow White*.

In my view, England will never live down its shame for its treatment of Turing. I know I should have compassion for the nasty bastards who did this to him, but compassion eludes me in this case. Fifty years earlier, England imprisoned one of its greatest writers, Oscar Wilde, for the same crime. Wilde died one year after completing his two years at hard labor. Jesus tells us that prophets are without honor in their own country. Indeed!

SPIRITUAL HEALING AND SPIRITUAL AWAKENING

Back in Palo Alto—while Joan was off in Hungary visiting Bobby—I was diagnosed with metastatic cancer of the liver. Spots appeared on the CAT-scan plates of my liver and intestinal cavity, and the radiologist told me that it was a recurrence of the colon cancer that I'd had eight years before. "It often happens that way," the doctor said. I looked sickly pale and had been losing weight. The concerned radiologist also told me that this would be a good time to call my two doctor children (Alex and Elisabeth), and "to put my affairs in order."

In response to this diagnosis, I called my friend Jane Katra, whom I knew as a spiritual healer with a PhD in public health from the University of Oregon, where she also taught. Jane came to Palo Alto to help me. She told the doctors that I was *not* sick and told me that I should not *say* I was sick, or that I had cancer! All we knew, she declared, was that there were spots on some film. By that time, I was already aware of the self-hypnotic effects that repeated affirmations of illness could produce in a person. Jane taught me to reframe the situation to one which posed a problem that I could learn to solve. She said that I was not powerless: There are always many things a person can do differently to enhance the activity of his or her immune system and strengthen the body's resistance to disease.

Jane wrote out a five-page prescription for me based on everything in the research literature concerning immune system enhancement, including diet. In addition, she did many healing meditations with me and taught me to do self-healing imagery, loving affirmations, and even prayer, which was an entirely new concept for me. Foremost among her recommendations was that I should get reconnected with friends and join a group involved in some sort of spiritual practice in order to create invigorating emotional and spiritual stimuli. I chose *A Course in Miracles,* which has become an important element in my life-after-Lockheed. This is partly because of the teaching, and partly because of the spiritual and emotional support of the little group to which I belong. Buddhists consider such a spiritual community (sangha) as essential to the life and mental health of every person. Jane found a *Miracles* group for me simply by walking up to a bookseller in a large Stanford Shopping Center bookstore, on a psychic hunch, and asking her if she knew of any local *Course in Miracles* study groups. The woman said—after some sputtering—that she was herself a member of such a group, with a number of people from Stanford. She was Phyllis Butler—a writer, who has become my good friend, movie buddy, and very conscientious editor of my last five books.

The idea of self-healing is that nourishing oneself with optimistic attitudes and goals, acts of service to others, and the cultivation of social and spiritual connections can disrupt the course of disease and invigorate the immune system even more than the physiological changes stimulated by megavitamins, fresh foods, and physical activity—which she also recommended. Jane spent the night of my most serious fever and crisis, mopping up and killing armies of ants that had taken over my kitchen! That was the symbolic turning point for my illness, whatever it was.

Jane's basic concept was to *change the host,* physically, mentally, emotionally, and spiritually, so the disease would not recognize me. We reduced or eliminated known sources of stress and depression in my life and replaced them with hopeful, peaceful, and empowering activities and environments. New clothes, new glasses, new haircut, and new behaviors to postulate a healthy future for a different person. These changes may seem to be superficial, but in fact, they are not at all. After these changes, I often did not recognize myself in the mirror. I *felt* like a new person, and this sensation initiated unfamiliar attitudes and perceptions. In addition, coworkers and friends noticed the changes and commented on them.

Although the doctors were planning to start chemotherapy in two weeks, at the start of the new year, I had surmised from reading the scant treatment literature that chemotherapy is rarely effective for tumors in the liver. After my last CAT scan, I felt I had a decision to make—I could either go home and get ready to die, or take this time to change everything in my life that could possibly need changing. I did the latter and told the doctors I would pass on the chemo.

In the healing literature, I found many different holistic and imaginative paths offering promising treatments for cancer. Some researchers described remarkable cures from the use of Laetrile from apricot pits. There were opportunities for coffee enemas in Mexico, and a healing retreat in the Alps run by the followers of the Austrian philosopher and founder of anthroposophy Rudolph Steiner, where the doctors played string quartets for the patients after dinner because they believed in the health-giving properties of the peaceful and harmonious setting—both the music and the mountains. I knew of a highly regarded healing center in Texas operated by Dr. Carl Simonton, who reported many remarkable cures of patients who took an active part in their healing through the use of self-healing visualizations.

In California, the Commonweal Foundation offered a variety of supportive and nurturing therapies. There was also the healing imagery approach of Jean Achterberg. One which seemed the most appealing to me had the patient visualize in his mind the bad cancer cells being consumed by the good white blood cells. From the patient's point of view, the good news was that each of these approaches offered a few examples of people with very advanced cancer who followed these procedures and were cured. From the scientists' point of view, the bad news was that not a single one of these healing modalities came with any statistics describing what percentage of the very sick people who were treated actually survived.

It looked to me as though coffee enemas, string quartets, and visualization could each claim a few astonishing cures, but the odds didn't look very good. Given the choice, as I sat in my easy chair surrounded by books, I thought that I might go with the string quartets. Would it work?

In *Healing: Doctor in Search of a Miracle,* Surgeon William Nolan describes a patient of his who had metastatic abdominal cancer that was so advanced and invasive that it was inoperable. Nolan sewed the man up and sent him home without telling him that he expected him to die. A year later he saw the man shoveling snow outside his home in Buffalo, New York, where they both lived. Nolan was shocked to see the man alive. When the doctor asked the man about his health, the man thanked Nolan for taking such good care of him. He reported that he had been feeling fine ever since the operation. This miraculous cure, probably the restimulation of the patient's immune system, stimulated Nolan to travel all over the world in search of other nontraditional healing. He visited many famous healers and healing centers but always came away disappointed. His book chronicles this unsuccessful search for nonmedical cures, although he still believed that his patient's personal miracle had actually occurred—because he had witnessed it himself.

My good friend Brendan O'Regan, Research Director at the Institute of Noetic Sciences, compiled an encyclopedic volume called *Spontaneous Remission,* which catalogues several hundred well-documented cases in which people recovered from metastatic cancer, despite having truly been at death's door. The following quotation by Dr. Lewis Thomas is from the introduction of this important book, and summarizes the healing opportunity:

> The rare but spectacular phenomenon of spontaneous remission of cancer persists in the annals of medicine, totally inexplicable but real, a hypothetical straw to clutch in the search for a cure. From time to time, patients turn up with far advanced cancer beyond the possibility of cure. They undergo exploratory surgery, the surgeon observes metastases throughout the peritoneal cavity and liver, and the patient is sent home to die, only to turn up again ten years later, free of disease and in good health. There are now several hundred such cases in world scientific literature and no one doubts the validity of the observations. . . . But no one has the ghost of an idea how it happens.

When the appointed time arrived for my checkup, I was already feeling much better under Jane's loving encouragement and ministrations. The doctors decided to take higher-resolution CAT scans to determine more precisely the nature and extent of my illness. The spots that had seemed so alarming from the initial pictures now appeared differently, and there seemed to be a question as to what was the correct diagnosis. Perhaps it was a hemangioma (a collection of blood vessels), and not cancer at all! They wanted to do a biopsy of my liver. Because of my bleeding disorder, I declined to do this quite risky procedure and waited for further developments, as I was feeling much improved.

At this critical point in my life, and living with a stressful and difficult marriage, Jane gave me the push, or the "spring" as psychologists say. I began to seriously think about a play I had seen almost forty years before. It was opening night of *Cat on a Hot Tin Roof,* 1955, and I was twenty-one. My mother was given tickets through her friendship and correspondence with the author Tennessee Williams. The great (300 pounds) folk singer Burl Ives played Big Daddy, who has most of the good lines, even though he is considered a supporting actor. I believe that his most famous line is something like: *"What's that smell in this room? Didn't you notice the powerful and obnoxious odor of mendacity in this room?"* (Today that smell is, of course, coming from Washington—but I digress.) The line that most affected me was the comment by Big Daddy to the effect that "When a marriage goes on the rocks, it's because there's rocks in the bed!"

In the spirit of changing everything in my life that might need changing, I left Joan and moved out of my beautiful house in the foothills overlooking San Francisco Bay and rented a 600-square-foot cottage on the edge of the Stanford University campus. I could walk to work from my new pad. It reminded me of being a graduate student again. I was now feeling much better, and it was the start of a new year. I spent Christmas week at my desk at Lockheed, writing a multimillion-dollar proposal to the Air Force, for an airborne wind detection system—a project that would keep my team busy for the next two years in case I died. For my whole research career, I was by no means the smartest scientist at Lockheed or at Sylvania, but I was always very successful at thinking of new things to do, and then selling that idea to the government. In a law firm, they would call me a rainmaker.

I have now been well for fifteen years since Jane did healing treatments with me. We will never know if I actually had metastatic cancer, or if it was a misdiagnosis. What we do know for sure is that Jane's interactions with me saved me from chemotherapy, which quite likely would have killed me. The hospital is left with a similar pair of possibilities: Did they tell a well man that he had a terminal disease, or did a man with a terminal disease recover through the ministrations of a spiritual healer and immune-system coach? Neither outcome is attractive to medical science at the present time. This is also the problem that always faces a healer. If the patient makes a miraculous recovery, everyone wants to say it must have been a misdiagnosis. It appears that healers learn to live with the important ever-applicable Buddhist teaching: "Don't expect applause."

As a reward for saving me, Jane got to keep me. We lived together and loved one another deeply for almost a decade. Between Jane and my teacher Gangaji, it was a period of intense transformation of consciousness and soul growth for me.

Jane and I went on to write two books together and had many other remarkable psychic adventures over the next decade. Just as I finished writing the above reminiscence, I heard the postman rattle the mailbox outside my study window, letting me know the afternoon mail had arrived. I went out into the sunshine, glad for a break from typing, and was happy to spy the *New Yorker* magazine peeking out from the pile of catalogs and tax letters. As I walked back into the house I was shocked to find that the lead article in the magazine was called "MEDICAL DISPATCHES: What's the trouble? The pitfalls of making medical diagnoses." It dealt with the difficulty doctors often have in remaining open to a wider possibility of illness, when faced with the bias of a familiar-looking situation. There is the medical aphorism, "When you hear hoof beats, don't look for zebras." The article illustrated some overlooked zebras. This kind of synchronistic event makes me feel that I am still in harmony with the universe.

As a result of our books, Jane and I were invited to teach remote viewing and healing workshops in Italy on four different occasions. In these weekend sessions, about thirty people would be introduced to their psychic abilities in many different formats. At the end of the workshop the group was divided into pairs of people. They would take turns being a viewer and then an interviewer. Each person was asked in turn to describe a picture of an outdoor scene in his or her sealed envelope. The viewer's partner (the interviewer) would then have to choose which one of four possible pictures the viewer partner was trying to describe. In all four workshops almost two-thirds of the people—all Italians—got the correct answer, where you would expect only one quarter by chance. The odds against such a result are 1 in 1000 for one occurrence. For this to happen in all four workshops is millions to one against chance. The very important corollary is that I have never had such good results with American students, in more than a dozen workshops with the same teaching materials, many of which I taught at the beautiful oceanside Esalen Institute. Even the hot tubs didn't help. Before the fourth workshop, I asked the Italians why they did so much better than their American sisters. A woman stood up in a big plenary session and explained that, "Italian women know that they are the most beautiful and the most sexy, so why shouldn't they also be the most psychic." I guess that about sums it up—identity, self-esteem, and intention!

On the afternoon of 9/11, we were at a conference on world peace in Assisi. We were standing in a big circle, holding hands in the plaza of the Basilica of Saint Francis, when a messenger came running into our circle and told us that planes had flown into the World Trade Center buildings. Since all the news was in Italian, it took the better part of that day to understand what had really happened—assuming we will ever really know. That was our last overseas time teaching together.

In 2009, I have finally carried out a workshop in the U.S., which was very successful and statistically significant. This was in Vermont, with 60 participants from the annual conference of the American Society of Dowsers. They were not stylish Italian women in black, but instead I had a room full of well-fed men in suspenders who psychically look for and find water for a living—remote viewing in a non-analytical way. People cannot psychically read, name things, or make numerical measurements. Dowsing, on the other hand, is principally analytical, reflecting what we think of as left hemisphere functioning. Dowsers use pendulums and dowsing rods to give precise information about data that has already been accessed by their subconscious non-local awareness. They can tell you how many yards the well will be from your house, and how many feet you have to drill before you hit water. They can do this using a map or by walking on the ground. The important observation that I was able to make from this conference is that remote viewing and dowsing are complementary approaches to gaining conscious access to subconscious information. The folks at this conference consider remote viewing to be a kind of "deviceless dowsing."

SHOCK AND AWE IN PALO ALTO

On a summer Saturday evening, Patty and I went to the movies in downtown Palo Alto, about half a mile from Stanford, where there is a little plaza and a theater surrounded by latte bars and gelato shops—just what you would expect to find in a West Coast college town. When we came out of the movie, we found a racketing helicopter with someone screaming something from its bullhorn over our heads in the darkened sky. Armed police on the streets. It felt like a rehearsal for life in Baghdad.

It was June 25, 2005, and a group of Palo Alto High school students, with a little help from their friends, became anarchists for a day. We knew from the local papers that the anarchists were coming to protest the Iraq war, capitalism, Bush, and military recruiters on campus. And indeed the message was pretty scattered. The protest was organized by a couple of small activist groups, Anarchist Action and Peninsula Anarchist Collective. Except for a few elderly hippies like Patty and me, the average age couldn't have been more than seventeen.

For us, the whole nighttime experience was quite frightening. The protestors were far outnumbered by a crowd of puzzled spectators and an imposing and quite intimidating police force. There were more than 300 police in full riot gear flanked by police horse units. They had automatic weapons, dark face-shields, and extra long batons. The side streets were abuzz with many police cruisers, motorcycles, an armored personnel carrier, and several buses with screened windows. A helicopter kept sweeping the area with its searchlight and booming the message: "This is an illegal assembly. Anyone who fails to disperse is subject to arrest." More police stood shoulder-to-shoulder across all the downtown intersections, confining the protestors and passers-by to the street, and forcing anyone who wanted to go home to walk many blocks, to the edge of the university. We had to walk two miles out of our way because we looked too dangerous to be allowed to cross the police line and enter the adjoining residential neighborhood where we live. *I don't know if you see what I see. I see the rehearsal for a police state.*

The night ended when the few remaining protestors, after a sit-down show of passive resistance singing, "Arise ye prisoners of starvation," meekly dispersed. The only violence was a little pepper spraying and a few baton pokes on the part of the police force. Not only was the police response vastly overkill, but most of the crowd inside the roadblocks was made up of spectators. The scene was downright hilarious. People at cafés alternated between watching the crowd and blithely sipping their wine and lattes.

Kids wearing black hoods and bandanas were followed closely by families with children, Häagen-Dazs in hand, trying to remember where they parked their cars.

A phalanx of the 300 Palo Alto police protecting us from our children

At the very next town council meeting, our police chief, Lynne Johnson, who had organized this $50,000 extravaganza, was petitioning the council for a new police station with *double* the present capacity to meet her expectation for the increased needs of Homeland Security for this 60,000 person college town. Her request was approved for a $50 million police complex. Is this what president George H. W. Bush meant in 1991 by "The New World Order"? In the meantime, our Palo Alto police have now been armed with 50,000-volt taser guns, so that they can, at their own discretion, try, convict, electrify, and stun any singers or protesters who don't disperse fast enough. *Whose reality is this?*

CHAPTER TWELVE

The Sun of the Orient

My next adventure is a little tale of sex, psi, and ice cream on the open sea. In January of 1994, I received a phone call from a wealthy Texas oil wildcatter named Al, who knew of my ESP work. This wily sixty-five-year-old prospector was a master at mounting huge projects with other people's money (OPM). He wanted to meet me at the Admiral's Club at San Francisco Airport to talk about how to apply remote viewing to a "unique, once-in-a-lifetime investment opportunity." And he needed my help. It was a Sunday, and he wanted to meet that afternoon. Since I am always happy to find a way to promote remote viewing and demonstrate its use for real-world tasks, I agreed to meet him. At that time I had no idea that I was about to be launched into a quite crazy two-year adventure that would end with my floating around in the South Indian Ocean for four weeks on a rusty salvage ship looking for the remains of a sunken wreck, *The Sun of the Orient (Le Soleil d'Orient)*—a Siamese ship that had been lost in a storm off the coast of Madagascar in 1681 with more than $200 million in gold and other treasures.

At the airport, Jane and I quickly spotted the Texan as I stood at the reception rail of the posh airport lounge. Al was about five foot six, with startlingly beautiful bright blue eyes, a string tie fastened with a turquoise clip, and a curled-up Stetson. He was sitting by himself in the corner of the bar drinking a whisky and reading Saturday's *Wall Street Journal.* It probably did not require ESP for me to spot him. Nor does this kind of thing require face recognition.

We introduced ourselves and sat down to join him as the cold January rain began to beat on the large plate glass windows in our corner. We snuggled in our coats; I was now sipping sherry as Al began his story—*after* I signed his non-disclosure documents.

He had made his small fortune, tens of millions perhaps, in a lifetime of speculating in the East Texas oil patch and investing in Denver, Colorado, real estate. But like every gambler, he was still looking for "the big one." To accomplish this lifelong goal, he had been carrying out a detailed investigation of sunken treasure ships with the idea of salvaging one. He had already chosen *The Sun of the Orient* as uniquely desirable—and clearly conveyed his excitement. It was well known in salvage circles that on a dark and stormy night in the 1600s, the ship of the French East India Company had left its port in southern Madagascar, on its way to France with a huge treasure from the King of Siam for King Louis XIV of France. The ship had been delayed by the need for repairs, and they were in such a hurry to complete their journey that they thought they could outrun the coming storm. In my experience, there have been many such disasters—to say nothing of the *Challenger* spacecraft, where money and schedule overtook common sense. The ship was never seen again after rounding the southern tip of the island. Al had navigation charts showing that the water in that location wasn't too deep for diving. He had already purchased a salvage lease from the crumbling Madagascar government.

Al had read my first book on remote viewing, *Mind Reach* with Hal Puthoff, and had even seen the *NOVA* television program describing our work. He offered me a generous 2 percent of the eventual winnings if I would help him. At this time, I had been at Lockheed for nine years with several successful projects behind me, and I had just won a big contract to keep my team busy. It was a purely military wind-measuring project, which I didn't want to work on anyway. So, this new adventure sounded promising and offered a welcome change for a few weeks. At Lockheed, people, including me, tend to accumulate many, many weeks of unused vacation time, rather than taking time off—it's an addiction.

What Al wanted from me immediately was to prepare a remote viewing briefing for his new young friend Peter, an investor from New York who had just moved to Berkeley with his wife. Peter would be the one who was actually putting up the money for the salvage operation. Basically, Al needed me as a shill for the operation. Helen Keller famously said: "Life is either a great adventure, or it's nothing." I told him I was in.

It sounded very exciting. So the following weekend, arthritic old Al, Peter, Peter's unnecessarily beautiful young wife Alice, and I climbed the somewhat shaky ship's ladder leading to the loft in my house, where I keep the television set and videotape player. I showed them eight tapes I had copied from TV shows in which remote viewers, with my help and guidance, had found and described, in real time, where the production crews were hiding. This was, of course, a replication of the remote viewing that we did for years at SRI. I also showed a tape of Stephan Schwartz's *Deep Quest* program, introduced by Leonard Nimoy, where my great friend, the alluring and highly intelligent psychic Hella Hammid, marked a map, on camera, locating the exact position of a previously unknown sunken ship in the Santa Catalina Channel off the coast of Southern California. She then personally guided the small research sub to find the wreck. That tape convinced Peter.

Over espresso and cookies at our kitchen table, Peter agreed to finance the initial reconnaissance operation, and I agreed to facilitate the remote viewing location and ask my friend, the renowned psychic and writer Alan Vaughan, to do the actual psychic dowsing location for us.

I telephoned Alan in February, and he was excited about the prospect of sharing a couple of million dollars with me. He generously came to my home from Los Angeles where he lived. Meanwhile, I had purchased a large navigational chart for our experiment. I guided Alan to remote viewing and dowsing over the chart to mark possible diving locations. After several viewing sessions, Alan settled on an area about fifteen miles off the southeast coast of Madagascar. Nothing really psychic was happening yet, because I had told him the story of *The Sun of the Orient,* as far as I knew it.

By November of that same year, Al and Peter had chartered a sixty-five-foot schooner and set sail with Alan, a photographer, and the ship's captain from Mauritius in the direction of Madagascar. The key man in my opinion, the oceanographer, had cancelled at the last minute. I never understood why, which means it was probably about money. On board, they had a GPS navigational sensor, an acoustic depth sounder/fish finder, and the map that Alan had marked up during his dousing session at my house. I would not be going along with them.

Alan reported the following to me upon his return. "As we approached the site that I had marked on the map, the depth sounder, which was operated by the photographer, registered a flat and featureless bottom, as shown by a flat line on the screen of the instrument. As the ship approached the site of interest, I psychically guided the ship to the left and right in accordance with my psychic impressions. As we came upon the exact latitude and longitude that I had previously marked on the map, I felt a tingling and called out, 'this is the place.' I didn't know at the time that the GPS instrument perfectly confirmed my feelings." (In a later conversation, Al excitedly confirmed this story, just as Alan related it.) "Within moments, the depth sounder started to chime and produced a unique spike on the screen of the instrument." That's the end of the really good news. The bad news was that no recording of this signal was made. This type of signal would normally be recorded on a paper chart or magnetic tape. In this case, the one experienced operator of the instrument was also the ship's captain, who was kept below decks and excluded from all observations, as Al put it, "for reasons of security."

The following day, the same instrument indicated a trench in the neighborhood of the spike. This corresponded well with Alan's written record and drawings of what he felt would be found at the site. Normally, such data would be corroborated before they would be accepted as a true physical feature. However, in this case, no other observations were made because of threatening weather and the small size of their craft. Also, the seventy-meter depth was too great for even a preliminary dive. Based on the remarkable coincidence of Alan's ability to guide the ship to the point of interest *and* the occurrence of a large and anomalous signal at that location, it was decided to revisit the location with a larger ship that could perform the salvage operations.

Although not an ESP buff, Peter was very excited by our preliminary results. Okay—based on this information, and the possibility of a $200 million payoff, how much would *you* invest to be part of this operation? This is the cost/benefit analysis that every investor has to make. Peter agreed to put up the $200,000 necessary to charter a 150-foot salvage ship—*The Scorpio.* It came with two experienced divers, a side-scan sonar, and a maneuverable underwater TV submarine with a camera (ROV). All of these were in perfect working order. There was no magnetometer, which I had requested. And only seven days were allotted for the reconnaissance and salvage phase of the operation. But, I agreed to go. How could I not?

The good ship Scorpio *on a test run off the port of Mauritius. Notice the large cutaway in the rail, for the unwary to slip overboard.*

We began what turned out to be a four-week expedition in January of 1996. We were not exactly a ship of fools, but certainly a rather motley crew. There were Alan and me for ESP and science, our ringleader Al, the investor's sexy wife Alice to watch how her husband's money was spent, a German society film-maker and her child-star son (friends of Al), a highly experienced and debonair English navigator, Gordon, who looked and sounded a lot like the famously handsome English actor Ronald Coleman, and Jack, a real oceanographer. We also had a retired English army general for security, along with the Swedish ship's crew of ten young sailors who wore skimpy Swedish bathing suits as they scurried up and down the ladders and ropes of the rigging. The general could call up troops from South Africa when we started pulling up old bullion! We were concerned about the notoriously violent pirates who also populate the shores off Madagascar. Peter, the investor, was not with us because he had an even more exciting deal cooking with Siberian oil (which, however, never came through) . . .

Our rusty salvage tub had been badly battered by a recent typhoon, so we started our voyage with a three-day layover in the crowded, bustling harbor of Mauritius to repair the engine and rudder. Apart from wandering briefly around the savory, rich-smelling port city, I spent a pleasant two days sitting on our gently rolling deck enjoying the balmy, salty air, while reading Patrick O'Brian's riveting novel, *The Mauritius Command,* describing Captain Jack Aubrey's thrilling adventures in the Indian Ocean— right where we were sitting. One of my most literate friends, Roy Kiesling, had given me this great read for the voyage. (By the end of the trip, everyone on the ship had enjoyed reading it.)

As I wandered around port, I was greeted with a miasma of pungent and unfamiliar odors all mixed together. I was surprised by the large piles of ginger root and vanilla beans being sold off blankets by wizened little sun-darkened street venders. Also, I could buy saffron for a few dollars an ounce, instead of the tens of dollars an ounce we see in the States. At once I started thinking of arbitrage, and I brought home enough saffron for several years of rice curry.

We were a relatively small ship bobbing at anchor in the busy global port. High above us was a huge Chinese freighter, whose sailors could not stop themselves from lining the rails over our heads to aggressively leer at the blonde wonder woman strolling our deck barely contained within the ruffles of her little peasant blouse. My job, entrusted to me by Peter, was to take care of his wife and to "keep her off the booze!" Alice was a sensitive and artistic woman, and we got along quite well. (The following year she won a year's scholarship to study painting in Rome, which she accepted. But, I am getting ahead of myself.) I told her that if she didn't like the boisterous sailors staring down her dress, she should change her outfit. I explained that she was what is called in legal circles an "attractive nuisance." She said, "I am paying for this voyage. I can damn well wear whatever I want." However, after our little discussion of freedom and responsibility, she put on a tee-shirt until we left port. I think part of her problem with the sailors was the strangeness of it all and the shouting in Chinese. I am guessing that if it had been a French ship, there wouldn't have been such an issue.

Our destination was 800 miles away to the west, and after three days of chugging along, we reached our site. I had hoped to get exercise by jogging around the deck, as I have done on ocean-going passenger ships in the past. No such luck here. The deck was crowded with cranes and winches used in the business of salvage at sea. Also, the food wasn't optimal for my health. We had a total abundance of sailor food: broiled beef, baked potatoes, strawberry, vanilla, and chocolate ice cream, and beer served in thick steins—the latter two, for both lunch and dinner daily. I gained ten pounds in the four-week trip.

Having reached our destination, we put out a bright yellow buoy to mark the site as indicated by our GPS from records of the previous voyage. We launched the ROV and carefully viewed and photographed the ocean's bottom in the neighborhood of the marker. We didn't see any signs of a wreck. We then undertook a systematic side-scan sonar investigation of an area approximately 1.5 miles square in the same area. The bottom was unusually flat and featureless. As a result of the earlier typhoon, we had continual problems with the ship's fore and aft anchors. Since the ship couldn't be stabilized, the divers were reluctant to dive from the ship to the seventy-meter depth required to reach the bottom. The ROV finally found a very suggestive 300-foot-long site that might have contained ballast rock—just what we were looking for. A magnetometer would have been very useful here, but we had none. The divers made two dives, but they were limited to fifteen minutes, and they didn't like the unstable conditions.

We continued to cruise the area for two more weeks, going all the way to Madagascar where another psychic had suggested we should look. By then, I was feeling very disappointed. I had thought we had this one in the bank, based on the previous data. Now, I realized that once Alan's map didn't pan out, we just became a small cork floating in a very big ocean.

But, once you open up your awareness to spaciousness in the sea air and the breathtaking intensely colorful orange, crimson, and bright yellow sunsets of the Indian Ocean, there's no telling what might happen. It was worth it to me to see the billowing waves of sunset fire extending from horizon to horizon—each evening I could just soak in the amazing penetrating color—like a bath in the luminous void. Of course, I wasn't paying for it.

We anchored a couple miles off shore of Madagascar, to allow people to swim in the lovely warm water. We could see that the crystal clear water was teeming with fish of all types and sizes—including sharks. We were told that the sharks were obviously well fed and therefore wouldn't bother us, but I was unconvinced. The only two of us who didn't avail ourselves of this delightful opportunity to swim with the sharks were Alice and me. She, because she was menstruating, and I because I had always warned my kids, never risk death by doing something really stupid. I could see that my new friend Alice was almost beside herself with the continual sight of the comely young Swedes climbing up and down the ladders almost unattired. But what I didn't know was that she was just about to have a passionate love affair with our handsome English navigator. This happened during the five uneventful days it took us to steam back to port against the wind with an overheating engine that had not been completely repaired.

In fact, when we finally returned to port in Mauritius, the two lovers ran away together for three weeks to the beautiful island beaches of the Seychelles. So, I had failed on both counts—ESP and Alice. But, I did keep her away from alcohol as I had promised. My only enduring souvenirs of the adventure are two humorous small brass dodos that I brought home with me from Mauritius. Dodos were large, edible, flightless birds, native to Mauritius, and hunted to total extinction by the Dutch in the 1650s. I named them *Moishe* and *Pipik*—after the Yiddish scapegoat.

Naturally, our nice young investor Peter was extremely distressed over the loss of both money and his wife on this caper. He came close to a nervous breakdown. And, through our continuing friendship, I encouraged him to find and become part of a spiritual community. After a year of struggle, he became a serious Buddhist practitioner. We neglected to tell him that sex and psi often go together. As to our sunken treasure adventure, my opinion is that the initial readings of the depth sounder were probably spurious. Others think that the initial schooner captain came back to the site in the intervening year, plundered the treasure, and neatly raked up the ocean bottom. We will never know.

For me, the moral of the story is that enlightenment is the thrill of not needing anything—that is, knowing when you have enough. I tried that concept on Al, but he seemed puzzled. "How can you ever have enough?"

Chapter Thirteen

Questioning Reality

Consciousness is a singular of which the plural is unknown.
There is only one thing, and that which seems to be a plurality is
merely a series of different aspects of this one thing, produced by
a deception, the Indian Maya, as in a gallery of mirrors.
—Erwin Schrödinger

So I had spent a decade sitting in the dark at SRI helping prospective remote viewers get in touch with their psychic selves. Since I don't drive a car, I was always the stay-at-home lab experimenter. I would help viewers in the lab at SRI describe their experience of the unknown location of a traveling experimenter—like a psychic travel agent. As I've told you, it was an unusual situation in that the CIA was paying for my spiritual development. What I found, after that ten years in the dark facilitating remote viewing, was that I could not possibly be just a physical body. If my awareness is able to participate in events far from my body or even in the future, it seemed obvious to me that a more accurate way of describing the situation was to say that *who I am* is nonlocal awareness residing (for a time) as a physical body. And *I am not my story* or my business card either.

When I quiet my mind, I can experience the flow of loving awareness—which is my nature. Knowing this prevents such familiar problems as "Looking for love in all the wrong places,"

205

as in the popular song. We can learn to be happy for no reason, other than our experience of our true nature. The teaching I've discovered can be characterized as *happy happy, empty empty.* Nobody can make me happy; I have to do it myself. Happiness is not achieved, it ensues. Luckily we have all been given the tools: mindfulness, emptiness, compassion, community, and gratitude—the Buddhist way—as I describe later. If we don't learn to use these truths, we will just go around driving ourselves and our friends crazy with our needs. It is clear to me that if you think that who you are is what you see in the mirror in the morning, you are in for a lot of suffering. It's no wonder you "feel bad about your neck."

In my years at SRI, I also discovered one of the most wrong places to look for love was on the couch in the Top Secret vault, where we did our remote viewing research—sex and psi again. It's amazing how quickly reality didn't get questioned when a red hot brunette with sparkly gold-rimmed glasses and a tangle of chestnut hair sprawled herself out with open arms on the coach. Even Magoo could understand this invitation, in spite of the fact that the potential bad outcomes could include the loss of my job, and even more seriously, the loss of my Top Secret security clearance. But, what's a poor forty-something scientist to do?

Let me explain. In the 1970s, the East Bloc was very active in international parapsychology. The CIA thought it would be a good idea for me to go to the biannual conference of the International Psychotronics Association in Tokyo in July of 1977. Hot, hot, hot—and humid too. I had never been to Japan and thought that it was an exciting idea. Before I left, our CIA contract monitor took me to lunch at our favorite Chinese restaurant near SRI. After lunch he counted out twenty-five $100 bills and handed them to me. He said, "I don't need a receipt. But, I expect you to take good notes and take photos of all the Russians." It was to be a conference that changed my life.

When I arrived at the conference hall, there was a beautifully decorated yellow and blue silk banner across the meeting hall proclaiming the goal of the meeting: "Science, Research, and *Integlity.*" (It was corrected the following day.) But *integrity,* however you spell it, quickly became my issue at the conference. In Japan, at this international conference, I encountered a brilliant, passionate brunette sitting quietly eating her apple. Each morning this beautiful "Eve" would show up with a big smile and her blue string bag holding an apple and an orange for her lunch. I had been sent by the CIA, and she was sent to represent Mensa, the smart people's international organization. She had degrees in physics, philosophy, and English literature, and remembered every word. At that time, she was working as a physicist—trying to manufacture efficient light bulbs—twenty years ahead of their time. And she was a talented musician and songwriter.

In the steamy Japanese summer and customary confusion of international conferences, there was an overpowering madness, like the irresistible pull of an electromagnet for iron filings, attracting the two of us to one another. At first, I had been concerned that the Agency or the Russians had conjured her up just to tempt me, to put me into a compromising situation. This is the well-known "honey trap" that we all learned about in our Top Secret briefing. However, that was not the case here, just my paranoia. But, it could have been true—it was a risk—and it illustrates just how crazy men can be with respect to sexual desire, in case there is anyone out there who doesn't know that.

I felt as though I were being swept up in an irresistible whirlwind to which I surrendered. The key fact is that I was trapped in the brain fog of passion and the syrup of love that I had read about and imagined all my life, but never before experienced. It was not a matter of my making a choice. I knew right from wrong but was unable to make any other choice. Thinking back on this now, I have new compassion for Bill Clinton, who also chose stupidly to gamble his career, marriage—and country—in order to satisfy the desire of the tiniest part of his brain.

I was once shopping for jewelry in the famous wholesale diamond center on Forty-seventh Street in New York, the origin of "I can get it for you wholesale." I laughed out loud when I overheard one bearded Hasidic Jew whisper to his counterpart, ". . . and remember, Abe, a standing penis has no conscience." I didn't get to hear the rest of the conversation.

Over the next several years, Eve and I arranged to find ourselves at similar international conferences in Bratislava, Rio, Vienna, Reykjavik, Quebec, Mexico City, Mykonos, Athens, and others. Eve even got to sing some songs in the ancient amphitheater at Delphi. Our meetings remind me of Alan Alda's popular 1979 film, *Same Time Next Year,* in which he has a rendezvous annually with Ellen Burstyn at out-of-town business conferences in romantic venues—as they otherwise continue their normal lives. So, two weeks of love in the cocoon of Japan led to almost a decade of passion and deception in the so-called real world. At the midpoint of his life, Magoo was finally freed from his chrysalis, to become an awakened, competent, and passionate man, by this experience of love between a man and a woman—no longer a befogged bumbling cartoon character. I had been married twenty years at this time and had three kids at home. Divorce was a possibility, but I didn't take it. In my experience, Jewish men don't like to leave their wives and children, yet, this self-serving betrayal of my marriage had a critical lifesaving, life-affirming importance for me in my non-affirmed life at the time. I felt that I had finally been sparked awake to life as an adult person through lovemaking that utterly stopped my mind, by overloading and electrifying my brain and my body. I believe that's why people like making love so much—it stops the mental chatter.

I had been looking for such a woman all my life, but I didn't know it until I found her. Or, more likely was afraid to admit it.

Everything was different from in my pre-Eve life—to finally experience the bliss of holding a happy woman silently asleep in my arms. This was my first encounter with "psychic energy" as a radiating force. Thank you, Eve. This eight-year manic phase of love, passion, vitality, joy, and understanding ended abruptly in 1985 when I had cancer surgery. As a result of my lengthy hospitalization, our clandestine affair surfaced—due to events which still remain classified.

It did not become reignited until a decade later, after the death of my wife. When Eve and I met again, we then devoted several years to producing half a dozen beautiful CDs of her music together in Nashville. We lovingly mixed, mastered, and recorded more than seventy of her songs, on six CDs. As I sat in the studio over many weeks, I watched these songs being recorded and engineered by a warmhearted and multitalented Nashville engineer named Sam Weedman, who operated the mixing board and computer with a pipe in his mouth and his big dog lying on his feet. In the mixing phase, Sam could pick up his guitar or mandolin and brilliantly improvise an additional harmony line right out of his head. And from my own amplifier-building days, I could correctly suggest how many decibels per octave the high frequencies should be cut to get rid of annoying inter-modulation distortion. For this, I received the greatest possible Nashville compliment when the engineer told me that I had "great ears." One disc includes a song that Eve and I co-wrote, called "I Am That Love." It is all about being freed from looking for love in all the wrong places. The verse and choruses go as follows:

> *I prayed to God, and searched the world,*
> *To find a lover passion filled.*
> *There'd be someone there for me,*
> *Who'd hold me close and leave me thrilled.*

But deep in prayer, there came the thought,
That I could give the love I sought.

I am that love beyond the sky.
My heart bursts open and I know why,
I was born to give away
The love I feel inside today.
I am that love.

Barriers fell, I could feel the joy,
Thankful tears fell from my eyes.
So this is what it's always been,
All this love was here inside,
A captive river, a
Pent-up dam
Broke, and out flowed who I am.

I think that Ramana Maharshi and H. W. L. Poonja (Papaji), great progenitors of Advaita Vedanta, would approve of the sentiment. Having demonstrated that I can be as crazy as anyone else, I would like to now share what I have learned in the *subsequent* thirty years. One of the advantages of being seventy-four is that you get to outlive some of your mistakes, unless you happen to be a mass murderer or a Klan member. Again, as Andrew Cohen teaches: Enlightenment is the thrill of not wanting anything. (I believe part of the problem with desire comes from advertising—whose purpose, especially on television, is to create *craving* for sex and "stuff" and to cause suffering by fostering attachment.) Leo Tolstoy perfectly summarized the situation in *Anna Karenina*. He wrote: "The eternal error is imagining that happiness is the realization of desires." The truth is that happiness *ensues*—it is a process. Empty, empty. Happy, happy.

QUESTIONING REALITY IN THE LABORATORY

One day in the spring of 1982, about five years into our relationship, I invited Eve to come to our laboratory to take part in a psychokinesis (mind over matter) experiment. There was so much loving energy between us—both psychic and sexual—that I thought she might be able to perturb our supersensitive strain gauge in its electrical shielded chamber. A strain gauge is a coil of fine wire whose electrical resistance changes when it is physically deformed. This experiment was carried out at the nice quiet end of the day, close to five o'clock. We sat very still collecting background, baseline data in the absence of any effort on her part. The sensitive, battery-operated chart recorder chugged along, drawing a slightly rippled straight line—just what one would expect.

At the appointed time, on the hour, I asked Eve to try to deform the little strain gauge and make the recording pen move, so that we would have a record. She closed her eyes and began to meditate with deep regular breathing. After less than a minute, we could hear the chart recorder's pen begin to chatter. Then came an even bigger signal on the chart paper. We were terribly excited. I began to think that we had proof that this girl is really charged. And then, about a minute after five o'clock, the chart recorder actually *said* the word "HELLO!" It was a miracle. I doubt that anyone in the world had ever seen such a thing. But, after all we were both scientists. We knew that chart recorders don't talk, although this one seems to have done just that. We were stunned!

I could tell you all the different things we looked at—but deep in our hearts we knew that it was probably radio-frequency interference from somewhere. In fact we didn't have to look far. We went outside into the courtyard and asked a security guard if anyone was using a radio transmitter. The guard said, "It's after hours, so there isn't much chatter on the walkie-talkies. But, the

SRI amateur radio club often comes on the air around five." And that was the answer. Our sensitive recorder with its long ink-pen stylus picked up (demodulated) the very strong radio signal, just a quarter mile from our lab. It didn't penetrate the shielded environment of the strain gauge, it was picked up directly by the chart recorder. Another reason to be careful what you wish for.

It's now thirty years since my fateful meeting with Eve in Japan. I have definitely said goodbye to Magoo. I relate these days instead to my hero, the Viennese physicist Erwin Schrödinger. He perfected quantum mechanics with the development of the wave equation that bears his name. He received the Nobel Prize for this achievement in 1933 and had already left Germany because of his opposition to Nazi anti-Semitism, though he himself was born Catholic. Schrödinger had to give up his Cambridge fellowship because the English administrators were not sympathetic with his ongoing love affair with the wife of his postdoctoral student, whom he had also brought to England. During the war he and his actual wife foolishly returned to Vienna and then had to flee, pursued by Nazis over the Alps to Italy, and then to the safety of Ireland, where he established a theoretical physics institute with the support of Ireland's president, Éamon de Valera.

Schrödinger was a lifelong student of Vedanta, which he learned about from his mother, who was an enthusiastic practitioner. In Ireland he wrote his influential book *What Is Life,* in which he was the first to introduce the idea of the "genetic code," which James Watson says in his memoir was influential to his imagining the double helix. At sixty, Schrödinger entered into a yearlong all-consuming tantric relationship with a brilliant Irish actress, Sheila May. According to Walter Moore's biography, *Schrödinger: Life and Thought,* he wrote in his journal that in Sheila he had finally found the answer to the question, *what is life?* But Sheila became pregnant, and with that the great man ended the affair! The Schrödingers, husband and wife, eventually returned in 1956 to Vienna where he became honorary chair of the physics department that he had left twenty years earlier. In a long heart-felt letter, his Irish sweetheart warned him that he would never find another one like her, who would take him the places they had been. And with that inspiration, I am happy to report that I have found continuing inspiration and surprises from my own Irish dharma buddy, my wife Patricia Kathleen.

LOOKING FOR BUDDHA

I began to wake up to the idea that I had other choices when I sat for the first time with my teacher Gangaji—an American mystic who teaches in the tradition of Ramana Maharshi. If one can actually quiet one's mind, I have found, it is possible at her intensive meetings in truth (called *satsang*) to experience the loving transmission of a centered and peaceful *Gangaji* (your own self).

As I have heard Gangaji say, we want to let go of our conditioning—what we have been taught—and let go of ego-based existence in which we spend our lives defending the story of who we think we are. In awareness conditioned by society, one regrets the past, fears the future, and never gets to experience the present. In order to end our ego suffering, the great eighth century Buddhist guru Padmasambhava taught *Self-Liberation through Seeing with Naked Awareness*—which is a translation of the title of one of his greatest books. The goal is to move from conditioned awareness of the ego, to freedom and spaciousness, or naked (unconditioned) existence. I could have written "unconditioned awareness," but what I really mean to say here is "unconditioned non-awareness." Surrendering our conditioning and our judgment is more non-awareness than awareness.

While studying all this, I was still working at Lockheed Missiles and Space Co. and becoming increasingly uneasy. Finally, Gangaji lovingly helped me to realize that it is mentally incoherent to be on a spiritual path while working at a weapons factory. After finally retiring and receiving my final Lockheed paycheck, I came home and cried with relief. Gangaji's advice is always something of the form: Be quiet and find out who you are. She writes:

> The meaning of your life depends on which ideas you permit to use you. Who you think you are determines where you put your attention. Where you direct your attention creates your life experiences, and brings a new course of events into being. Where you habitually put your attention is what you worship. What do you worship in this mindstream called your life?

After spending two years under the beneficent thrall of Gangaji, I was invited to Los Angeles by my friend Suzanne Taylor. She has a beautiful home high in the hills above Sunset Boulevard. Many well-known teachers, especially her good friend and teacher Lex Hixon, have taken part in her evening salons. Her current houseguest was a cheerful, very good-looking, forty-something Japanese-American *adviata* teacher named Yukio Ramana. He had just returned to the United States from a year in India, where he had a full-fledged awakening experience with H. W. Poonja (Papaji), who gave him his highly esteemed name, Ramana. Yukio had been a classmate of Gangaji's and then spent six months meditating in Ramana Maharshi's cave at the holy mountain Aranachala, where the Ramana ashram is located.

Eight of us were sitting around Suzanne's coffee table in her high-ceilinged living room overlooking the lights of the city.

Yukio, bursting with energy, wanted all of us to help him in figuring out how to set up a school or teaching center in L.A. Always
trying to be helpful, I asked him, "What do you do?"—sort of asking, "What's your gig?" He started describing his experience sitting with Papaji at the ashram in Lucknow. Then he described,
rather matter-of-factly, his change of consciousness from months
of meditation in Ramana's cave. As he went on, I gradually began
to feel my chest being filled with love—like warm loving syrup—
it was a shocking and not entirely pleasant experience. It was
completely overpowering. As I looked around our little group, I
had the startling experience—an epiphany—of seeing everyone
through eyes of love. There was absolutely and literally no separation
between them and me. We were one being, one awareness, one
consciousness. I was overcome and started weeping uncontrol-
lably. Yukio looked over at me and said, "Russ, that's what I do."
If I had been in a Christian revival meeting, I probably would
have felt that I had been "born again."

It is very important for all religions, spiritual paths, cults, and
teachers to realize that no one owns the experience of transcendence and the flow of loving awareness—whatever one wishes to
call it.

The following summarizes my own simple five-step path to
experiencing unity, peace, and spaciousness. It describes basically
what I have done. We can think of it as the "Five Keys to Liberation."

1. Mindfulness: It is essential to find some kind of meditation practice that will allow you to stop the ongoing chatter of
the mind. If you don't like what you are experiencing you must
find the off switch. Meditation can do this. *Vipassana,* or insight
meditation, is one that is well suited to the Western mind. That
is to say, it works for me and many other fugitives from Silicon
Valley. The quiet mind has access to transcendent knowing,
transcendent doing, and transcendent being. Historically, people have used many different types of practices to alter their

state of consciousness and to enable them to access a nonlocal transpersonal realm. They include Buddhist and Yoga meditation methods, as well as rhythm techniques such as those involving sound or rhythmic body movements. Examples of these are the chanting of mantras, prayers, or songs; the beating of drums; and the movement practices of Yoga, Tai Chi, Anthroposophist Eurythmics, and Hassidic and Sufi Dervish dances. Other types of consciousness-altering techniques that have been used are the more physiological methods, such as fasting, the use of psychedelic and other pharmacological agents such as LSD and psilocybin, and entheogens like MDMA (Ecstasy). This latter particularly facilitates *empathy,* heart opening, oceanic, or even orgasmic feelings for nature (or the Divine), spaciousness, and loving awareness—(no wonder it's illegal).

There are various methods of asceticism and ritualistic breathing patterns such as the Pranayama Yoga breathing techniques. Unlike MDMA, LSD can be either beautifully transcendent or terrifyingly frightening—definitely not for everyone, because you never know what you are going to get. Much better, and often equally transformative in my experience, is a ten-day silent meditation retreat. Ten days are necessary, because the first three days are used principally for processing mental garbage—a frequently painful, but essential process. Often, people want to flee during this initial period. My opinion is that everyone should do such a retreat at least once. I am reminded of the quote attributed to fellow writer, explorer, and motorcyclist Hunter S. Thompson, "I hate to advocate drugs, alcohol, violence, or insanity to anyone, but they've always worked for me."

Transcendent knowing is the opportunity to in-flow information from the distance and from the future. (Remote viewing is not a spiritual path. But, it can indicate that you are achieving some level of mind quieting.) Knowing also includes intuitive or psychic diagnosis, which is even easier than remote viewing.

Transcendent doing, which the Buddhists call skillful means, is the outflow of your loving intentionality. It includes distant or spiritual healing, relieving the pain and suffering of a distant person. *Transcendent being,* or enlightenment, is the awakening experience, however fleeting, of residing in spaciousness and experiencing the flow of loving awareness that is always available. The ancient Hindu teaching that *Atman* equals *Brahman* means that our own soul or center of awareness is coincident—one with—the entire physical and nonphysical universe. Erwin Schrödinger, in his little book *Mind and Matter* refers to this as "the greatest principle in all of metaphysics."

2. Emptiness: Nothing is happening, or even there, except for the meaning I give it. There are indeed things in this room, it is just that they are empty of meaning. Suffering comes from *personalizing* events which are actually random, such as being cut off on the highway, or being knocked over by a wave. Cars aren't cutting you off. They don't even know that you are there, any more than the wave does. Nobody would ever give the finger to a wave! The Ego is self-centered, self-pitying, and lonely. The "self" is an illusion, or a story. You need never fear embarrassing yourself, because the teaching is that there is no self to be embarrassed. But it is essential to have a well-esteemed self before you can give it away.

3. Compassion: Spaciousness is generous, flexible, loving, and joyful. *Experiencing the Divine in yourself and others, and then teaching that experience, gives meaning and purpose to our lives.* This leads to the experience that separation is an illusion. There are many bodies and one consciousness, as Schrödinger writes in the epigraph to this chapter. The woman at the checkout stand is not just a mirror of yourself, she *is* part of your greater Self. When that is recognized there will be less suffering in the world.

4. Community: It is essential—critically important for peace of mind—to be part of some kind of a safe spiritual community.

Buddhism teaches that there are three jewels: the Buddha, who is the teacher, the Dharma, which is the teaching, and the Sangha, which is the spiritual community. Of the three, the Sangha is considered the most important. The greatest "sin" is creating dissension in the Sangha.

5. Gratitude: Gratitude is the recognition of undeserved gifts, such as a good mind, being born in a safe country, or having a healthy body. These are unearned gifts—like Grace. When we wake up in the morning and go to bed at night, a way to center your thoughts is to thank the universe, or God, for your remarkable good fortune. We have a whole continuum of possibilities on which to focus. These range from desperation, judgment, fear, and resentment—to gratitude, peace, love, and bliss. And you get to choose each time you put your head on the pillow. I recommend gratitude for a daily starter. Unity Church teaches, "Let go. Let God." When you allow yourself to wake up in gratitude, it puts a positive glow on everything you experience the whole rest of the day. That glow disperses the cloud of mind-fog that could have prevented you from seeing the oncoming bus. That is—a positive grateful attitude can save your life.

One final version of reality I have learned to question is the teaching of Aristotle that happiness comes from health, wealth, fame, and beauty. I can hardly imagine advice more likely to cause suffering. We need only look again at some of our celebrated stars, such as Marilyn Monroe, "the king" Elvis Presley, Janis Joplin singing the blues, Jimi Hendrix with his guitar, and Jim Morrison of The Doors. All these immensely talented and financially successful people took their own lives either accidentally or deliberately, while searching for a Self or trying to ease the pain. How could that be? It is as though the "self" were sucked out of them by their Dionysian fans. They began to think that who they were was the picture on the album cover—once again their story. The spiritual path known as *A Course in Miracles* teaches, "I am not a body. I am free, as God created me." Sad to say, Princess Diana must also be added to this tragic list of people who had no idea who they were. If Diana had had a single trustworthy, spiritually minded friend at court, she wouldn't have been keeping such questionable company and might well be alive today. She is one more example of a person utterly trapped by her story. If you have any doubts, read the recent horrendous biography of Diana by Tina Brown.

Aristotle also taught us to exclude the middle. "A thing is either true or it's not true." This dualistic division is most clear in the Judeo-Christian teaching of the Divine. The problem with this was made clear to me several years ago by one of the great spiritual teachers, Monty Python, in *The Meaning of Life.* As John Cleese goes into the large church, he looks up at the ceiling and says, in effect, "God you are so high, so big, so omniscient, and so powerful; and I am so low, so weak, so ignorant, and so puny; won't you help me?" This destructive and false dualistic split between you and your Divine nature has been taught for millennia. I believe it is a false teaching that if you wish to reach God the Father, you have to pray, pay, and obey. A mystic, such as a Gnostic Christian, a Kabalistic Jew, a Sufi, or a Buddhist, would say *there is no separation between you and the Divine*—which is your own loving spacious nature. A mystic will never ask you to believe anything. They will invite you *to have an experience.* That's my invitation. The flow of loving awareness is who you are— Who I Am. So, in the end if we are still suffering, don't blame George Bush. Blame the dead Greek guy.

Poles apart from Aristotle, the ancient philosopher that I have found most helpful and inspiring is the second-century Buddhist dharma master Nagarjuna. Quite contrary to dualism, Nagarjuna encourages us to follow "The Middle Way," in which we recognize that most ideas we hold and encounter are *neither true, nor not true.* This is a nondual path much more likely to lead to peace and love than is Aristotle's path of judgment. In addition to my book celebrating these teachings, *The End of Suffering,* a clear and very inspiring little book on Nagarjuna is *Verses from the Center: A Buddhist Vision of the Sublime*, by Stephen Batchelor. You won't be sorry.

RETIREMENT

After retiring from Lockheed and SRI, I returned to my roots. Before lasers and before ESP, there was publishing. I grew up surrounded by piles of books and *Publishers Weekly* magazines all over our house. Wherever we lived my father had familiar little flat boxes containing manuscripts, stacks of galley proofs bound and unbound, which he read lying on the couch and dropping the finished pages on the floor, just as I am doing today as I edit this manuscript. When he retired in 1978 from Putnam's Publishing as editor-in-chief, he created Targ Editions, which allowed him to personally publish fine autographed editions (printed by letter-press) of specially written books by the authors he had worked with in the past. These books are now valuable collector's items. In his memoirs, he wrote about the making of a book. "Binding, paper, type arrangement, dust jacket: These elements are not accidents in the making of a book. Each calls for expertise and taste. I must know how a book feels in the hand, how it rests on the shelf in the company of other books."

So, it is no wonder that in 1998, when I finally said goodbye to aerospace, I thought about doing something in publishing. I decided I wanted to reprint my lifetime favorite classic books in parapsychology research. Some of the twentieth century's most profound metaphysical texts were out of print, hard to find, and unknown to most readers; yet they are still of importance and full of exciting stories and information. Their insights into the dynamic world of metaphysics and parapsychology are valuable and vital. So, I proposed to Frank DeMarco of Hampton Roads that I would like to co-publish (cost share) with them and bring some of these groundbreaking texts back into print. He responded to this cold call with an amazing, "Yes, I had been thinking of doing just such a series." We brought back classics in the fields of metaphysics, consciousness, and ESP research to a new generation of readers, in attractive and inexpensive editions. The Studies in Consciousness series covers such perennially exciting topics as telepathy, astral projection, after-death survival of consciousness, psychic abilities, and long-distance hypnosis (see bibliography for complete list).

CHAPTER FOURTEEN

Exploring the Survival of Bodily Death

We now have, for the first time in the history of our species, compelling empirical evidence for belief in some form of personal survival after death.
—Robert Almeder, PhD, professor of philosophy, Georgia State University

It is no more surprising to be born twice than to be born once.
—Voltaire

Throughout my life and my work, I have continually been impressed by the evidence, everywhere I turn, that awareness, which is what we are, can in-flow information from all of space-time and out-flow healing intention to the present, and perhaps the future and the past. This all happens because space-time is nonlocal, and there is no separation in consciousness.

The Buddhist Four Noble Truths teach: *First,* that there is suffering in the world, and *second,* we don't like it. I have not found any disagreement with this so far. *Third,* the source of that suffering is said to be impermanence, craving, and the fear of death. That's the one that we all are principally worried about. The fourth Noble Truth teaches that there is a path to the end of suffering—it is called *The Eightfold Way.* But, regarding impermanence, there is evidence from many sources that something does indeed survive death. This includes F. W. H. Myers's mediumistic studies and a very exciting, recently published scientific paper that indicates how much of our personality may indeed survive death and bodies.

Twenty years ago a chess match was apparently played between living and deceased chess grandmasters. A German psychologist and a Swiss investor were involved in this remarkable investigation of survival. Wolfgang Eisenbeiss and Dieter Hassler published this grandmaster game from the beyond, "An Assessment of Ostensible Communications with a Deceased Grandmaster as Evidence for Survival," in the British *Journal of Psychical Research* in April 2006. The trance medium, Robert Rollans, who worked with the researchers, was asked to psychically find a deceased grandmaster who was willing and able to play a match with the living grandmaster Victor Korchnoi. He found the Hungarian grandmaster Geza Maroczy who had died in 1950. I sent the reported final chess score to Bobby Fischer—who, as I mentioned earlier, lived in Iceland, having been rescued from a Japanese jail by the kindness of the Icelandic government. Bobby wrote to me saying that "anyone who can go fifty-two moves with Victor Korchnoi is playing at a grandmaster level." This case is of great interest to survival researchers, because it shows that a medium can demonstrate a *skill* of the deceased communicator, in addition to just information. Grandmaster Maroczy provided, through the medium, all sorts of personal, intimate, and humorous information about his life and his interactions with the grandmasters of his day, including the Cuban José Raul Capablanca and the Russian, Alexander Alekhine (both world champions). Korchnoi said that Maroczy played the same kind of intensely complicated middle game he was famous for in the 1920s. In his prime, Maroczy was the second strongest player in the world, just as Victor Korchnoi was. It was a hard-fought match. But, in the end the living player won. Incidentally, the match was held in the late 1980s, when there was no computer that could have stood in for Maroczy.

The nineteenth century English scholar F. W. H. Myers spent a good part of his life investigating mediumistic evidence for survival of human personality after death of the body. His great book, *Human Personality and Its Survival of Bodily Death,* gives many examples of spirit communications that sound surprisingly like long-distance phone calls from the dead. Nonetheless, he felt that the only way one could be certain that a spiritual communication could be *definitely assigned to a previously alive person, rather than just clairvoyance* on the part of the medium, would be for the spirit to communicate information that the medium could not know, even psychically. That's why the previously described post-mortem chess game is so important. This would be the only way to falsify the so-called super-psi mind-reading/clairvoyance hypothesis. After Myers died, he apparently carried out this experiment posthumously. The deceased Myers sent independent fragmentary messages to three well-known and widely separated mediums—in England, India, and the United States. The messages made sense only when they were combined and analyzed at the Society for Psychical Research in London. These celebrated communications are known as the "cross-correspondence cases." They are like three meaningless pieces of a jigsaw puzzle that show a recognizable picture only when all three are put together. Many of these complex transmissions were drawn from Myers's extensive knowledge of Classical Greek and Roman plays and poetry, described in Francis Saltmarsh's fascinating analysis of this cross-correspondence material in his book, *The Future and Beyond.*

The following remarkable story of Haley and her Spirit Friend was related to me at a book signing event, by the grandmother of the lost and found little girl. Grandma was the mother of one of my laser colleagues in Boulder, where the event was held.

For years I had no reason to believe in a spirit world, but I had no reason not to, either. Circumstances have a way of introducing new thinking. My granddaughter Haley had just turned six. She was a bright only child with a reserved personality. Her grandfather and I thought she would enjoy a spring wildflower walk and so we joined forces with three other adults for an outing.

On the way we decided to take a side trip to the Ozark Mountain Wilderness, one of our state's most photogenic places. Haley managed the easy downhill trail but resisted leaving when she wanted to go to a small waterfall partly down the cliff and high above the river below. In typical pouty child fashion she insisted on being carried up the hill as we hurried her to stay on our schedule. In equally authoritative adult fashion, we resisted and announced that we were leaving. Three adults went ahead while a friend stayed with me to move at a pace Haley could easily overtake. A couple of glances back indicated she was coming our way, but not wanting to start the pout again we stayed out of her view. However, when I looked back a third time, she was not visible, nor did she come along after a short wait.

Though I still could not see her, I decided she must have gone back to the falls, so I quickly headed back. When I came to a previously unnoticed side-trail, I decided to take it, figuring she might have wandered that way, but soon I saw forking paths and dense foliage and I now knew she was dangerously separated from us.

Not long after, a massive search of the wilderness area began, including its many cliffs, tangled brush and waterfalls. It involved dogs, helicopters, and hundreds of people who were organized by the search-and-rescue officials in authority. Prayers were offered, and help of every conceivable nature was put into play. It was hard to believe that all this effort produced nothing, leaving us drained by the third day. I went to a meeting of the American Society of Dowsers in nearby Fayetteville.

There, one of America's great dowsers, Harold McCoy, considered our desperate situation. He said that the little girl was "being taken care of by a kind woman," and she would be "found by two men on horseback within the day." [These facts were confirmed to me at a recent national dower's conference, by Gladys McCoy, Harold's wife.]

On the afternoon of the third day, two local residents who knew the country well and owned mules had a hunch where she might have gone, and they decided to make their own search rather than be part of the large, organized effort. After some time, just as they were about to give up, they found Haley lying exhausted on a boulder at the edge of the river at the bottom of the cliff. After a very difficult trip out, they brought her to the hospital and safety.

As one might imagine, this story brought Haley and her family a great deal of attention, so they decided to take a little vacation to escape the glare of publicity. It was not until this time that Haley started talking about the friend she had made while lost. She said the little girl's name was Elisha and that she was five years old. Elisha had come to Haley as soon as she was lost. Together they sang songs and played games, and Elisha acted as a guide to lead Haley down the bluff trail to the river through a very challenging ravine. Authorities had thought it was too difficult for a small child to manage this route wearing only a tee-shirt and flip-flops, and left it out of consideration.

While some children are known to have imaginary friends, this had never been the case with Haley. Nonetheless, Haley went on to describe her new playmate's hair and clothing and drew pictures of her. I began to wonder if there had been an incident with a lost child in that remote area before, and if there was a possibility of a spirit connection. After checking with authorities to learn about any legends or stories, I discovered that a child had been murdered and buried two decades earlier quite near to where Haley had been found.

Fascinated by this information and wanting to know more, I searched old newspapers and court records to learn the details. Among the items in the possession of the authorities was a picture of the child's mother along with other photos of a religious cult. They were accused and convicted of killing the child because the leader of the group, considered to be the "prophet," had declared her possessed.

Something about the mother's expression made me think she was as much a victim as the child. I became determined to learn more about her and to let her know about Haley and her spirit friend. My search led me to the man who had served as the mother's attorney. To my surprise, he had maintained contact with her, and he agreed to put us in touch with each other. The e-mails that followed were amazing to both of us. I learned that the very month and day that Haley was lost was the exact month and day that Elisha was buried. The name Haley gave for her friend was very close to a name Elisha had called herself. The hair and clothing styles Haley had drawn were distinctive of Elisha and the styles of the time at which Elisha had died.

Haley also told us about a silver flashlight that Elisha had at night, and that Elisha had refused to let Haley hold it. I asked the mother if her daughter had had a flashlight, and she startled me with the following account:

Elisha had a Raggedy Ann doll that she always slept with. [A woman in the cult] took it away from her. I had a small silver flashlight that I kept in my room because Elisha was afraid of the dark. I had to work three jobs from early morning till late at night and I found out later that [the woman] would put Elisha in the room in the dark. After her doll was taken, Elisha began to sleep with the flashlight. I would wake up at night and find that she had it with her under the covers. She would cry when I would try to take it, and most of the time I let her have it....

It is a tribute to the human spirit that this young mother was able to survive the terrible loss of her daughter, the accusation of being part of her murder and the unjust imprisonment which followed. She rebuilt her life but has kept this story from many who know her now. I wanted to let her know that if her child had indeed been in contact with my lost granddaughter, there was some positive outcome to her tragedy that might bring some peace to her torment. This was her response:

I have had thoughts and dreams of things that I could not explain. I guess now I can finally put those to rest. I know now that she is okay, but oh just to hug her one more time, hold her hand and tell her I love her. To know she saved someone else is beyond happiness and I am so thankful she was there for Haley. Being in that area myself, I know there was no way Haley could have survived her ordeal alone. I suppose one aspect of all this is that Elisha was destined to die to save Haley, and Haley had to live to save me in some sort of way.

After thinking about this possibility of a spirit child, I have wondered if Elisha was, in fact, the lure to attract Haley away from the adults and off the right path. Could this have been a child who missed the company of other children and drew her away? Or was she fulfilling a purpose for her own grieving mother as well as for my granddaughter? The joy of finding our granddaughter without physical or psychological injury is still amazing to everyone. The possibility of her being guided by an innocent spirit from a previous horror takes it to a whole new level of awe.

This story has now been described in a privately published book, *The Search for Haley: An Insider's Account of the Largest Search Mission in Arkansas History,* by photographer and trail guide Tim Ernst, whose main interest was to determine how the little girl got from the top of the cliff to the river below.

Here's a case from the 1930s that is remarkable as much for the passion exhibited by the deceased communicator as for the information he provided. It is a complex case involving a communicator who pleaded with the participants sitting with a medium in Iceland to help him find his missing leg! The séance circle had been meeting from time to time during 1937 and 1938, when this uncouth spirit named Runolfur Runolfsson, or "Runki," appeared. Runki was totally unknown to anyone in the circle.

The case, known as "Runki's Leg," is significant for several reasons: The material that appeared could not have been clairvoyantly perceived by the medium from any single document or obituary, nor telepathically obtained from a single living person. Even though these events occurred in Reykjavik in the 1930s, they were investigated by two of the world's most experienced and knowledgeable psychic researchers, American Dr. Ian Stevenson and Dr. Erlander Haraldsson from Iceland. These scholarly researchers were not thrilled with a drunken bum looking for his lost leg. Author Alan Gauld writes in *Mediumship and Survival* that Runki "showed a yearning for snuff, coffee, and alcohol, refused to give his name, and kept reiterating that he was looking for his leg. Asked where his leg was, he replied that it was 'in the sea.'" I spoke with Haraldsson recently at an international parapsychology conference, and he reaffirmed his confidence in the accuracy of this amazing case.

In 1939, a new sitter named Ludvik joined the circle and became the focus of questions from the communicator, Runki, speaking through the medium. Runki revealed that he had been drinking with friends in October of 1887—more than fifty years earlier. On his way home from the party that night, Runki said, after he lay down and fell asleep on the rocky seashore, he was swept out to sea and drowned. [Later] "I was carried in by the tide, but the dogs and ravens tore me to pieces." He told the sitters that the remnants of his body were buried in a nearby graveyard, but his thighbone was missing. The bone "was carried out again to sea, but was later washed up at Sandgerti. There, it was passed round, and now it is in Ludvik's house."

Ludvik, the new sitter, knew nothing about the bone. But inquiries among the oldest people in the community turned up memories of a very tall man's leg bone that had been found on the beach. For reasons that no one could remember, the bone had been put into the interior wall of the house now occupied by Ludvik. The bone was then retrieved from inside the wall of Ludvik's house, and it was verified that Runki had indeed been a very tall man.

Most astonishing is the passionate purpose of the communicator. No mere phantom appearing at the foot of your bed, he appeared to a specific sitter with a purpose. However, one of many interesting questions still remains to be answered. Why was the spirit of Runki still looking for his leg fifty years after his death? We could conjecture that he is caught in some kind of transition, because although he is in the world of spirit he's still interested in his previous body.

Before we are overwhelmed with the idea of born-again souls, it would be wise to define reincarnation with what we observe, to separate it from all the different belief systems that lay claim to it. Philosopher Robert Almeder has minimally defined the term in the 1997 *Journal of Scientific Exploration:*

> There is something essential to some human personalities . . . which we cannot possibly construe solely in terms of either brain states . . . or biological properties caused by the brain. . . . [F]urther, after biological death, this non-reducible biological trait sometimes persists for some time, in some way, in some place, existing independently of the person's former brain and body. Moreover, after some time, some of these irreducible essential traits of human

personality . . . come to reside in other human bodies, either some time during the gestation period, at birth, or shortly after birth.

Another aspect of these communications that had interested Myers was *xenoglossy,* in which the medium brings a message from a dead person and speaks it in a foreign language to which she has never been exposed. I experienced such a case one week after the tragic death of my daughter Elisabeth in 2002, when her husband Mark received a letter from a woman in Seattle. The writer, a nurse, had been one of the twenty spiritual healers in Elisabeth's successful experiment on distant prayer. In the woman's dream, a few days after Elisabeth's death, Elisabeth came to her with an urgent message for her husband. But, the Seattle lady could not understand it at all. She thought the message was nonsense syllables. Elisabeth kept repeating them, over and over again, and then woke up the woman, so that she could write them down phonetically.

At dinner, Mark opened the letter containing the message, which was two rows of English letters, with each row arranged in four three-letter groups—like a code. As he tried to read the message, I recognized the first group of syllables as the Russian words for "I love you." I didn't recognize the second group. A native Russian speaker has told me that they say, "I adore you," in idiomatic Russian. The Seattle lady claims not to know or have been exposed to Russian, or any language other than English. Elisabeth, of course, as I mentioned earlier, was a translator and fluent in Russian. We believe that this is just the sort of message that Elisabeth would send to establish that she is still present somewhere.

The following night three of us were sitting on the wooden deck outside my hillside home in Portola Valley, looking out across San Francisco Bay, watching the airplanes fly by the crescent moon on their way to the airport. As we discussed the previous day's mysterious letter, the foyer lights in the nearly darkened house flashed off and then on again. Since these were the only lights that had been on, this was very striking for us all. As we wondered aloud if it could be a signal from Elisabeth, the lights then flashed off and on two more times. Since we were sitting just outside the room in which Elisabeth had passed away the previous week, we were all silenced and overcome with awe. I like to believe that she is still trying to keep us in touch with the truth, much as Myers did a century earlier.

The important thread running through all these examples is that awareness persists, and that our minds are *powerful and nonlocal*. And above all, we are more than just a body. Our memories and our present thoughts affect the thoughts and experiences of ourselves and others now and in the future. Our memories, emotions, and intentions create information that can be accessed in non-ordinary states of awareness, such as dreams and remote viewing.

I believe dreams can be a most valuable source of information about who we are and what we can expect to see in the future. According to Luisa Rhine's vast collection of spontaneous psychic experiences, dreams are the most common pathway for a person's initiation to the world of psi—so happy dreaming.

Of all the approaches to survival I've discussed thus far, I am probably most comfortable with the succinctly expressed views of the Indian sage Ramana Maharshi:

> The real Self is continuous and unaffected. The reincarnating ego belongs to the lower plane, namely thought. . . . On whatever plane the mind happens to act, it creates a body for itself; in the physical world, a physical body; and in the dream world a dream body . . . .

It should now be clear that there is neither real birth, nor real death. It is the mind which creates and maintains the illusion of reality in this process, till it is destroyed by Self-realization.

The cases I have described in this chapter, taken together with the precognition experiments described previously, offer strong evidence that we each stand at the center of a vast personal coordinate system like a spider web, in which we can see in all directions and remember both the past and the future, because it keeps tugging on us. The future, in particular, keeps tugging to become realized. As we learn to participate in this expanded awareness of space and time, past and future, we create the opportunity to experience the transcendence described by the world's mystics.

In the end, after decades of study, philosopher Stephen Braude concludes in his deeply analytical book, *Immortal Remains,* that the super-psi hypothesis requires what he calls a "crushing burden of complexity." This leads him to decide very reluctantly in favor of the proposition that some aspect of awareness or personality does indeed survive. And it's *not* just some kind of "super-psi"—a combination of particularly outstanding telepathy combined with clairvoyance—which would allow a medium to know everything about a deceased person. Nor would it be explained by one's venturing into Jung's *collective unconscious.* I believe that this demonstrates that we possess not only limitless mind, but the possibility for limitless love, as well—since that's who we really are.

It is my pleasure to end this chapter with a quote from the greatest of Dzogchen masters, Longchenpa (Longchen Rabjam). He reminds us again that we already have everything we could possibly want. "There is only self-knowing awareness, the blissful place of rest, extending infinitely as the supremely spacious state of spontaneous equalness" (emptiness). Ultimate reality or ultimate truth is non-conceptual and non-dual, what Longchenpa calls the "basic space of phenomena" in his sublime book of the same name. I experienced this remarkable book as a direct transmission into my soul. The ineffable nature of ultimate reality is expressed in the aphorism, "The Tao that can be spoken is not the true Tao." Our naked, *unconditioned* awareness—non-dual intuition—gives us access to this basic space of phenomena.

In Longchenpa's powerful transmission known as *The Jewel Ship,* he gives us a meditation called, "Making Your Free Behavior the Path."

> *Listen great being [that's you]: do not create*
> *duality from the unique state.*
> *Happiness and misery are one in pure and total presence.*
> *Buddhas and beings are one in the nature of mind.*
> *Appearances and beings, the environment*
> *and its inhabitants, are one in reality.*
> *Even the duality of truth and falsehood are the same reality.*
> *Do not latch onto happiness; do not eliminate misery.*
> *Thereby everything is accomplished.*
> *Attachment to pleasure brings misery.*
> *Total clarity, being non-conceptual, is self-refreshing pristine awareness.*

POSTSCRIPT

One last thought about things seldom being what they seem: Here we have a case of "skim milk masquerading as cream." The picture on the next page is an actual photograph of the blind biker, who's the author of this book, and his wife, Patty. They walked into a "Photo Magic" studio on a recent trip to Las Vegas and came away with this photographic sleight of hand as a memento. This offers another opportunity for our continuing questioning of reality.

The principle teaching in the pre-Buddhist *Advaita Vedanta* is to discover—who am I? Gangaji has told me in more than one of our meetings, "What a lucky life you have had, Russell." I laugh as I tell her, "Wait. It's not over yet!"

I will leave you with my favorite Buddhist *Prayer of Loving-Kindness:* unconditional love and regard for yourself as well as others.

May you be in peace.
May your heart remain open (to give and receive love).
May you awaken to the light of your true nature.
May you be healed (from all fear, separation, and judgment).
May you be a source of healing for all beings.
May you never feel separate from the source of loving-kindness.
May you be happy.

EPILOGUE

The Return of the Bobby Snatchers (or Bye-Bye Bobby)

I played my first game of chess with Bobby Fischer more than fifty years ago. I was courting his sister, Joan, and he was fourteen. He beat me, even though he was playing blindfolded, eating a bowl of chicken soup in the kitchen, and I had the pieces and the board right in front of me. But it took him more than five minutes. The greatest chess player the world has ever known died on January 17, 2008. After traveling around the sun once for each of the sixty-four squares on his chessboard, Bobby Fischer died of kidney failure, after many months of distress, in a Reykjavik, Iceland, hospital. He refused medical treatment until the very end. In death, as in life, he wanted to do it his own way.

Although there have been many fabulously brilliant chess players, such as Alekhine, Capablanca, Gary Kasparov, and the astonishing American Paul Morphy, none have ever shown the analytic genius and demonic will to win that Bobby showed in his brief career. On my way home to America from Bobby's funeral in Iceland, I had a chance to discuss this with Icelandic grandmaster Throstur Thorhallsson, who happened to be sitting just in front of Patty and me on the plane. (Little Iceland with 300,000 people, has nine grandmasters.) In the 1971 Candidates Tournament leading up to his world championship bid, Bobby cleanly knifed through his grandmaster opponents Mark Taimanov and Bent Larsen with the unprecedented and likely unrepeatable scores of 6–0 and 6–0. This would be like winning a Grand Slam tennis tournament without your opponent ever hitting the ball—like a match between Targ vs. Federer. Fischer went on to beat the great Tigran Petrosian 6.5–2.5 and qualified to challenge Boris Spassky for the World Championship in 1972.

That so-called Match of the Century, possibly the most famous match in chess history was played in Reykjavik. It had a shaky start. Bobby lost the first game. He then forfeited the second, complaining about the large canvass-wrapped TV tower on the stage creating visually distracting playing conditions. But he turned up for the third game and won it brilliantly. The great Spassky, then World Champion, won only one more game in the rest of the match and was eventually beaten by Fischer by a score of 12.5–8.5. Bobby thereby crushed the Russian chess machine at the height of the Cold War, and became an enduring world celebrity.

Many years ago, I was standing in Washington Square Park with the renowned mathematician Prof. Kurt Friedrichs, who was cofounder of the New York University Math Institute. I asked the young man standing next to me if he was in Prof. Friedrichs's class. He said, "No. I'm Professor Kranzer. Professor Friedrichs is in a class by himself!" Similarly, it is generally agreed that even among the great grandmasters of chess, Bobby Fischer was in a class by himself.

Bobby's last years were, in their own way, as spectacular and bizarre as his earlier years of glory. In July of 2004, Bobby was at Narita airport outside Tokyo on his way to visit his (we believe) daughter, Jinky, and her mother, Marilyn Young, in the Philippines. As I described earlier, his passport was grabbed by Japanese Immigration officials because it had been declared invalid by the U.S. government, who wanted him in the U.S. for a show trial just before the 2004 presidential election. Bobby was taken to a Japanese jail where he languished for he next eight months, "because he was in the country without a passport!" Just before he was to be deported to the U.S. in March of 2005, to be tried for playing chess in Yugoslavia, he was generously granted Icelandic citizenship, so that he could leave prison and move to Iceland, where he remained for the next three years. He lived in an apartment overlooking the Reykjavik harbor, where he frequented the nearby restaurants and bookstores.

Late in the evening of Thursday, January 17, 2008, I received a phone call from Gardar Sverrisson, Bobby's neighbor and one of his closest friends of the last few years. He told me that Bobby had died in the hospital that evening. I knew that Bobby had been very ill. The previous week, our family had sent him photos of his mother Regina at his request. I told Gardar that my wife and I would come to Iceland that Sunday to help arrange the burial and put Bobby's affairs in order in a respectful manner. Patty and I took the red-eye and arrived at Reykjavik airport early Monday morning. We visited a lawyer that my son had found and then took a nap.

At two o'clock that afternoon, we were awakened by the lawyer to learn that Bobby's body had been taken from the hospital at midnight by Miyoko Watai (a Japanese woman's chess champion) and Gardar. Miyoko was waving a Japanese document which she claimed was a Japanese marriage license and consequently the hospital released the body to the pair. The document turned out to be her Japanese identity papers. With the body in the back of his station wagon (hopefully in a coffin), Gardar and Miyoko drove to the town of Selfoss, 60 km south of Reykjavik. According to the lawyer, the grave was dug secretly in the darkness of the white frozen landscape—ready for Bobby Fischer's last getaway. All this covert rush made it impossible for our family to participate, which was probably their desire. Not even the minister, whose churchyard it was, knew of the burial planned for the following morning.

According to the news reports, only five people attended that brief service early on Monday, conducted in darkness before the short Icelandic day had properly begun. Among them was Gardar, who had organized the digging of the grave, bypassing the customary process of requesting permission of Iceland's Lutheran Church or of the State authorities. Recent reports in the press suggest that the legality of Bobby Fischer's quiet burial in the small cemetery at Laugardalur church may be called into question. Gardar had also secured the services of a Roman Catholic priest from Reykjavik. Bobby was not a Catholic, of course. Another mourner, who may or may not have been Fischer's wife, was Miyoko Watai. Canadian journalist John Bosnitch, who worked tirelessly to free Bobby from jail, swears she was indeed Bobby's wife. However, the people I talked with in Iceland all claimed that Bobby said he wasn't married nor did he intend to be married. I trust we will know soon enough.

The following day, Tuesday, Patty and I met the very congenial Lutheran minister Kristinn Agust Fridfinnsson, in whose front yard Bobby had been planted. Rev. Fridfinnsson conducted a very thoughtful and moving memorial in English for Patty and me and three members of the Reykjavik Spiritual Association. These three men, who surprisingly located us the day we arrived, had been of enormous help to us in understanding what was going on and dealing with the impossibly difficult Icelandic language. (They have six more consonants than we have in English and they use every one of them.) Rev. Fridfinnsson said that although he had no prior knowledge of the burial right in front of his church, he was happy to take good care of Bobby, who is a hero in chess-crazy Iceland. Although a peaceful man, he wasn't thrilled that a Catholic priest from Reykjavik had performed a service in his churchyard without asking.

As we sat in the little church listening the service conducted for our group, artist Patty noticed that the large oil painting behind the alter contained a figure of a man who greatly resembled Bobby, looking adoringly at Jesus. The photo below, shows Bobby shortly after he arrived in Iceland from the Japanese prison and the head of the Bobby look-alike in the painting. We all thought that this striking likeness was a good omen for his happy resting place.

Bobby Fischer in Iceland, shortly after being freed from a Japanese jail in 2005 and an image in the altarpiece of the rural Icelandic church where Bobby was buried, January 21, 2008

Patty, me, and the minister, Rev. Fridfinnsson, standing in front of the altarpiece which includes the Bobby figure

Churchyard in Selfoss where Bobby is buried

The following day, we attended an art opening at the Reykjavik Art Museum, where the president of Iceland, Ólafur Ragnar Grímsson would formally open a new exhibition. I was happy to have an opportunity to express our family's gratitude to him and the people of Iceland for generously providing Bobby sanctuary from the Japanese jail. I also wanted to discuss a concern I had over the proposed grave marker, which was to be a crucifix. Since at least one of Bobby's parents was Jewish (another contentious issue we won't dwell on here), I thought that this was not an appropriate memorial, although it was approved by the Catholic priest who buried him and the Lutheran minister who owns the churchyard where he is buried. I proposed to President Grímsson that, in the interest of religious harmony, a chess king would be a more suitable marker. Since that chess piece already has a little cross on top, it should be acceptable to all factions. Grímsson said that religious peace between Lutherans and Catholics had been an issue for hundreds of years in Iceland, and my proposed solution might be just the thing. What a wonderful country where the President has time to try to soothe

Patty, Russell, and Icelandic President Grimsson at the Reykjavik Art Museum

everyone's sensibilities! Finally, what we remember is that Bobby had an inventive and brilliant mind, which was the hallmark of his genius. As a chess player and an American, he achieved real victories and, for a moment, carried the freedom torch during the Cold War when he won the World Chess Championship. Unmistakably, he also faced some great personal challenges. He had a wonderful sense of humor and was capable of great warmth. Bobby was a loved part of our family and he will be deeply missed. May he finally rest in peace.

BIBLIOGRAPHY

What follows is a list of books that have informed
my life and this memoir.

A Course in Miracles. Los Angeles: Foundation for Inner Peace, 1975–1992.

Abhayadatta. *Buddhist Masters of Enchantment.* R. Beer, illustrator, and K. Dowman, editor. Rochester, Vt.: Inner Traditions, 1998.

Allen, M. *Visionary Business.* Novato, Calif.: New World Library, 1996.

Almeder, Robert. *Death and Personal Survival: The Evidence for Life after Death.* Lanham, Md.: Rowman & Littlefield, 1992.

———. "A Critique of Arguments Offered against Reincarnation." *Journal of Scientific Exploration,* vol. 11, no. 4, 1997.

Anonymous. *Bhagavad-Gita.* Translated by Swami Prabhavananda and Christopher Isherwood. New York: Harper, 1951.

Asimov, I. *Foundation.* New York: Avon, 1974.

Ayer, Alfred. *Language, Truth, and Logic.* New York: Dover Publications, 1952.

Batchelor, Stephen. *Verses from the Center: A Buddhist Vision of the Sublime.* New York: Riverhead Books, 2000.

Beer, R., and K. Dowman. *Buddhist Masters of Enchantment.* Rochester, Ver.: Inner Traditions, 1998.

Bell, J. S. "On the Einstein, Podolsky, Rosen Paradox." *Physics* 1, (1964):195–200.

Bem, D., and C. Honorton. "Does Psi Exist? Replicable Evidence for an Anomalous Process of Information Transfer." *Psychological Bulletin,* vol. 115, no. 1 (January, 1994): 4–18.

Benor, Daniel J. *Healing Research,* vol. 1. Munich, Germany: Helix Verlag, 1992.

Bernstein, Morey. *Search for Bridey Murphy.* New York: Doubleday, 1955.

Besant, A., and C. Leadbeater. *Occult Chemistry.* Wheaton, Ill.: Theosophical Publishing House, 2000.

Blavatsky, H. P. *Secret Doctrine.* Wheaton, Ill.: Quest Books, 1993.

Bohm, David, and Basel Hiley. *The Undivided Universe.* New York: Routledge, 1993.

Boorstein, Sylvia. *It's Easier Than You Think: The Buddhist Way to Happiness.* San Francisco: Harper San Francisco, 1995.

Bradbury, R. *The Martian Chronicles.* New York: Bantam Books, 2006.

Brandon, Nathaniel. *My Years with Ayn Rand.* San Francisco: Jossey-Bass, 1999.

Braude, S. *Immortal Remains.* Lanham, Md.: Rowman & Littlefield, 2003.

Brown, Tina. *The Diana Chronicles.* New York: Doubleday, 2007.

Clarke, A. C. *Childhood's End.* New York: Harcourt Brace, 1954.

Cohen-Solal, Annie. *Sartre: A Life.* New York: Pantheon Books, 1987.

Cooper, David. *God Is a Verb.* New York: Riverhead Books, 1997.

Cranston, Sylvia, and Carey Williams [compiled by]. *Reincarnation: A New Horizon in Science, Religion, and Society.* New York: Julian Press, 1984.

Crowley, Aleister. *The Confessions of Aleister Crowley.* London: Penguin Books, 1979.

de Beauvoir, Simone. *The Manderins.* New York: Harper Perennial, 2005.

Doore, Gary. *What Survives? Contemporary Explorations of Life after Death.* Los Angeles: Jeremy Tarcher, 1990.

Dossey, Larry. *Meaning and Medicine: Lessons from a Doctor's Tales of Breakthrough and Healing.* New York: Bantam Books, 1991.

Dunne, B. J., R. G. Jahn, and R. D. Nelson. "Precognitive Remote Perception." Princeton Engineering Anomalies Research Laboratory (Report), August 1983.

Eisenbeiss, W., and D. Hassler. "An Assessment of Ostensible Communication with a Deceased Grandmaster as Evidence for Survival." *Journal of Psychical Research,* April 2006.

Evans-Wentz, W. Y. *The Tibetan Book of the Dead.* New York: Galaxy Books, 1960.

Farrell, J. T. *Studs Lonigan.* New York: Penguin Classics, 2001.

Forwald, H. *Mind, Matter, and Gravitation.* New York: Parapsychology Foundation, 1969.

Frankl, Viktor. *Man's Search for Meaning.* New York: Simon & Schuster, 1984.

Freedman, S., and J. Clauser. "Experimental Test of Local Hidden Variable Theories." *Physical Review Letters* 28 (1972): 934–941.

Freeman, L. *Killers of the Mind.* New York: Random House, 1974.

———. *Fight against Fears.* New York: Crown Publishing, 1975.

Gangaji. *You Are That!* vol. I and II. Boulder, Colo.: Satsang Press, 1995.

———. *A Diamond in Your Pocket.* Louisville, Colo.: Sounds True, 2005.

Gardner, M. "Notes of a Fringe Watcher: Distant Healing and Elisabeth Targ." *Skeptical Enquirer Magazine.* March/April 2001.

Garrett, Eileen. *Many Voices.* New York: G. P. Putnam, 1968.

Gauld, Alan. *Mediumship and Survival.* London: Paladin/Granada, 1983.

Gisin, N., et al. "Violation of Bell Inequalities by Photons More Than 10 km Apart." *Physics Review Letter* 81 (1998): 3563–3566.

"Healing Happens." *Utne Reader,* no. 71 (September–October 1995): 52–59.

Hearst, Patricia C. *Every Secret Thing.* London: Methuen, 1982.

Inglis, Brian. *Natural and Supernatural.* London: Hodder and Stoughton, 1977.

Jampolsky, Gerald. *Love Is Letting Go of Fear.* Berkeley, Calif.: Celestial Arts, 1979.

Kaku, Michio. "Techniques of Discovery." The Prophets Conference, New York: May 18–20, 2001.

Kantor, MacKinlay. *Don't Touch Me.* New York: Random House, 1951.

———. *Andersonville.* G. P. Putnam, New York, 1955.

————. *Spirit Lake.* G. P. Putnam, New York, 1961.

Katra, J., and R. Targ. *The Heart of the Mind: How to Experience God without Belief.* Novato, Calif.: New World Library, 1999.

Kelly, Edward F., Emily Williams Kelly, and Adam Crabtree. *Irreducible Mind.* Lanham, Md.: Rowman and Littlefield, 2006.

Kiesling, Brady. *Diplomacy Lessons.* Washington, D.C.: Potomac Books, 2006.

Kipling, R. *Just So Stories.* New York: Gramercy Reprint, 2003.

Korzybski, A. *Science and Sanity.* Fort Worth, Tex.: Institute for General Semantics, 1995.

Krishna, G. *The Awakening of Kundalini.* Ontario, Canada: Institute for Consciousness Research, 1989.

LaBerge, Stephen. *Exploring the World of Lucid Dreaming.* New York: Ballantine Books, 1990.

Larson, Erik. "Did Psychic Powers Give Firm a Killing in the Silver Market?" *Wall Street Journal,* Oct. 22, 1984.

Longchenpa. *You Are the Eyes of the World (The Jewel Ship).* Ithaca, N.Y.: Snow Lion Publications, 2000.

Lusseyran, Jacques. *And There Was Light.* Parabola Books, 1994.

Maharshi, Ramana. "Who Am I?" in *The Collected Works of Ramana Maharshi.* Translated by T. Venkataran. Sri Ramanasramam, India: Tiruvannamalai, 1955.

————. *The Teachings of Bhagavan Sri Ramana Maharshi in His Own Words.* Edited by Arthur Osborne. London: Rider and Co., 1962.

————. *Be As You Are: The Teachings of Sri Ramana Maharshi.* Edited by David Godman. New York: Arkana/Penguin, 1985.

————. *The Spiritual Teaching of Ramana Maharshi.* Boston: Shambhala, 1988.

————. *Talks with Sri Ramana Maharshi.* Sri Ramanasramam, India: Tiruvannamalai, 2000.

Mansfield, K. *Collected Stories of Katherine Mansfield.* London: Penguin Ltd., 2001.

McMoneagle, J. *Mind Trek.* Charlottesville, Va.: Hampton Roads Publishing, 1993.

————. *Remote Viewing Secrets.* Charlottesville, Va.: Hampton Roads Publishing, 2000.

————. *The Stargate Chronicles.* Charlottesville, Va.: Hampton Roads Publishing, 2002.

————. *Memoirs of a Psychic Spy.* Charlottesville, Va.: Hampton Roads Publishing, 2006.

Mitchell, Edgar. *Psychic Exploration.* New York: G. P. Putnam, 1974.

Monroe, Robert. *Journeys Out of the Body.* Main Street Books, 1973.

Moore, Walter. *Schrödinger: Life and Thought.* Cambridge University Press, 1989.

Muldoon, Sylvan, and Hereward Carrington. *The Projection of the Astral Body.* London: Rider and Paternoster House, 1929.

Murphy, Michael. *The Future of the Body.* Los Angeles: Jeremy Tarcher, 1992.

Myers, F. W. H. *Human Personality and Its Survival of Bodily Death.* Edited by Susy Smith. Hyde Park, N.Y.: University Books, 1961.

Nolan, W. A. *Healing: Doctor in Search of a Miracle.* New York: Random House, 1974.

Norbu, Namkhai. *Dream Yoga.* Ithaca, N.Y.: Snow Lion Publications, 1992.

O'Brian, P. *The Mauritius Command.* New York: HarperCollins, 1955.

O'Regan, B. *Spontaneous Remission.* Petaluma, Calif.: Institute of Noetic Sciences, 1993.

Orloff, Judith. *Second Sight.* New York: Warner Books, 1997.

Ostrander, S., and L. Schroeder. *Psychic Discoveries behind the Iron Curtain.* New York: Prentice Hall, 1970.

Padmasambhava. *Self-Liberation through Seeing with Naked Awareness.* Translated by John Myrdhin Reynolds. Ithaca, N.Y.: Snow Lion Publications, 2000.

Patanjali. *How to Know God [The Sutras of Patanjali].* Translated by Swami Prabhavananda and Christopher Isherwood. Hollywood, Calif.: Vedanta Press, 1983.

Poomja, H. W. L. *The Truth Is.* New York: Weiser Books, 2000.

Puharich, Andrija. *The Sacred Mushroom.* New York: Doubleday, 1974.

Puthoff, H. E., and R. Targ. "A Perceptual Channel for Information Transfer over Kilometer Distances: Historical Perspective and Recent Research." *Proceedings IEEE,* vol. 64, no. 3 (March 1976): 329–354.

Puthoff, H. E., R. Targ, and E. C. May. "Experimental Psi Research: Implication for Physics." *AAAS Proceedings of the 1979 Symposium on the Role of Consciousness in the Physical World,* 1981.

Puzo, M. *The Godfather.* New York: J. P. Putnam, 1969.

Radin, Dean. *The Conscious Universe.* San Francisco, Calif.: HarperCollins, 1997.
———. *Entangled Minds.* New York: Pocket Books, 2006.

Ram Dass. *Be Here Now.* New York: Harmony Books, 1971.

Rand, Ayn. *Atlas Shrugged.* New York: Random House, 1957.

Report of the Presidential Commission on the Space Shuttle Challenger Accident (In compliance with Executive Order 12546 of February 3, 1986).

Rhine, Louisa. "Frequency and Types of Experience in Spontaneous Precognition." *Journal of Parapsychology,* vol. 16 (1954): 93–123.

Richards, R. *No Way Renée.* New York: Simon and Schuster, 2007.

Robinson, C. A. "Soviets Push for Beam Weapon." *Aviation Week,* May 2, 1977.

Saltmarsh, F. *The Future and Beyond.* Charlottesville, Va.: Hampton Roads Publishing, 2004.

Sartre, Jean Paul. *Intimacy.* Berkeley, Calif.: Berkeley Books, 1968.

———. *The Age of Reason.* New York: Vintage, 1992.

Schrödinger, Erwin. *What Is Life?* Cambridge, England: Cambridge University Press, 1945.

———. *Mind and Matter.* Cambridge, England: Cambridge University Press, 1958.

———. *My View of the World.* Woodbridge, Conn.: Ox Bow Press, 1983.

Sheehan, D. "Frontiers of Time." *Proceedings of the American Institute of Physics.* New York, 2006.

Smith, Paul H. *Reading the Enemy's Mind.* New York: Forge Books, 2005.

Stapp, H., R. Nadeau, and M. Kafatos. *The Nonlocal Universe: The New Physics and Matters of the Mind.* Oxford University Press, 1999.

Stevenson, Ian. *Twenty Cases Suggestive of Reincarnation.* New York: American Society for Psychical Research, 1966.

———. *Children Who Remember Previous Lives.* Charlottesville, Va.: University Press of Virginia, 1987.

———. *Where Reincarnation and Biology Intersect.* Westport, Conn.: Praeger, 1997.

Sylvia, Claire. *A Change of Heart.* New York: Little, Brown, and Co., 1997.

Targ, R. *Limitless Mind: A Guide to Remote Viewing and Transformation of Consciousness.* Novato, Calif.: New World Library, 2004.

Targ, R., and K. Harary. *The Mind Race: Understanding and Using Psychic Abilities.* New York: Villard Books, 1984.

Targ, R., and J. J. Hurtak. *The End of Suffering: Fearless Living in Troubled Times.* Charlottesville, Va.: Hampton Roads Publishing, 2006.

Targ, R., and Jane Katra. *Miracles of Mind: Exploring Nonlocal Consciousness and Spiritual Healing.* Novato, Calif.: New World Library, 1998.

Targ, R., J. Katra, D. Brown, and W. Wiegand. "Viewing the Future: A Pilot Study with an Error-Detecting Protocol." *Journal of Scientific Exploration* (1995): 67–80.

Targ, R., and H. E. Puthoff. *Mind Reach: Scientists Look at Psychic Ability.* New York: Delacorte Press, 1977.

———. "Information Transfer under Conditions of Sensory Shielding." *Nature* 251 (1975): 602–607.

Tart, C., H. E. Puthoff, and R. Targ. *Mind at Large: Institute of Electrical and Electronics Engineers Symposium on the Nature of Extrasensory Perception.* Charlottesville, Va.: Hampton Roads Publishing, 2002.

Tolstoy, Leo. *A Confession.* New York: Penguin Classics, 1988.

———. *Anna Karenina.* New York: Penguin, 2004.

Ullman, Montague, and Stanley Krippner, with Alan Vaughan. *Dream Telepathy.* New York: MacMillan Publishing Company, Inc.,1973.

Vallée, Jacques. *The Heart of the Internet.* Charlottesville, Va.: Hampton Roads Publishing, 2003.

Van Vogt, A. E. *Slan.* Berkeley, Calif.: Berkeley Re-Issue, 1940, 1982.

Wittgenstein, L. *Tractatus Logico-Philosophicus.* London: Routledge, 1961.

Wright, R. *Black Boy.* New York: Harper Perennial, 2005.

———. *Native Son.* New York: Harper Perennial, 2007.

Zimbardo, Philip. *The Lucifer Effect.* New York: Random House, 2007.

STUDIES IN CONSCIOUSNESS

In addition to authoring or co-authoring five books this past decade, I have had the privilege of co-publishing the following dozen books with Hampton Roads, with the great support and encouragement of Frank DeMarco, a co-owner of the firm at the time.

1. *Mental Radio,* Upton Sinclair (1930). Carefully conducted ESP experiments by the famous muckraking writer and his psychic wife. Preface by Albert Einstein.
2. *An Experiment with Time,* J. W. Dunne (1927). Detailed reports of a scientist's precognitive-dream journal and theories. Preface by Russell Targ.
3. *Human Personality and Its Survival of Bodily Death,* F. W. H. Myers (1903), ed. Susy Smith, 1961. Myers's landmark work in the theory of psychology, psychic research, and survival. Preface by Jeffrey Mishlove, introduction by Susy Smith.
4. *Mind to Mind,* René Warcollier (1948). Detailed description of psychic capabilities and the sources of mental noise limiting such perception. Preface by Ingo Swann.
5. *Experiments in Mental Suggestion,* L. L. Vasilliev (1963). Including his famous experiments in long-distance hypnosis. Preface by Arthur Hastings, introduction by Anita Gregory.

6. *Mind at Large: IEEE Symposia on the Nature of Extrasensory Perception,* eds. Harold Puthoff, Charles Tart, and Russell Targ (1979). Preface by Russell Targ.

7. *Dream Telepathy: Experiments in Natural ESP,* Montague Ullman, Stanley Krippner, and Alan Vaughan. This pioneering and highly successful telepathic study was conducted at Maimonides Hospital in the 1960s. Preface by Stanley Krippner and Montague Ullman.

8. *Distant Mental Influence: Its Contributions to Science and Healing,* William Braud. A new book describing pioneering research on how the thoughts of one person can affect the physiology of a distant person. Preface by Larry Dossey.

9. *Thoughts through Space: A Remarkable Adventure in the Realm of the Mind,* Sir Hubert Wilkins and Harold Sherman (1931). True psi adventure involving a downed plane in the arctic. Preface by Ingo Swann.

10. *The Future and Beyond: Paranormal Foreknowledge and Evidence of Personal Survival from Cross Correspondences,* Harold Francis Saltmarsh (2004).

11. *Mind Reach: Scientists Look at Psychic Ability,* Russell Targ and Harold Puthoff (1977, 2005). The first book describing remote-viewing research at Stanford Research Institute. Preface by Margaret Mead.

12. *The Secret Vaults of Time,* Stephan A. Schwartz (2005). A comprehensive account to the present time, describing the use of psychic abilities to aid classical archeology.

INDEX

Hampton Roads Publishing Company

. . . for the evolving human spirit

Hampton Roads Publishing Company
publishes books on a variety of subjects,
including spirituality, health, and other related topics.

For a copy of our latest trade catalog,
call 978-465-0504,
or visit our website www.hrpub.com